Hausa Architecture

J.C. Moughtin

First published 1985
by Ethnographica Ltd
19 Westbourne Road, London N7
in association with
Institute of Planning Studies, University of Nottingham

Designed by Edgell Marland
Typesetting in Itek Bookface by TNR Productions, London N7

ISBN 0 905788 40 0

Hausa
Architecture
J.C. Moughtin

Ethnographica, London 1985

Contents

To Nell and Jim,
Kate, Mark, Nick and Tim.

Acknowledgements

I wish to express my gratitude to my old friend and teacher, 'Mek', Professor McCaughan, whose guidance and inspiration led to the writing of this book. The approach and method adopted for the study are both based upon 'Mek's' teaching: any quality it may have is due to his guidance, the faults however are my own.

During the course of this study I have been employed by three Universities: Ahmadu Bello University, Zaria, The Queen's University of Belfast and the University of Nottingham. Through their current Vice Chancellors, Professor Abdullahi, Dr Froggatt and Dr Weedon I wish to express my thanks to those Institutions for their support. I also thank Alan Leary for his companionship on our many visits to Hausa cities, for his help in measuring some of the buildings and for the ideas he has contributed to this study. Amongst the many colleagues with whom I have worked over the past twenty two years and from whom I have gained so much, two stand out as being particularly supportive in my studies of Hausa architecture. They are Professor Alex Potter and Professor Gerald Dix. To them for their encouragement and help I am also very grateful. My thanks are due also to Lynne Bellamy who not only typed the manuscript for this book but also organised my professional life making it possible for me to devote time to writing. I wish also to thank Gill Thomas for preparing the maps for Chapters 1 and 2 and for advising on presentation techniques for the remaining drawings.

Lastly but by no means the least, I shall always remain indebted to my wife Kate McMahon who made me sit down and finish the book; she also edited the numerous drafts and advised on style of writing, an aspect of the work which gave so much trouble.

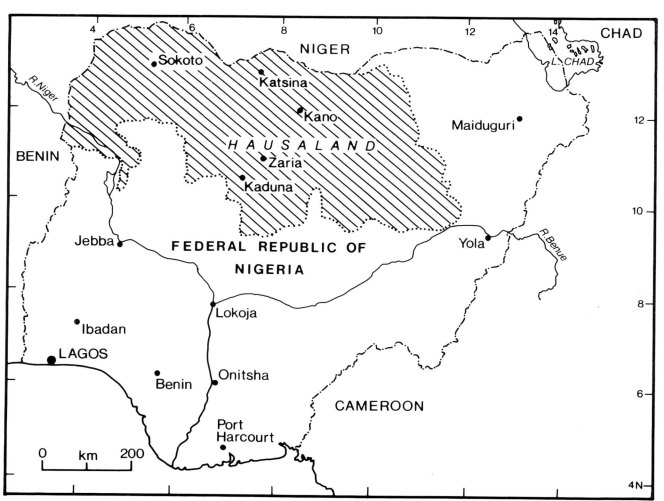

1.1 *The Location of Hausaland*

Introduction

My first view of Zaria in 1961 left such a profound impression that I decided, there and then, to study the architecture of the Hausa. This study has continued ever since. Return visits to the Hausa settlements still leave me with that sense of excitement and deep respect for the culture which gave birth to such a wonderful art form.

I was inspired by the beauty of mud architecture. The immediate questions raised by the buildings surrounding me in Zaria were quite straightforward: how and why did they acquire their distinctive form? I set out to try to answer these questions, but in the twenty years or so that I have continued the study, the original focus has evolved. The last two decades have seen momentous changes in the developing world, to which Nigeria is no exception. A population explosion, coupled with rapid urbanization, has brought about a qualitative cultural change and a physical change to the urban structures. Hence the original stimulus of the study, which stressed the outward visual impact of a period of great mud building, has been modified by a growing interest in trying to appreciate the current dynamic in Hausa society and the fundamental unchanging meaning of built forms, in an effort to determine those elements of urban structure which seem to be of more lasting importance to the Hausa than the transitory beauty of architectural fashion. It is, in Alexander's terms, these fundamental architectural 'patterns' which outlive a particular architectural fashion and which are important in guiding future development.[1]

Earth or mud architecture is often described as impermanent and therefore as an inferior method of building. Yet unbaked earth has been used for many thousands of years, not only for housing, but for some of society's most prestigious developments: great ziggurats, pyramids, religious and public buildings have all been constructed from this material. About 9,000 years ago Babylon was composed of earth constructions, and many of its buildings were magnificent engineering feats. The great terraced tower close to the Temple of Marduk (Baal), sometimes assumed to be the Tower of Babel, may have been equivalent in height to a thirty-storey office block. Records exist of many great earthworks constructed to defend important cities and even whole civilizations. Large parts of the Great Wall of China, built of unbaked earth, have managed to survive from the third century B.C., testifying to the importance of this material in architectural development. The present study outlines the use of earth or mud by one group of prodigious builders—the Hausa.

Over one third of the world's population lives in structures made from mud.[2] Despite the best efforts of governments and aid agencies to build modern, permanent homes, a majority of the urban population in developing countries relies upon its own efforts to house itself.[3] Such 'self built' housing is often of traditional materials, although many urban poor live in shacks made from packing cases and other oddments. These 'packing case' homes, and those built of more permanent materials such as iron sheets and concrete blocks in the expanding informal housing areas, have few of the qualities of traditional architecture. Vast squatter areas of abysmal environmental quality grow daily around major urban centres in the developing world. Since the formal building industries supported by governments and international development agencies have a poor record in trying to solve the housing problems of the urban poor, it may be apposite to examine the architectural traditions of the developing world to see if any are useful for this purpose. Hassan Fathy is one architect who has tried to harness traditional methods for modern developmental purposes, but such experiments are all too rare.[4]

The subject matter of this book is the changing architectural traditions of the Hausa people. The term architecture is not used here in the narrow sense of building types, form, construction and detailing; but is widened to include the arrangement of buildings in space as functioning elements within a settlement. Architecture, then, is a people's use of an accumulated technological knowledge to control and adapt their environment for social, economic, political and religious requirements. This study looks at the ways in which the Hausa have learned to solve the total programme of requirements for the built environment. Their architecture is viewed as an element of their spiritual and physical culture.[5]

The book begins with an outline of the physical environment of Hausaland set within the broader framework of West Africa. Chapter 1 emphasizes the effect of the environment on settlement patterns. For this the work of Mabogunje was particularly illuminating.[6]

Chapter 2 looks at the evolution of settlement from the emergence of the Hausa states to the effects of rapid urbanization and development since independence. The strongly fortified Hausa settlements resulted first from the revolutions in agriculture and iron smelting, and secondly from the pressure of population caused by a southward immigration of peoples into the region. The communities gathered within these highly nucleated settlements were further stimulated to develop complex political and administrative structures of city and state government by expanding trans-Saharan trade connections. Though polarized between powerful neighbouring states the Hausa, on sites with a plentiful water supply, good agricultural land and a defensible position imbued with ancient religious meaning, have built great fortified mud cities dominating a landscape of dependent settlements. Their territorial organization closely mirrors, or is mirrored by, their political and religious structures. It was this organization which enabled them to take advantage of the inherent qualities of the environment.[7]

The morphology of Hausa settlements is discussed in Chapter 3. Development within the walls of the old cities is the main concern, although it is examined in relation to the later, colonial and post-independence urban growth, most of which has been outside the traditional settlements. This chapter analyses the relationship between the main elements within the old city, that is, the organization of traditional structure in terms of the location and form of residential areas, the market, mosque and palace.[8]

Chapter 4 analyses Hausa buildings in terms of the functional arrangements of accommodation and the symbolic meaning of spatial form. The buildings studied are the residential compound, the palace and the mosque. It was found that the implicit architectural programme of Hausa society, disciplined as it is by Islam, results in a unified and highly organized spatial structure which expresses in built form the significant features of Hausa culture. For example, the Friday Mosque, *Shari'a* court, palace and *dendal* are sited at the centre of the city and together symbolize the power of Allah, Islamic law, government, state and community solidarity. The city is divided into wards, each of which has at its centre the ward head's house, a meeting space and neighbourhood mosque. At the hub of the extended family house is the *shigifa*, *kofa gida* and prayer mat which complete the city structure, binding citizen and state into a cohesive society with Islam as the governing discipline.[9]

Chapter 5 describes and analyses the method of architectural construction. The modular nature of the constructional system is shown to be an outcome of the structural limits of the building materials used, while the development of the reinforced 'mud arch' is seen to be a simple, though ingenious extension of this system of trabeated construction.[10]

In Chapter 6 Hausa architecture is analysed in terms of its ability to control or mitigate the effects of the harsh climate in Northern Nigeria. Hausa buildings are designed to resolve the conflicting requirements of two broad climatic conditions: a hot, dry climate and a warm, humid climate. The solution is based upon the use of a range of building types and outdoor spaces. It is interesting to note, however, that whatever the building elements used by the Hausa, whether they be indigenous, North African or European in origin, climatic control as a determinant of form takes second place to cultural, social and economic factors.[11]

An important feature of Hausa architecture is internal and external decoration. Chapter 7 traces the development of decorative style over the last two hundred years. Decoration is analysed in terms of symbolism, its relationship to the building process and the origin of the motifs used.[12]

In Chapter 8 the possible derivatives of architectural form are outlined. The development of architectural forms is presented as a long process of acculturation whereby new ideas are introduced slowly into the vocabulary of the builders. Among the Hausa, building is a family concern, knowledge being passed down from father to son. Such lineages of builders are responsible for developing the structural and decorative techniques of a distinctive architectural form, with influences from North Africa being assimilated over a long period. The process of change has accelerated in the last twenty years, and a fine environment built entirely of mud is in danger of being lost. Will there be time to create a new architectural synthesis of the elements of traditional architecture and the built environment and desirable features associated with modern construction?

Chapter 9 is a short conclusion which attempts to identify those features of Hausa architecture which transcend the whims of fashion. Such enduring features of the built environment could form the basis of a visual language useful in planning future urban development.

Measured drawings of buildings and a photographic study are the main sources of information used throughout this book, but in terms of documentary evidence it is based largely upon secondary sources. Most of the drawings were made between 1961 and 1963 although from 1978 to 1981 additional surveys were carried out, and some buildings remeasured to discover the changes made to them over the twenty-year period. A large selection of building types have been included, many from Zaria, but some from other settlements. Interviews were conducted with builders and householders and detailed observations of activities in and around buildings were observed and recorded. Aerial photographs taken at different intervals have been used to examine recent detailed physical changes in settlement patterns. Apart from the buildings themselves the greatest stimulus for this study has been the writings of the travellers and explorers of the nineteenth and early twentieth centuries. It is the curiosity of such people at Barth, Clapperton, Staudinger and Lugard which aroused my own interest in this subject, as well as providing fascinating insights into the way of life and the architecture of the Hausa.

Nottingham, 1985

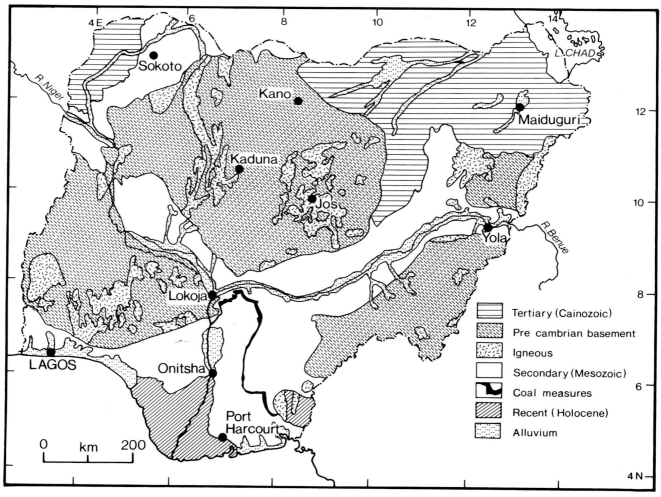

Legend:

- Tertiary (Cainozoic)
- Pre cambrian basement
- Igneous
- Secondary (Mesozoic)
- Coal measures
- Recent (Holocene)
- Alluvium

1.2 *The Geology of Nigeria*

6 HAUSA ARCHITECTURE

1. Environment and Settlement Pattern

Location

Kasar Hausa, Hausaland, the present heartland of the Hausa people is situated between the confluence of the Rivers Niger and Benue, in the Federal Republic of Nigeria.[1] It extends approximately from latitude 3.5° east to latitude 11.0° east, or 844km.; and from longitude 10.5° north to longitude 14.0° north, or 400km. (See Figure 1.1.)

Geology

The basic geological structure of Hausaland, from west to east, consists of Tertiary sediments to the west of Sokoto, which overlie Lower Cretaceous sedimentary rocks. Further east, in the Sokoto and Katsina provinces, these Lower Cretaceous rocks themselves form the surface material. However, the major part of Hausaland consists of the 'basement complex' of pre-Cambrian rocks, which give way in the extreme east to Tertiary sediments. (See Figure 1.2.)

The rounded domes of bare rock known as inselbergs, a distinctive feature of the Hausa landscape, are outcrops of the pre-Cambrian 'basement complex' of crystalline rocks underlying Hausaland, and, indeed the whole of West Africa.[2] These pre-Cambrian rocks, consisting of granites, gneisses and schists, are sources of minerals such as tin-stone, columbite and gold. The sites of early settlements are often found where such mineral-bearing rocks come close to the surface. For example, Dala Hill, an inselberg within the walls of the ancient city of Kano, is the site of an early iron-smelting furnace dating back to the seventh century.[3]

The land-forms of Hausaland consist of mature, or 'old-age' plains upon which the process of erosion operates slowly; so that weathering has taken place to a great depth, and to such an extent that the rocks have been decomposed to a degree where it is not possible to identify the original type. Therefore, despite the variety of underlying rock structure, wide areas of Hausaland are covered by a common end product, laterite, with exposures of fresh rock of limited extent.[4] This geological structure has influenced the development of traditional building techniques, for laterite is the single most important material used. The walls of the great emirate cities rise out of the laterite plain as naturally as the massive ant hills which stud the landscape. The mud architecture is organic in every sense of the word, being built from the earth, eroded, repaired and demolished — an extension of the process that forms the landscape structure.

Topography

The high plains of Hausaland may be subdivided into a number of erosion surfaces, at 610-752m.; at 488-610m., with younger surfaces at lower levels. These wide and magnificent tree-studded plains are separated by steep scarps. Towards the margins the plains are more broken and terminate abruptly against the scarps that mark the Jos Plateau, which rises to over 1,769m.; the Mada Hills and the Liruein-Kano Hills. Hausaland terminates to the west in the Sokoto plains, while in the east the land falls to the vast featureless plain of the Chad basin.

This is an extensive and expansive country: one which invites movement, conquest and large-scale acquisition of land. The land form is ideally suited to the use of the horse as a means of transport, allowing a relative ease of movement which facilitated both the policing of a large territory and the collection of agricultural and trading products into market centres. It is ideal territory for the growth of centralized states.

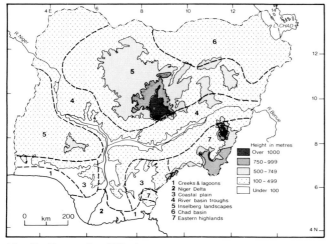

1.3   The Topography of Nigeria

The upland area of Hausaland is separated from the two other main upland areas of Nigeria, in the south-east and south-west of the country, by the Niger-Benue trough. (See Figure 1.3.) This trough is composed of sedimentary rocks laid down during the Lower Cretaceous period (Albian), in a long arm of the sea which followed the valleys of the Niger, Benue, Cross and Gongola rivers. The lowland runs from west to east across the country in a wide curving belt, merging with the lowland coastal region and mainland margins, south of the Benue and east of its confluence with the Niger. It is this trough which separates the Hausa of the northern highlands from the two powerful culture groups of the south, the Yorubas and the Igbos. The lowland area is noted for the prevalence of the tsetse fly and its hard covering of lateritic crust. For these reasons it is sparsely populated;[5] a contrast to the high densities associated with the highland zones of Nigeria.

Climate

Climate is an important factor in both the location and form of Hausa settlements. West Africa has a tropical climate with wet and dry seasons. It is characterized by broad east-west belts in which the duration of the seasons depend on proximity to the sea or the Sahara. Broadly speaking, the length of the rainy season decreases from south to north and the length of the dry season increases. Three main climatic patterns are distinguishable in Nigeria: tropical wet in the south-east, with uniformly high temperatures and heavy rainfall evenly distributed throughout the year; tropical wet and dry, or savanna, in the north and west: and dry steppe in the extreme north. The northern areas of Hausaland fall within the latter classification; its southerly fringes approximate more closely to savanna. (See Figure 1.4.)

The climate of Hausaland is influenced by two principal wind systems. From November to April the Harmattan, a hot, dry, north-easterly wind, brings dust from the Sahara, accompanied by high temperatures in the afternoon and low temperatures in the morning and at night. Low humidity and haze which may reduce visibility to less than half a mile are

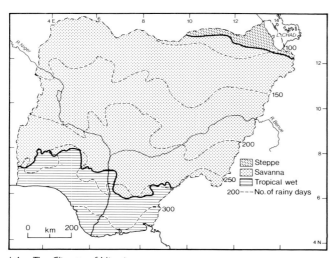

1.4   The Climate of Nigeria

characteristic of this time of year. It is the period for building, general maintenance and repair. From May to September, a south-westerly wind brings moist, warm air from the southern Atlantic Ocean. Most of the rain falls at this time of year and the humidity is high. Surface winds are generally light; in Kano, for example, 72 per cent of all air movement is below seven miles per hour. At times of high humidity, air movement through buildings is very important for bodily comfort. The only exception to this wind pattern is the occasional line squall which may reach speeds of up to 145km. per hour and can cause havoc to poorly constructed roofs. Line squalls occur mainly at the beginning and end of the rainy season.[6] (See Figure 1.5.)

The highest recorded air temperatures in Hausaland are normally in April; minimum air temperatures are usually recorded about December. (See Figure 1.6.) Mean maximum temperatures increase from the south to the north of Hausaland from about 95° to over 105°F; mean minimum temperatures, on the other hand, are fairly constant at about 60°F. Figure 1.6 illustrates the contrast in temperature regimes between Hausaland, which in general terms has a wide range of temperatures, and the southern regions of Nigeria, which do not exhibit the same variations.

Figure 1.5 shows the distribution of annual rainfall in Nigeria, which, broadly speaking, decreases with increasing distance from the coast. The rainfall in Hausaland varies from about 127 cm. per year in the south, to about 50cm. per year in the north. Such annual rainfall totals, however, have little meaning, the seasonal nature of precipitation being of greater significance. Figure 1.5 illustrates the seasonal pattern of rainfall in Nigeria and shows clearly that, with the exception of its southern fringes, the rainfall in Hausaland is confined to the wet season. Over the greater part of Hausaland there are five months without rain; along its southern borders there are only three or four such months.

It is evident, therefore, that despite wide variations from north to south, buildings in Hausaland must resolve the incompatible requirements of two broad climatic conditions: a hot humid climate and a hot dry climate. How the traditional

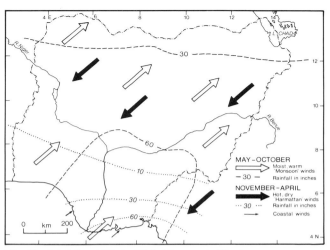

1.5 The Rainfall and Principal Wind Systems in Nigeria

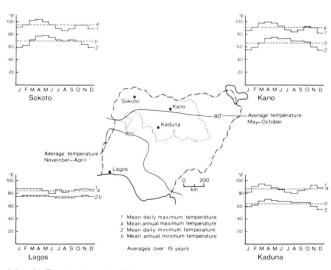

1.6 Air Temperatures in Nigeria

builder attempts to resolve these conflicting design requirements will be discussed later.

The climate necessitates the location of settlements close to the river systems; the main ones being the Sokoto and Kaduna which flow into the Niger, the Gongola which flows into the Benue and the Hadejia which drains into Lake Chad.[7] Population is concentrated close to these rivers and their tributaries or in areas with reliable sources of potable water during the dry months. Settlement in the region is by no means uniform, varying from densities as low as 20 persons per square km. in the 'middle belt', to over 160 persons per square km. close to Kano. This is explained to some extent by environmental differences within the region. Because the Hausa did not develop techniques for the storage of large quantities of water, and because 20.0m. is the maximum depth of traditional well digging techniques, permanent settlement is restricted to those areas where the water table is no lower than 20.0m. at the height of the dry season.

Although for part of the dry season many rivers are dry, water can be found close to the surface in their sandy beds. So it is not surprising that many major settlements are sited close to a river. For example, in Sokoto Province, Prothero found that between 75 and 85 per cent of the total population and all but three of the towns with populations of over 5,000 are located near rivers.[8] Although the average rainfall in all parts of the province is sufficient to support successful crop cultivation during the four-month wet season, its incidence is badly distributed throughout the year, making permanent settlement difficult. In the north and west there are good supplies of water in the perched aquifers of the sedimentary rocks, usually at a maximum depth of 15.0 m., and so within the range of traditional well-digging techniques. But this cannot be guaranteed to last the full dry season; hence there is shifting settlement, villages in the area being abandoned in the dry season. Water is even more difficult to find during the dry season in the southern and eastern parts of the province, where it occurs only sporadically in the older crystalline rocks, often masked by a thick covering of drift. In contrast, areas of Hausaland supporting high densities of population, such as the Kano close settled zone, have a plentiful supply of portable water. Here it is usual to find a high water table throughout the year with wells varying in depth between 4.5m. and 12.0m.[9] 12.000m.[9]

A comparison of the distribution of inselbergs and settlement sites in southern Hausaland suggest a link. Zaria and Kano, for instance, both ancient cities, are close to inselbergs. Kano encloses two prominent rocky outcrops within its walls; some smaller settlements stand at the foot of other similar formations, while inselbergs not associated with settlements today show evidence of earlier occupation. One reason why such sites have proved important for the location of settlements, is the modifying effect they have on local groundwater conditions. These large granite masses are capable of storing considerable quantities of rainwater, releasing it either in the form of springs at their base or by lifting the level of the water table in the surrounding area.[10]

A further factor limiting both the density and distribution of population is the location of fertile soils. On the whole, Hausaland is better endowed in this respect than neighbouring areas, being covered by a veneer of sandy drift derived from the north during a former encroachment of the desert.[11] The depth of this drift varies, but the texture of the soil becomes finer towards the south.

There are two main soil types in Hausaland, giving rise to two main crop systems. (See Figure 1.7.) In the Kano area, on the interfluves and less eroded valley sides are loose brown and orange soils (known as *jan kasa*) which support, among other crops, ground-nuts for the export market.[12] To the south, in the Zaria area, these red laterite soils are replaced by more fertile, blackish soils (*bakin kasa*), a product of the deeper, finer drift where cotton and tobacco are extensively grown.[13] In the valley floors of both areas are grey soils, of partly alluvial origin, with a high clay content and fine-grain structure. This lowland soil (*fadama*) is extensively cultivated throughout the year.

The different soil types in Hausaland have encouraged the growth of local trade: foodstuffs cross the line of soil change while trade flourishes between the major settlements such as

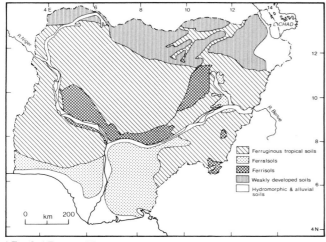

1.7 Soil Types in Nigeria

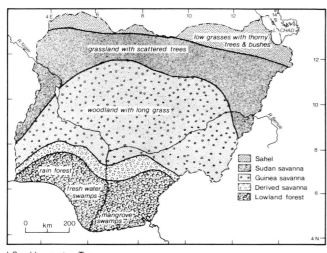

1.8 Vegetation Types

Kano and Zaria and their surrounding countrysides. Hausaland is one of the two major zones in Nigeria where the peasant economy is capable of producing a substantial agricultural surplus, a valuable national export. It is this economic activity, stimulated by a favourable environment, which has supported the development of densely settled communities.

Vegetation and Landscape

Hausa cities, towns and villages seem to grow organically from the sweeping savanna parkland, built from the laterite on which they stand, and using local vegetation as a source of materials for roofs and fences. They are in complete harmony with the environment. The ecological result of the interaction of climate, geological structure, topography, soils and drainage is a vegetation cover which is the base from which man develops his agricultural technology: a limiting factor in the development of settlement.

West African vegetation may be classified into a number of broad zones, which run in roughly parallel lines from east to west. The major climatic factors affecting this zoning are the variation in mean annual rainfall (which decreases with distance from the coast), and, consequently, the severity of the dry season. The resulting vegetation is a band of forest near the coast and broad bands of savanna, which become progressively drier northwards until the desert is reached.[14]

In Nigeria, as elsewhere in West Africa, man has radically changed the landscape. Although high forest forms the climax vegetation over most of the humid south, it has been extensively modified. Large areas of original forest have been destroyed and replaced by oil-palm bush. In the less humid northern fringes of the forest zone, abandoned fields have been invaded by grasses and fire-tolerant trees, resulting in a zone of derived savanna. (See Figure 1.8.) The northern limit of derived savanna is the probable climatic limit of high forest. Beyond this stretches the southern Guinea zone, the transition between forest and savanna. Transition woodland is the climax vegetation of this area, but it has been degraded by fire and farming into savanna woodland, with tussocky grasses 1.5 to 3.0m. high, and short-boled trees up to 15.0m. high.[15]

There are two main vegetation zones in Hausaland: the northern Guinea and the Sudan, with a zone of transition between them, running broadly east-west through northern Zaria Province. The climax vegetation of the northern Guinea zone is a western extension of the great *miombo* woodlands (*Isoberlinia-Brachystegia*) of East, Central and South tropical Africa. The well-developed woodland of this zone consists of broad-leaved trees from 9.0 to 12.0m. high, with crowns more or less touching, in places dense enough to cast deep shade that suppresses grass. As a result of extensive cultivation and grazing it is usual for the vegetation to be relatively open, with shorter grass than in the southern Guinea zone.

Land in the vicinity of towns and larger settlements is permanently cultivated and natural vegetation completely suppressed. Beyond the permanent farmland is a zone of low regrowth savanna which has been alternately cultivated for short periods, then grassed. Beyond this, if the settlements are far enough apart, is an area of open and very irregular savanna woodland.[16] For example, there are four concentric zones surrounding each smaller walled settlement (*gari*) in the Zaria area. Within the walls of the *gari*, land is cultivated on an annual basis, with heavy fertilization for garden crops. The innermost fields outside the walls receive regular manuring, being cultivated annually for grain crops and ground-nuts. Beyond this, land is cultivated for four years with a fifth year fallow. In the outlying bush are scattered, self-contained isolated farms. The fifth zone is a belt of *fadama*, following the valley floors, which in contrast to the surrounding upland soils can carry crops throughout the dry season using irrigation.

Close to Zaria the smaller *gari* settlements are more numerous; the zones of annually cultivated farmland merge into a greater zone centred on Zaria. This tendency towards a concentric arrangement of land use, based on a gradation from more to less intensive usage, is reminiscent of von Thunen's model of German settlement in the last century, being determined largely by transport costs; although in this instance, political security may also have been important. Areas close to the emirate city, *Birni*, being the safest, were also the most densely populated and most intensively farmed.[17]

Moving northwards, as the annual rainfall decreases and the dry season becomes longer, Guinea savannas give place to Sudan savannas. It has been suggested that the climax vegetation of this zone was probably similar to the *mutemwa* vegetation of Zimbabwe, consisting of larger emergent trees with open canopy, an understorey of deciduous shrubs, with little or no grass.[18] The natural vegetation has been modified as a result of many centuries of human occupation, the bush having been cleared and burnt for cultivation, hunting and cattle grazing. In the areas around larger settlements, such as Kano and Katsina, natural bush vegetation is almost completely absent, but trees for shade and fruit have been planted, including *Acacia albida Tamarrind indica* and *Butyrospermum parkii*. Natural vegetation occurs in areas remote from human settlement and marginal areas unfit for cultivation, yet even here grazing and bush fires restrict matured woodland to a few rocky areas, including forest reserves. Compared with the Guinea savanna, the grass in the Sudan savanna is shorter and more feathery, while the number of thorny plants, usually species of acacia, is greater. Trees of the small-leaved varieties are more numerous than the broad-leaved ones associated with the northern Guinea zone. An important species of tree here, which is used extensively for building purposes, is the dum palm (*Hyphaene thebaisa*), which occurs singly or in dense groves.

To the north of Hausaland, and beyond the Nigerian frontier, the climate becomes drier, and Sudan savanna is replaced by a broad zone of Sahel savanna. Typically, Sahel vegetation consists of open thorn savanna, with trees some 4.5 to 9.0m. high, short, sparse grass cover, and *Acacia seyal* forming almost pure stands in low-lying areas.[19]

The Heartland of the Hausa

The present heartland of the Hausa people is an area of Sudan savanna, one of the great east-west ecological zones of West Africa which run parallel to the coast. There are Hausa-speaking people to the north, in the Sahel zone just south of the Sahara, and important outlyers in the south, in areas such as Zaria which encroach into Guinea savanna.

To understand how the Hausa came to occupy their present territory we shall consider how environment has affected settlement patterns in West Africa as a whole.

Man and Environment

The tropical rain forest, which separates the inland areas of West Africa from the coast, inhibits dense human settlement. This was particularly true during man's early development, but even today large stretches of this zone are occupied by small populations. Where there are large populations at high densities, there are traditions of the people having moved into the area, replacing or absorbing indigenous, more primitive peoples. So it seems that the forest formerly provided a refuge for weaker peoples, giving some security against stronger, better organized groups from the grassland region.[20]

The Guinea savanna (immediately to the north of the high forest and derived savanna), in which lies the middle-belt of Nigeria, as was mentioned above, is noted for the prevalence of the tsetse fly and its hard covering of infertile, lateritic crust. Hence it is sparsely populated. Its rough and broken topography inhibited the movement of horse-riding invaders, and the hilly outcrops in the region were a refuge for weaker and more primitive groups. The Guinea savanna, today known as the 'middle belt' of West Africa, is occupied primarily by small groups of people who have remained relatively independent of mainstream development. In no other part of West Africa is there such extreme ethnic and linguistic fragmentation.[21]

Further north are the Sudan and Sahel savannas: areas of lower rainfall, shorter grasses and large, sweeping plains. It is possible that this zone is the birthplace of agriculture in Black Africa with major crops such as pearl millet, sorghum, cowpea, bambara ground-nut, calabash and cotton being domesticated here.[22] Hausaland lies in this area which, as was indicated above, is easily traversed and so open for conquest and large-scale state formation. Being relatively free from tsetse fly, it is the zone in West Africa most suitable for rearing the major beasts of burden. The horse, the donkey, goats and cattle were probably first introduced into this part of West Africa from Asia, via Egypt, in the early neolithic period at a time when agriculture was beginning to develop.[23]

It was in the Sudan-Sahel region that the first large West African states were formed, made possible by the horse, and later the camel, which allowed owners to conquer, rule and police large areas of land. However, it was the cattle, the smaller livestock and the development of agricultural technology that ensured the concentration of sufficient people to make urban and then state government possible.

The climate and vegetation of West Africa have not always been as they are today. In prehistoric times the Sahara may have passed through several dry and humid cycles.[24] The last humid period, when the vegetation of the Sahara was more steppe than desert, occurred during the Quaternary. Concurrent with the closing phases of the last ice age in Europe there was a gradual change in the Sahara; its present dry climate was established several thousand years before the Roman period. Since that time human activities rather than climatic change have been the most potent factor in altering the environment of West Africa.[25] It is the destruction and neglect of man, not the lessening rainfall, which has caused desiccation since Roman times. Overgrazing, over-cultivation and the loss of centralized authority resulting in the collapse of dams, aqueducts and defensive walls, all contributed to the encroachment of the Sahara on to previously rich and fertile lands. These momentous ecological changes may have been one of the causes which stimulated population movements into the Sudan-Sahel regions, so triggering the changes in Sudanic society which resulted in the foundation of the great West African empires.

2. The Evolution of Settlement

West African Prehistory

The Sahara may not have been an insuperable obstacle at any time, but from about 3000 BC onwards it began its final desiccation. From then until the camel became common, West Africa lost contact with the Nile and was unable to derive any benefit from the Bronze Age civilization in Egypt. (See Figure 2.1.) The area was virtually isolated and West Africa entered the mainstream of development with the introduction of iron smelting.

Iron smelting in West Africa is associated with the Nok culture which probably flourished in an area to the south of Jos Plateau from about 500 BC to AD 200. It is possible that it was a West African development, but more likely that it spread into the area either from the kingdom of Kush—which lasted for nearly a thousand years in the area of the great bend of the Nile south of Dongola—or from Carthage in the north. According to Shaw: 'It seems probable on present evidence that the knowledge of iron metallurgy reached West Africa, not from Meroe as has often been proposed, but from the area of Carthaginian influence in North Africa.'[1]

The introduction of iron smelting and the agricultural revolution which preceded it were both significant developments in the prehistory of West Africa. It is known that the Nok people possessed the knowledge of iron-working which enabled them to make tools to increase agricultural productivity and weapons to subjugate neighbouring communities. There is little evidence of the Nok people after AD 200 and it is not known where they went nor who supplanted them. Yet despite our lack of knowledge of this formative period in the development of the political organizations and administrative systems necessary to support the growth of large states, it is evident that their development was made possible because of the spread of iron technology throughout West Africa. The possession of the horse and camel provided the necessary mobility for policing large territories. However, the key to the whole process of urbanization was the development of the organizing ability to gather agricultural surplus into a few key centres.

Urban development in West Africa

Two models have been put forward to explain the social process that led to the first urban revolution in West Africa. One explains state formation as a result of largely external influences, the other in terms of the development of indigenous traditions. The first is called the Hamitic hypothesis and suggests that the process by which the great Sudanic empires evolved was stimulated by invasions of Arabs and Berbers from the north who brought with them the military skills and social disciplines of the mobile band. This view places the formative influence for state building with non-Negro desert people who themselves had been in close contact with centres of higher culture. In contrast the role of the indigenous and sedentary farming population is seen very much as that of a junior partner, wholly passive during these momentous social changes.[2]

The alternative and more reasonable explanation is based on the hypothesis that stateless societies, which define their solidarity by co-residence on a clearly defined tract of land, rather than by a genealogical link, contain in their cultural systems the germs from which state organization can develop. Stateless societies of this type which still survive in West Africa are of two variants: either they are dispersed, or the settlement pattern has clotted into large compact villages. In

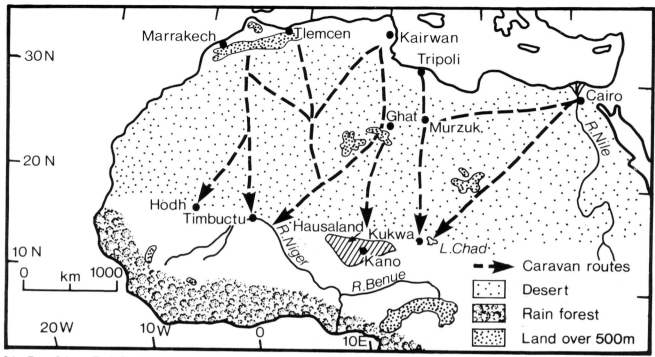

2.1 *Trans-Saharan Trade Routes*

both variants the important principles of political organization are co-residence on common territory and submission to the laws sanctioned by the spirit of the land. These ideas are very close to the concept of sovereignty and to a body of laws to which all comers are automatically subject. The first occupants of the defined territory have a closer and more intimate relationship with the land than late comers which provides for a potential differentiation between royal and non-royal lineages. The main lineages, too, are complementary to each other; different lineages performing different functions for the community, which may be seen as a direct link to the political, administrative and economic specialization found in urban communities.[3]

The Hamitic hypothesis is based mainly on legends that depict white strangers coming from the north and founding great states. It may be argued that this evidence is fragmentary and ambiguous, and was recorded by Arab chroniclers many years after the events. It might also be said that it was prepared by writers trying to explain their own dominant role in West Africa, and was later interpreted by European scholars to show that all institutions of value in West Africa were introduced by non-Negro invaders. In other words, the Hamitic hypothesis is ethnocentric.[4]

The process of state formation can no longer be regarded as the grafting of complex political structures on to a previously simple rustic society, by a more progressive group. Yet there is evidence of outside intervention in West African affairs which cannot be ignored. For example, in the Nile valley and North

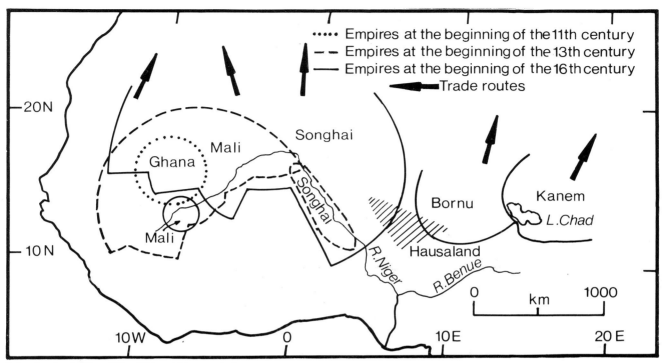

2.2 *Empires in West Africa (11th to 16th centuries)*

Africa there were a series of high cultures; and there has been contact across the Sahara over many centuries.[5] The scale and efficiency of government in some of the early states at some stages of their evolution may have been due in part to literate Muslim chamberlains from north of the Sahara.[6] Nevertheless indigenous traditions appear to have been more important in state development and trans-Saharan influences were of lesser significance.

The Growth of States in West Africa

The early years of the first millennium AD may have been the period in which some rural communities in West Africa began to emerge as urban settlements, stimulated by the possibilities of trade across the Sahara with North Africa, and by the grow-

ing need to aggregate into walled defensive settlements as a precaution against the pressures of marauding desert peoples. This implosion of people and the growth of commerce may well have provided the sparks which triggered off the political changes resulting in the growth of a succession of mighty empires in the West African Sudan.

The succession of empires which rose and fell in the Sudan between the fourth and the nineteenth centuries AD established their capitals at the terminus of one of the great trans-Saharan trade routes. (See Figure 2.2.) Until the coming of the European to West Africa and the opening up of trade along the coast, all trade and all culture contact for the West African Sudan was via the routes across the Sahara. To the west of Hausaland, at the northern bend of the River Niger, was centred a succession

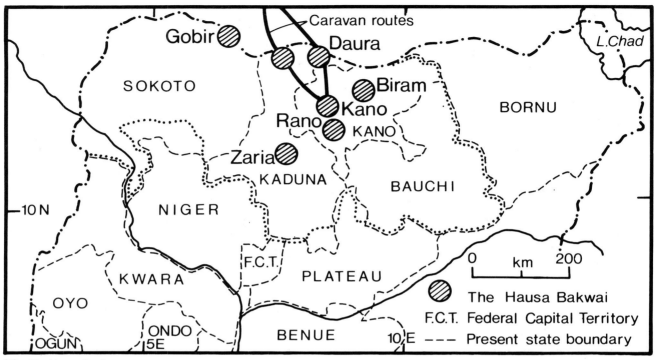

2.3 *The Hausa City States*

of empires: Ghana, Mali and Songhay,[1] which were in close contact with and influenced by Morocco and Algeria. To the east of Hausaland was the equally powerful state of Kanem-Bornu, centred on Lake Chad, whose trade routes gave it close connections with Tunisia.[8]

The Hausa City States

In the savanna land between the great northern bend of the Niger and Lake Chad were founded the Hausa city states. (See Figure 2.3.) A legend of unknown antiquity, current in the southern part of Hausaland, suggests that a group of seven related states, the *Hausa bakwai* (the Hausa seven), were founded by a common family.[9] According to this legend a man named Bayejida came to Daura, where he killed a snake that

had long prevented people drawing water from a well; he then married the Queen of Daura and became the new ruler. Biram, a son of Bayejida, was founder of Garun-Gabas near modern Hadejia, and Bawo, another son, was father of the remaining founders: Gazaura in Daura, Kumaiyu in Katsina, Baganda in Kano, Zamagari in Rano, Gunguma in Zazzau (Zaria) and Duma in Gobir.

The Bayejida legend has been interpreted as evidence of the invasion of Hausaland by politically organized warrior folk from the north who subjugated the indigenous tribes and imposed on them a new structure of government which provided the impetus for urbanization.[10] While there is evidence of population movements into Hausaland, and this legend may indicate structural changes in society and the replacement of a matriarchal system by a patriarchal one, the legend is disputed by the folklore of Gobir which disassociates its dynasty from the sons of Bawo. Until the fifteenth century the centre of Gobir was at a considerable distance to the north of the territory of the other six, and it did not come into contact with them until the end of that century. Kano, Katsina, Zazzau, and Gobir are the only states mentioned in the legend which may be described as powerful; the remaining three played little or no role in interstate relations before the nineteenth century. In addition, the Bayejida tradition mentions an earlier dynasty at Daura, and a powerful pre-Bayejida dynasty at Kano which ruled over a large area of surrounding territory. State formation and urban settlement in Hausaland, therefore, probably pre-date the Bayejida invasion. The formation of the Hausa city may, in fact, be due to causes other than or in addition to the invasion of powerful groups.[11]

For an understanding of the institutions of present Hausa society and the development of technology we must first trace the great climatic changes that have affected the environment in which these developments occurred. 20,000 years ago present day Hausaland, and the area immediately north of it, as far as the Azben Plateau, was a swell of land traversed by rivers flowing either south-east from Azben to Chad, or from the watershed stretching between Azben to the Jos Plateau south-west to the Niger. During this early period, the upland area is believed to have supported a parkland flora merging into denser vegetation in the south-west. (See Figure 2.4.) To the east of this region, at this time, stretched the Mega Chad, a vast expanse of water stretching from Bilma and Gashua in Nigeria to the foothills of Tibesti.[12]

The Mega Chad may have remained full until about 3000 BC, but the climate had already started to change dramatically from a warm humid one to its present hot dry state. It is impossible to trace the desiccation in detail, but over a period of about 7,000 years the great Chad dried up, leaving the present shallow lake. The dense vegetation of the southern edge of the region retreated, leaving the present Guinea Savanna, and the northern half of the region suffered extreme dessication to produce what is now known as the great erg of

2.4 *The extent of the Mega Chad (after Grove and Warren)*

Tenere, a desert of sand dunes stretching from Agades into the Jurab depression.[13]

The new regional pattern affected human settlement in several ways. Firstly, there developed a large stretch of country, Azben-Borku-Chad, which was practically uninhabitable. Secondly, there was a thinning out of population in the northern part of the region, in the territory to the west of the great erg, and as a consequence of this, a concentration of population in the southern part of the region. This population movement to some extent corroborates Hausa legends which suggest ancient migrations from this direction. Thirdly, a barrier to human contact was formed between the territories to the east and west of Lake Chad. It consisted of the great erg to the north of Lake Chad, Lake Chad itself, and the swampland to the south of the lake. Until the fifteenth century, therefore, independent states developed separately on either side of Chad: the great state of Kanem to the east and the Hausa states to the west. The area to the west (present day Hausaland and Bornu) is linguistically homogeneous, being occupied by people speaking Chadic languages. To the east, people speak Teda-Daza languages, to the south, Niger-Congo languages (perhaps as a result of a southern movement of Niger-Congo speaking peoples in face of an invasion of northerners). The desiccation of the Sahara may therefore be seen as having produced a concentration of Chadic-speaking people to the west of Lake Chad, a settlement pattern that emerged somewhere between the last millennium BC and the first millennium AD.[14]

The origins of the Chadic-speaking people are unknown, but by the early centuries of this millennium their greatest population concentration was established on the well watered areas around the Gulbin-Kebbi and its tributaries, and on the newly formed lands left by the retreat of the Mega Chad. The population movements left the Hausa-speaking community in the west of the region—in an area bounded roughly by a line running from Azben southwards as far as the north-eastern corner of the Jos highlands; and from there, westwards to the great bend of the Kaduna River, then north-west to the valley of the Gulbin-Kebbi and north-eastwards to Azben. The remaining area, between Hausaland and Lake Chad, is occupied by other Chadic-speaking peoples, including the Bolewa, the Ngizim, the Manga, the Margi, the Buduma and the Kotoko.

Organization of the pre-Urban Hausa

In the period between the desiccation of the northern part of Hausaland and the rise of cities, *birane* (s. *birni*), Hausa people probably lived in small agricultural communities known as *kauyuka* or *unguwoyi* (s. *kauye, unguwa*).[15] According to Abdullahi Smith these early communities were likely to have been independent family groups practising communal shifting cultivation, but unlike the present close-settled zones of Kano and Zaria, the nucleated groups were separated by uncultivated land (*daji*).[16] Political authority was vested in the family heads (*masu gida* s.; *mai gida* pl.); communal agrarian pursuits were organized by the *sarkin noma*, king of farming; *sarkin ruwa*, the water-king and *urban farauta*, father of hunting.

Yet even at this time it is possible that Hausa society did not consist entirely of such small hamlets and may have supported larger settlements, market centres where trade and other non-agricultural pursuits were practised. Trade and the introduction of iron smelting in the early part of the first millennium AD would have stimulated the growth of such centres, so that before the formation of states, the picture is one of settlements of various sizes scattered throughout Hausaland, some devoted entirely to agriculture, others having markets and workshops. In those favourable locations where the *unguwoyi* clustered to form towns, *garuruwa* (s. *gari*), political authority came to be vested in *sarkin gari*, king of the town. All settlements, however, were politically quite independent of each other.

When the *sarkin gari* extended his authority over substantial territory beyond the immediate town and its lands, including other *garuruwa*, he became *sarkin kasa*, king of the country; his citadel, *birni*, took on new physical dimensions, matching the growing political power. The social and political revolution by which a system of very small and mutually independent political units was replaced by a much smaller number of larger units, some with governmental and organizational functions, probably occurred in the early centuries of this millennium. The evidence indicates that the movement towards statehood did not proceed uniformly over the whole region, but that it occurred earlier in the south. It seems too that in some places the process was a lengthy one; in Kano, for example, it took two hundred years of conflict to establish the state government. Some states and their capital cities failed to achieve a permanent government; others, such as Rano, appear to have lost their political independence, and to have been absorbed within the sphere of influence of a neighbouring state, which in the case of Rano was Kano.[17]

The new capital city differed from earlier types of settlement in several ways. First, it was a cosmopolitan centre: a place, which because of some special feature of its location, attracted foreigners of diverse origins who had no kinship ties with the indigenous population or with each other.

Secondly, it was heavily fortified, being surrounded by a wall and ditch. Thirdly, behind the protection of its defences, it developed into the seat of a new kind of political power, which it exercised over the population in surrounding dependent lands. This political power was managed by a complicated local government consisting of a hierarchy of officials with specialized functions. The plain of Zazzau is a good example of the process of state building, for here two ancient cities, *birane*, have been identified: one at Kufena, adjacent to present day Zaria, and one at Turunku (34km. south of Zaria). Both settlements appear to have been in existence during the fifteenth century; both covered extensive areas, each having great defensive walls encircling the largest inselbergs on the plain. At the end of the fifteenth century, Bakwa, the ruler of Turunku, siezed power at Kufena, and Turunku *birni* ceased to be an independent centre. The kings of Zazzau who now ruled the territories of Kufena and Turunku moved the capital to a new citadel at the eastern end of the *birni* of Kufena, calling it 'Zaria' after a daughter of Bakwa.

It is not possible to say with certainty what conditions facilitated the dynastic change at Zazzau. However, traditions in Kano allege that *Sarkin* Kano Kanajejidan Yaji, who ruled early in the fifteenth century, fought and defeated *Sarkin* Zazzau, killing him at Gadz, then occupying the town of Kufena for eight months. This destruction of government in northern Zazzau may have given Bakwa of Turunku the opportunity to move to Kufena. The change in dynasty, whatever the cause, heralded a new era of development in Zazzau. The next three centuries saw the final stage in the evolution of the socio-political structure of the state, paralleling developments in other parts of Hausaland.

The extent of the authority of Bakwa, *Sarkin* Zazzau, his descendents and the kings of the other great *birane* of Hausaland was dependent upon the support of those who wielded power in the subordinate *gararuwa*. The monarchy was supported by, and in return supported, in feudal relationship, a ruling class of office-holders, *masu sarauta*, possessing territorial fiefs. The most powerful members of the ruling class were *galadima, wambai, dallatu* and *madawaki*—the chief

public officers and advisers of the *sarkin*. Of these, the most powerful were the *galadima* and the *madawaki*, both of whom controlled a group of junior fief-holders. There were other fief-holders, including the *dangaladima* (heir apparent to the throne), and *sarauniya* (a daughter of the *sarkin*), and the *iya* (a wife of the *sarkin*'s father). Important groups of government officials in the administration of the state were the Islamic office-holders (*malamai*) and the slave-officials (*baya sarki*). Outside the office-holding lineages and royal families, the *masu sarauta*, were the peasants, *talakawa*, largely indifferent to politics so long as they were permitted to pursue their livelihoods in peaceful conditions. The authority of the *sarkin* lay in the support of the office-holders, the rulers of the ordinary people. Even the choice of a new king from among the competing claimants was decided by the *galadima, madawaki* and *limamin juma*, chief of the order of *malamai*, and was a reflection of the distribution of power among the fief-holding class.[18]

This feudal hierarchy of fief-holding rulers is reflected in the settlement pattern. The *birni* was at the top of the scale, the *sarkin* at its centre; wards of the *birni* were controlled by important office-holders, while *garauwa* and *unguwoyi* were held by lesser fief-holders on their own behalf or on behalf of a higher power. The whole pattern was one of political and territorial dependence; territorial organization being based upon the local chieftainship of community units.

Settlement pattern was strongly influenced by the need for water, good farming land and defence, the result being a compact distribution of population within walled towns. Each walled town was surrounded by smaller satellite settlements owing their allegiance to the village chief of the area, who in turn paid allegiance to the *sarkin*, or to him through one of his close advisers. M.G. Smith suggests that in Zaria the towns were strung out along the principal caravan routes. However, the availability of water was of the first importance and the caravan routes were probably considerably influenced by this factor. It is likely that they connected good watering places around which markets grew.

At the centre of this web of influence the *sarkin* was obliged continually to seek means to maintain power. This was achieved by further conquest of territory and by developing the capital city as a centre of commerce under his control. The wealth so generated could be used to pay for the loyalty of clients. For example, from the sixteenth to the eighteenth centuries the kings of Zazzau constantly expanded southwards until the influence of Zaria was extended over a vast area as far as the Niger-Benue rivers. A popular folk story in Hausaland is of Amina, daughter of a ruler of Zazzau, renowned as a lover, warrior, builder of great defensive structures, and for making Zazzau the most powerful of the Hausa states.

> Strange things have happened in the history of the seven Hausa states and the most strange of these is the extent of the possessions which God gave to Aminatu, daughter of the ruler of Zazzau. She waged war in the Hausa lands and took them all, so that the men of Katsina and the men of Kano brought her tribute. She made war in Bauchi and against the other towns of the south and the west, so that her possessions stretched down to the shores of the sea (i.e. the Niger).[19]

The slave raids provided people to farm the lands in the central state, and an entry for southerners into the ruling class; a number of great *sarauta*, of the state in Zazzau, for example, became posts held exclusively by slaves (eunuchs) from the south who dominated government through their power in the southern territories. According to M.G. Smith the chief method of capital investment open to the noblemen of Hausaland during the nineteenth century was the buying of slaves and their employment as farm labourers on the family lands (*gandu*).[20] The slaves, for the purposes of organization and also for their protection, were settled on the family lands in small walled villages (*rinji*). They were permitted to marry and were allocated land which could be farmed during free time. (See Figure 2.5.) The slave villages, *rinji*, were sited where water was plentiful and land fertile. Bassawa, a slave village belonging to the Mallawa family of Zaria, was sited close to a tributary of the River Gulma and close to areas of *fadama*. The walls of the settlement which were standing in 1963 can still be traced. They were probably 6 to 9m. high, and would have presented an attacker with considerable difficulty.

Religion and Early Settlements

The importance of religious factors in the early development of Hausa cities is difficult to determine precisely, although some of these cities were established close to the rocky outcrops which were the dwelling places of the spirits, *iskoki*. It is hardly surprising that the inselbergs, the great 'black hills' of central Hausaland, strategically dominating the landscape and having a constant water supply, should take on a religious significance and attract settlers from the surrounding country-side. For example, the abandoned city of Turunku was located at Dutsen-Turunku and Kano at Dutsen-Dala. In the immediate vicinity of Zaria there are three such inselbergs: Kufena Hill (710m.); Tukur Tukur (710m.), and Madarkaci Hill (693m.), once enclosed by a single wall. An old legend tells of the hills being occupied by three *iskoki*, who ate from a common bowl placed between them. Mardarkaci is named after Madara who was asked by the other spirits, '*Madara ka-ci?*'—'Do you want to eat Madara?'.[21]

The development of the city states from the fourteenth century onwards is closely connected with the progressive Islamization of the people. The spread of Islam appears to have taken the form of a gradual modification of the ancient religion of the Hausawa, centred on a high god, *Ubangiji*, who did not interfere in the day to day affairs of men. The direction of human affairs was thought to be through the agency of supernatural forces, or spirits, the *iskoki* of the inselbergs. The maintenance of the correct relationship with the spirits, of whom there were many thousands, was left to the *mai-gida* in each compound; the *sarkin noma* and *sarkin ruwa* for agricultural rituals, and the kings themselves on behalf of the state. There was also a priest class, *bokaye*, skilled in contacting the spirits (*bori* in this condition), who would speak through them. This religious structure with its strong emphasis on ritual, both supported and was part of the political organization of Hausaland; it is, indeed, still practised by the Magazuwa, a non-Islamic Hausa group, and underlies current Islamic traditions.[22]

2.5   *Aerial photograph of Bassawa*

The Growth of Islam

Islam seems to have taken the form of a gradual modification of the old beliefs of the Magazuwa; *Ubangiji* having greater significance in the affairs of man than the *iskoki* who were relegated to the harmless position of jinn. In political terms, the *bokaye* came to share power with the Islamic *malamai* the *sarkin* occupying the position of leader of both groups.

During the early centuries of Islam, the Hausa appear to have had little or no contact across the Sahara with North Africa. In both Katsina and Kano the introduction of Islam is traditionally associated with the eastward migration from the Upper Niger of a people called the Wangarawa some time in the last half of the fourteenth century. It seems likely, therefore, that early contact of the Hausa states with more advanced cultures in North Africa was via the Western Sudan.[23] The ancient kingdoms of Ghana and Mali had close contacts with Islamic areas in North Africa, and indeed their main cities had Islamic quarters from early times. Many rulers of the ancient kingdoms made pilgrimages to Mecca, but for students of West African architecture the most important pilgrimage was made by Mansa Musa, the ruler of Mali from 1312 until 1337.

Musa returned from Mecca bringing with him many Muslim scholars, one of whom was a poet and an architect, Abu-Ishaq al-Sahili, who was reputed to have introduced burnt brick architecture into the Sudan and also to have built great mosques at Gao and Timbuktu.[24] Islam has greatly affected many aspects of Hausa culture, and architecture is no exception. Imported ideas in the field of building design and construction have progressively changed the indigenous architecture of the Hausa to one more suited to the arid climate of the Sahara. During the formative years of city development in Hausaland North African architectural practices came to the region from a secondary source in the Western Sudan, but how far these ideas had penetrated Hausa building practice by the fifteenth century is not known.

It was not until the late fifteenth century that Islam began to spread rapidly throughout Hausaland. Its spread is associated with Muhammad Korau of Katsina, Muhammad Rabbo of Zazzau and Muhammad Rumfa of Kano, all of whom ruled their respected territories for about twenty-five years at the end of the fifteenth century. It was during their reigns that important changes occurred in the organization and structure of the Hausa community, whereby Islam was institutionalized and affected state government. For example, Muhammad Rumfa governed according to Islamic law, consulted with the Islamic jurist Muhammad b'Abd al-Karim al-Maghili who wrote a treatise for him on the art of government.[25] Al-Maghili then settled in Kano and established there a Muslim community of North Africans. Under the influence of al-Maghili, Muhammad Rumfa made changes to his governmental structure, built mosques in the city and established his own seat of government in the form of a *qasba* outside the walls of the old city. At this time, too, the office of *sarkin* acquired the form of a sultanate in Katsina, Kano and Zazzau, with a class of *'ulama* emerging as patrons of the emir. In addition to social changes in the city this period saw the start of Islamization of the countryside.

Towards the end of the fifteenth century important political changes were also taking place in the north-east of Hausaland. A Tuareg sultanate was established at Agades in the traditional homeland of the Gobirawa which resulted in a southward movement of this important Hausa people until they occupied their present location.

During the sixteenth century Hausaland lay between the two powerful empires of Songhay to the west and Bornu to the east. Bornu, after a century of fratricidal succession struggles by Mai Ali Gaji and his descendants, established a new capital at Ngazargamu (Birnin Bornu), on the banks of the river Yo, to the west of Lake Chad.[26] The homeland of the Songhay people stretched from Dendi, through Kukiya to Goa along both sides of the River Niger, so that the centre of the empire which replaced Ghana and Mali was closer to Hausaland than either of its predecessors. Consequently the Hausa states were under the influence of Songhay for the first part of the sixteenth century, but after this time Kebbi, one of the *banza bakwai* (upstart, or bastard Hausa states), broke free and became a buffer between Hausaland and the Songhay empire.[27] Katsina and Kano, two of the most important Hausa states of the time, entered a period of major economic and military growth, and until the middle of the seventeenth century were constantly at war with each other. From the time of the Moroccan invasion of the Songhay empire in the late sixteenth and seventeenth centuries, trade was diverted from the western to the central Saharan caravan route, and the Hausa states prospered, Katsina and Kano becoming important West African cities.[28]

The growing prosperity of the region stimulated competition for the control of the central Saharan trade routes, and also for larger shares in the profits of this trade. In the seventeenth and eighteenth centuries there was growing conflict among the main contenders for control of the savanna lands west of Lake Chad. These years saw wars between the growing power of the Tuareg sultanate centred at Agades in the north, the Bornu empire, now centred to the west of Lake Chad at Ngazargamu, the older established Hausa states and the ring of 'upstart' Hausa states to the south and south-west of the heartland of the Hausa. For most of the seventeenth and eighteenth centuries, the Hausa states, particularly Kano, were under the hegemony of the more powerful Bornu. Bornu's influence in Hausaland varied from time to time but was never completely dominant. The many bitter conflicts in Hausaland at this time were symptomatic of the move towards ever larger states, which was the main theme of the period.[29]

One of the dominant themes of Hausa history is closely related to the problems of state building, partly to guarantee the safety of individual polities and partly for economic reasons. Important too in this process were the developing religious institutions and the contact and fusion of different groups and sub-cultures. It is impossible to reconstruct the details of many of the major developments, but two elements were the spread of Islam and the immigration in large numbers of the Fulani people into Hausaland.

The Fulani are now scattered throughout West Africa and number about six million. Although their origins are unknown, they are now a clear ethnic group whose expansion is thought to date from the twelfth and thirteenth centuries when they spread eastwards across the Sudan, probably taking over at first only the lands not suitable for agriculture on which they maintained their herds. Many sedentary Fulani accompanied the migration of their kinsmen, and it was this group who tended to be sophisticated in political matters, learned in Islamic law and intolerant of the infidel. During the seventeenth and eighteenth centuries there was an increasing migration of Fulani into Hausaland, some of the newcomers even holding important posts in the governments of the Hausa states. This group of learned Fulani, under the leadership of Uthman dan Fodio, declared a jihad or holy war against the traditional Habe rulers of Hausaland in 1804. Within a decade the Hausa states were united into a Fulani empire, ruled by a series of Fulani emirs paying temporal and spiritual allegiance to the *Sarkin Musulmi* in the new capital at Sokoto.[30]

The Jihad

The jihad of the early nineteenth century saw a consolidation of Islam as the force permeating government, law and administration. The jihad resulted in the old Habe ruling dynasties in the main Hausa states being replaced by a new ruling elite, the Fulani. Though Islamized, the state government retained its old forms, many of the titles and functions of the offices remaining the same. The same feudal territorial system was in force, and followers of the new regime took over the lands and the roles of the dispossessed. The process of Islamization introduced many social and institutional reforms to a previously *laissez-faire* system of government, in which injustices and oppression had alienated the Hausa peasants and small traders, and which had relegated the Fulani to the role of second class citizens. The new administration and overall control of Hausaland did much to increase internal security and, in consequence, the volume of trade.

An important consequence of the jihad of Sheikh Uthman dan Fodio was the creation of the Sokoto caliphate in which all the emirs (*sarki*) paid allegiance to the Amir al-Mu'minin of Sokoto. According to Adeleye, 'the most significant result of the creation of the Sokoto Caliphate was the supra-ethnic ethos which the Islamic ideology of the *Umma* brought to the fore as the strongest agency for large-scale political integration'.[31]

Constant wars with neighbouring states changing territorial boundaries and Sokoto's extending influence were all features of the caliphate in the nineteenth century. Pre-jihad Hausa, Habe administrative structure and territorial organization remained largely unchanged, with the need for retaining the highly nucleated and easily defended settlement system. New *ribats*, or walled towns, were built along the frontiers of the Sokoto empire as armed bases and rallying points. The *ribat* was introduced into Hausaland by Muhammad Bello, son of Uthman dan Fodio, and was based on the strongholds established by the Arabs in the conquests of Syria and North Africa. Two such *ribats* were Sokoto and Wurno which acted alternately as the capital of the caliphate until the British occupation of Nigeria, when Sokoto became the main spiritual centre of the caliphate and the residence of the Amir-al-Mu'minin.[32]

Bauchi and Yola were cities founded by flag-bearers of Uthman dan Fodio in areas where no major urban centre had previously existed. Both cities are evidence of the expansionist policies of the caliphate during the nineteenth century. To this day most of the population of Yola still speak Fulfulde, while in Bauchi many city-dwellers also speak Fulfulde.

The occupation of Nigeria in this century by the British and their adoption of a policy of indirect rule tended to strengthen the power of the Fulani ruling classes of Hausaland. Independent Nigeria's regional pattern of government gave these traditional rulers greater power over provinces they had only marginally influenced since the jihad. Recent revisions to these regional boundaries follow more closely the pattern of ethnic groupings.

Population dispersal

A constant theme of this chapter has been the need for defence in the location of settlements, resulting in a highly nucleated and hierarchical pattern ranging from *gararuwa* to *birni*, the great walled city and last refuge for the countryside. The effect of the unsettled times was noted by Barth who travelled in the area during the last century; he found many parts of the region depopulated, and settlements, both large and small, abandoned and falling into ruin.[33] The nucleated pattern is evident today, but with peaceful conditions this century the need to live in fortified settlements is no longer necessary, and in some areas there has been a general dispersal of population.

Re-orientation of trade towards the coast

An important change in West Africa in this century has been its orientation away from the Sahara towards the coastal trade routes. Whereas Hausa trade was formerly with North Africa, via the Saharan camel routes, today it is with Western Europe, via Lagos and the coast. This has had far-reaching effects on human settlement in Hausaland. Settlements on the new trade routes have acquired an added importance, and the change in mode of transport from camel to train and lorry has increased efficiency and brought changes to the economy.

Kano, for years the railhead and main collecting and distributing centre for the north has expanded more rapidly than other cities. Its growth has necessitated a greater production of food, which in turn requires not only additional farmland, but more efficient means of farming. The manures for increased agricultural production are provided by the city's waste material, and McDonnell, writing in 1964, suggested that Kano had reached the technological limit of its agricultural system, which is dependent on donkey transport to bring manure from the city to the farm and to take crops back from the farm to the city.[34] The mushrooming of population in the Kano area which is proceeding despite McDonnell's warning is the most remarkable feature of the changes in population patterns. It is due mainly to the adaptation of the environment to suit the growing needs of a great city which developed initially from an admirable location.

The railway line brought trade to those settlements through which it passed, giving towns like Zaria and Gusau added importance as centres of the regions they serve. These towns were thus favoured with a greater prospect of growth. Zaria has become the main centre in the north for learning, having such institutions as Ahmadu Bello University and several large schools and colleges; Gusau is a focal area for economic development. Those settlements not connected directly to the coast by rail or metalled roads have declined and stagnated. For example, Katsina's fall from being one of the great trading cities of West Africa in the seventeenth and eighteenth centuries with its own seat of Islamic learning to its present rather sleepy position in the backwater of development, started with its stiff resistance to the jihad and was completed with the building of the railway to Kano.[35]

New settlements like Kaduna, one time capital of the north, and primarily an administrative centre; and Jos, which has grown up around the tin mines, are important railway junctions. They were founded by the British and are outside the scope of this work, but their detailed layouts are an interesting contrast to the traditional Hausa settlements.

Conclusion

The Hausa states emerged as a result of, first, revolutions in agriculture and iron smelting, and secondly, the population movements from the north to Hausaland which, in turn, caused the pressures that led to the development of strongly fortified centres. The communities thus gathered within highly nucleated settlements were further encouraged to develop complex political and administrative structures of city and state government by the expanding trans-Saharan trading connections. While these structures were forming, that is, between the last centuries of the first millennium AD and the first centuries of this millennium, Hausaland was polarized between the powerful states to its east and west.

However, because of the great distances from the heartland to the western states, and because they were effectively cut off from the Kanuri empire of Kanem by Lake Chad, the Hausa states developed for long periods in relative isolation from their powerful neighbours. On sites with a plentiful water supply, good agricultural land nearby and a defensive position, which are imbued with ancient religious meaning, the Hausa have built great fortified mud cities, dominating a landscape of smaller dependent settlements. The territorial organization closely mirrors, and is mirrored by, the political and religious structures of the Hausa community, enabling them to take advantage of the inherent qualities of the environment.

28   HAUSA ARCHITECTURE

3. The Structure of Hausa Settlements

Introduction

The Daura legend tells of the Hausa *bakwai*, the seven city states of Daura, Gurum-Gabas, Katsina, Kano, Rano, Gobir and Zaria, allegedly founded by a common family.[1] Each state was said to have a special duty. Gobir, on the fringe of the desert, was the outpost guarding Hausaland against attack from the north; Zaria, to the south, was the slave-raider, providing the group with slaves; Daura and Katsina were occupied with trade, while Kano and Rano were industrial centres.[2] Kano, Katsina, Zaria and Gobir became powerful, the other three played little or no role in interstate relations.[3] After the jihad (holy war) of Uthman Dan Fodio in the first decade of the nineteenth century, additional caliphate cities were established; the important ones being Sokoto and Wurno, twin capitals of the caliphate, and Bauchi and Yola.[4] The displaced Habe rulers of Gobir, Kano and Katsina fled after the jihad establishing cities at Maradi, Tsibiri, Tessawa, Madawa and Sabon Birni in the present territory of the Niger Republic. The deposed habe *sarki* of Zaria, Makau, moved south to Abuja and established his capital there.[5]

The fortunes of the Hausa cities have waxed and waned through the centuries, but since British occupation and independence it is those linked to the new transport networks which have flourished. Kano is by far the largest Hausa city, and in 1963 had a population of about 300,000. It is now (1985) the regional economic centre with a population in excess of one million. Zaria, as an important educational centre, had a population of 166,000 in 1963, and now has an estimated population of 250,000. Both Katsina and Sokoto had populations of about 90,000 in 1963, while at the other end of the scale are Wurno with 23,000 and Daura with 20,000.[6]

The cities of Hausaland share common features. In the centre is the old walled city inhabited by the Hausa and Fulani. Surrounding this are a number of well defined 'strangers' quarters inhabited by Nigerians from other parts of the country and by people of other nationalities. Zaria is typical of such cities, comprising *birnin* Zaria, the home of the true citizens of Zaria, and colonial and post-colonial suburbs outside the city walls. (See Figure 3.1.) The main areas outside the walls are the Government Reservation Area (G.R.A.), planned as the seat of colonial administration and the residential area for British administrators; the commercial area; *Sabon Gari* (new town), for non-Hausa Nigerians; *Tudun Wada* (hill of wealth), an area for Muslim strangers, and *Samaru* which has grown as a residential area for the university. In Zaria the suburban quarters are physically separated from each other and from *birnin* Zaria by topographical elements; the barriers between the quarters being the city wall, the railway track, the river and the remains of the landscaped building-free zones.[7] Each sector or quarter has its own centre and its own architectural character; the settlement as a whole resembles a cluster of independent urban centres rather than a single unit.

Similar patterns of development are exhibited in other cities. Kano, for example, consists of the old city, *Fagge*, a district occupied by Arabs, Tuaregs and Lebanese, as well as Hausa and Fulani; a British colonial town with numerous physically separated functional elements including *Tudun Wada* for Muslim Northerners (i.e. Nigerians) and *Sabon Gari* for other Nigerians. (See Figure 3.2.)

The 'strangers' quarter, an area set aside for non-natives, is found in many West African settlements, even small Asanti villages have their *zongo* area, and Ibadan, one of the largest settlements in West Africa, has a Hausa village and a Nupe

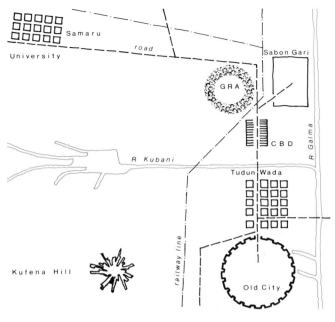

3.1 *Greater Zaria*

village which, although parts of the city, are communities in their own right. The source of this sub-division of African settlements into an area for residents and an area for strangers (usually outside the walls) is lost in antiquity. Barth, travelling in the last century, made notes and sketches of settlements of two communities formed in this way.[8] El Bekri, describing the ancient capital of Ghana in the eleventh century, also wrote of a town consisting of two parts, in this case, six miles apart.[9] According to him, the basis of the division of the capital was religion: the Muslims occupied one sector, the non-Muslims the other. The non-Muslim sector was the oldest part of the town and seat of government; the Muslim sector was a later addition and may have developed from a simple strangers' quarter.

Urvoy has suggested that the Zaghawa, a nomadic desert tribe who conquered the people of the Chad area, ruled their subjects from camps sited outside the main settlement.[10] There is no evidence to support this theory, but the usual division of West African settlements into areas for residents and strangers may well be rooted in the traditional system of land tenure. Traditionally, Hausa, in common with most West African peoples, have no concept of 'ownership' of land, in the Western sense. They enjoy only usufructuary rights to the land they farm: all land belongs ultimately to the community and alienation of land is not on a permanent basis.[11]

The site of a settlement may or may not have been chosen for the fertility of the soil in its immediate surroundings, but by its very proximity the area close to the settlement has special value, being intensively used for agricultural purposes and heavily fertilized with local waste material. Usually all the land close to a settlement is used by the local inhabitants and not available for temporay alienation to outsiders. As the distance from the settlement increases, so there is more land not in use which, although strictly still the community's property, is not 'owned' and is therefore available for use by outsiders. Apart from the benefit to the community in the reduction of friction between foreigners and local people because of their physical separation, this means that the strangers establish themselves close to their newly-acquired land. This results in the creation of a sub-settlement a short distance from the main settlement.

The underlying reasons for the division of Hausa settlements, including the *birni*, into areas for different communities may have been present from early times, but the polynucleated form of today is due mainly to later influences. When Barth visited the area in the nineteenth century, conditions were unsettled and he noted Hausa settlements containing strangers' quarters within the walls.[12] Yet even then communities were segregated, for within each settlement were separate quarters for the ruling Fulani, the subject Habe, and Arabs and other strangers. It would seem that the building of suburban areas outside old cities like Zaria and Kano is due largely to the imprint of colonial rule, the administration conveniently following natural trends. Lugard's policy of indirect rule which emphasized maintaining established traditions and

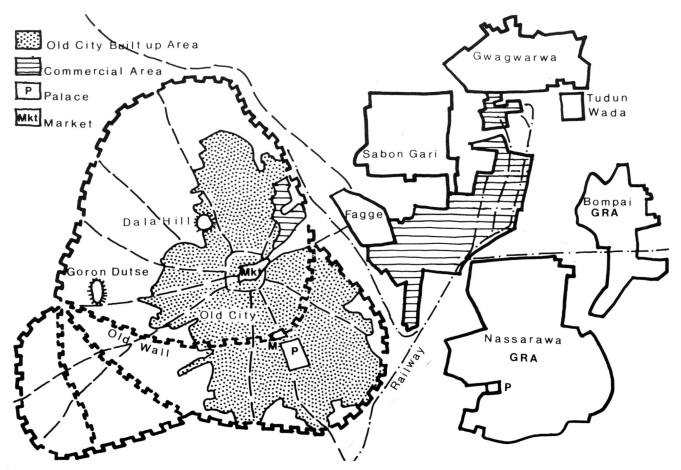

3.2 *Greater Kano (after Urquhart)*

non-interference with Muslim settlements, was an important factor in the evolution of the present structure, particularly the larger Hausa settlements, the emirate cities.[13]

The effects of the changes in the economy of Hausaland which have taken place this century can be seen most clearly in developments outside the walls of the old cities. For it is here that the railway, the new suburbs, the commercial and administrative areas and the educational establishments have been sited. It is here too, outside the walls of the cities, that most population growth has occurred. In contrast, the old walled cities remained in a cultural backwater until the end of colonial rule and independence, and appear to have been in virtually the same condition then as they were prior to colonization. Since the 1960s changes have been caused by the acceptance of new technology: the use of concrete-block construction and the ubiquitous tin roof, the installation of piped water to some properties and, above all, by the effect of providing access for the car. It is the incorporation of such technological innovations into an otherwise conservative and traditional society that is of extreme interest to the planner and architect. This process of acculturation whereby a society changes is of the utmost importance to those attempting to control and direct physical changes in the environment.

General description of the Old City: *Birni*

Surrounding the old city, or *birni*, are the remains of the city walls, *ganuwa*, which even in ruined condition give a clear picture of what was formerly an impressive defensive structure. (See Figure 3.3.) In 1904 Sir Frederick Lugard estimated that there were forty walled towns within a 48km. radius of Kano, and a total of one hundred and seventy in the whole of the province of Northern Nigeria.[14] Barth commented upon the size and scale of the defensive structures of Kano,[15] which consisted of a mud wall 9 to 12m. high surmounted by a battlement; in places it had two moats and an encircling road on the outer face. The wall is approximately 16km. in circumference; it now has thirteen historic gates and three recent ones. This formidable wall was described in 1885 by Paul Staudinger, a German traveller:

At no other town in Hausaland have I seen a similar fortification. These smooth clay walls probably twenty metres high, flanked by a protective moat approximately fifteen metres deep, as well as the formidable and sinister gate-house, called forth an almost uncanny feeling in the traveller who had to trust himself within them.[16]

3.3 *The Kano wall*

3.4 Birnin *Zaria*

Now the great fortified structures are fast disappearing, being
used as a quarry for building materials or, since maintenance
has ceased, eroding naturally in the rainy season and returning
to the lateritic plain from which they were raised. In Kano and
Zaria, however, it is still possible to imagine the grandeur of
this remarkable pre-industrial, earth-moving enterprise.

The main routes from the once heavily fortified city gates
pass through a broad belt of agricultural land to either of the
twin focal points in the city—the market, centre of commercial
life and the *dendal*, the main civic, religious and ceremonial
focus. (See Figure 3.4.) At the edge of the *dendal* are the emir's
palace, the main city mosque and the administrative buildings.
The *dendal* and market are within the residential area which is
encircled by agricultural land and the city wall. The residential
area breaks down into wards, *ungugoyi*, which are sometimes
associated with a particular gateway and usually occupied by a
group of people practising the same trade. (See Figure 3.5.) The
focal point of the ward is the home of the ward head, a small
neighbourhood mosque and possibly a street market. The
wards are made up of groups of family compounds whose
members share a common ancestor and a communal open
space onto which the compound doors open. The family
compounds are connected by pathways to the market, civic
and religious centre and the gateways.

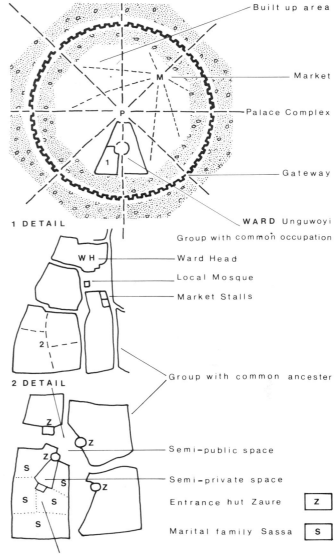

EXTENDED FAMILY COMPOUND

3.5 *Structure of the Old City*

The development of City form in Hausaland

Before colonial rule and the current process of modernization, there were two main influences on Hausa settlements: the indigenous, or Habe traditions and those of Islam and North Africa. It would be an oversimplification to assume that Islamic and North African traditions in city planning were introduced with or since the jihad: the ideas of Islam have been incorporated slowly into Hausa culture over many generations, and this is probably true of city building too. The process of Islamization was not uniform throughout the Hausa-speaking region, nor did it affect all aspects of culture to the same degree: society in the emirate cities was most influenced by the ideas of Islam; the rural areas often remained outside these mainstream developments.[17]

City planning before the jihad

An understanding of the present form and structure of Habe–Hausa cities like Kano and Zaria, as distinct from caliphate cities like Sokoto, is incomplete without a recognition of the effect of earlier, non-Islamic traditions of spatial organization. Three sources of information throw light on these traditions. The rural Hausa among whom Islamic ways have not penetrated deeply, particularly the Magazuwa, the pagan Hausa; the urban forms used by the Hausa people who fled north after the jihad and who now occupy the Mardi Valley in the Republic of Niger, and the evidence from the ancient Hausa settlements themselves, complicated as it may be by developments which post date the jihad.

The holy war of Uthman dan Fodio was wholly successful in the Hausa states now in the Federal Republic of Nigeria. But in the northern part of Hausaland the Fulani conquest met stiff resistance. The deposed rulers of Gobir, Katsina and Kano and their followers settled as refugees in the wooded valley of Maradi, and with the *Sarakin* Anna they built armed bases in Maradi, Tsibiri, Tessawa, Madawa and Sabon Birni. From here they and their descendants carried on a war of reconquest which was finally rendered impossible by the colonial subdivision of the territory; the area occupied by the older Habe-Hausa being allocated to the French and the Fulani-Hausa states to the British.

As a result, the more ancient elements of Hausa culture have been preserved in Niger. Here too, Islamization has made recent progress, but pre-Islamic practices persist in the courts of the rulers and in the bush hamlets: the people have retained the traits and characteristics of ancient Hausa culture alongside practices resulting from Islamic influences. For example, in 1945 the French administration moved the sites of the capitals of the rulers of Katsina and Gobir from areas liable to flooding to high land. Although the new areas were laid out by an engineer the inhabitants insisted on superimposing their ancient sacred plans on the European ones, claiming that theirs constituted the most efficacious defence against all the evils threatening them, such as epidemics, thieves or malevolent acts of gods and sorcerers.[18] It is the rights and symbolism associated with these ancient beliefs which may have influenced the structure and built form of Hausa cities in Northern Nigeria.

In traditional Hausa society the layouts of fields, houses, granaries and towns are governed by an ancient cosmology which regulates numerous facets of daily life. This ritual for structuring space exists side by side with later symbolism inherited from the Arabs and Islam. Nicolas has found that, to the majority of the inhabitants of the Maradi valley, each important activity is an occasion for a preliminary ritual, more or less exclusive to the activity in question, and designed to set limits to it. An activity may only be undertaken in a limited and defined space protected from the malevolent spirits which inhabit the world. This space when defined correctly and orientated within a precise schema becomes the domain of favourable forces.[19]

The critical points of the Hausa spatial schema are on a boundary defined by the cardinal points, axes which run east-west, north-south, north-west-south-east and north-east-south-west. At the centre point, where these axes meet, is a vertical axis linking heaven and earth at that space. This geometrical schema and its variations stem from a view of man and his relationship to the cosmos. (See Figure 3.6.).

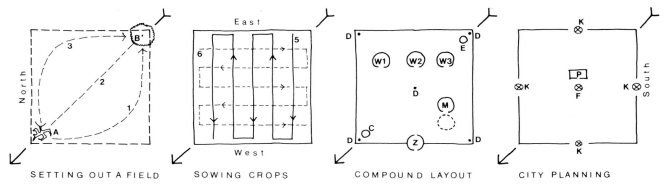

| SETTING OUT A FIELD | SOWING CROPS | COMPOUND LAYOUT | CITY PLANNING |

3.6   *Hausa Spatial Schema*

In Hausa mythology the eastern and southern cardinal points are masculine, the western and northern ones are feminine. In ritual these cardinal points become personified; for example, when sacrificing, the priest invokes the gods: 'You, East, South, West, North, sons of Dodo', sometimes varying the formula to: 'Sons of the East, sons of the South, sons of the West, sons of the North', as though addressing a common father, 'Dodo', and four children. By nature every being is situated facing east. He is born into the world facing east, enters his home facing east and makes sacrifices facing east. He is surrounded by four beings or groups of beings: male in front of him and to his right; female to his left and behind him. His strong sides, the front and right, are male and his weak sides, the left and rear, are female. Thus every being on earth seems to be surrounded by four beings or groups of beings, linked like the four arches of the dome which dominates Hausa building, by a celestial main point at the crossing of the arches.

Every being and all the space surrounding him is divided into four equal spheres or domains, each of which belongs to one of the four major 'spatial owners'. The four spatial zones are not comprised of the axes which join east to west and north to south, but by those formed by the bisectors of the right angles which they form in cutting each other at the centre point of the space, that is, by the north-west-south-east and the north-east-south-west axes.

The four major spaces are divided into two sexual components: east and south are male; west and north are female. Certain couplings of the spaces are permitted and others forbidden. The relationship between the cardinal points is experienced as a matrimonial alliance: the line linking north-east and south-west being a line of sexual exclusion, the axes joining north with south and east with west being the coupling or copulating axes. Space in traditional Hausa cosmology appears to be a field of convergent and divergent forces which maintain an equilibrium between the four elements. In setting out a field, a house, a market or a city, the Hausa, through geometrical ritual, attempt to maintain this delicate balance with the forces of the cosmos.

Most Hausa fields are square or rectangular, the important axis facing northwest–southeast. The ritual for setting out new fields is clearly described by Nicolas, while Polly Hill's study of rural Hausa provides additional evidence for a rectangular field system.[20] According to Nicolas, crops are sown in a rectangular pattern: where millet and sorghum are planted together in the same field they are sown in rows at right angles to each other. Millet, because of the phallic shape of the seed, is thought to be a masculine crop, and is sown in an east-west direction; sorghum, a feminine plant, is sown in a north-south direction. The field thus resembles a piece of weaving, the warp and weft interlacing. After such a 'marriage' the millet and sorghum become fertile.

In Niger the traditional Hausa compound, unlike its Muslim counterpart in Nigeria, is laid out like the field in a quadrilateral arrangement, according to the four cardinal points. In order to establish a new dwelling, the head of the household (*maigida*) buries five pots containing charms (*magunguna*), one each at the four cardinal points and in the centre of the site which is then surrounded by a boundary wall. Each adult member of the family arranges his own hut within the compound, the entrance facing west so that entry to the hut is eastwards. Houses of the spouses of each man are arranged in a line along a north-south axis: the first wife has the house to the north, and the last, the one to the south. This physical arrangement reflects the social hierarchy of the wives: the first wife (*matar jari*) is the mistress of the house (*uwal gida*) and is often called the 'woman of the north' (*matar arwa*).

When in 1945 the French administration moved the capitals of Katsina and Gobir, the local inhabitants superimposed their own cosmic structure upon the plans of the engineer, insisting that nobody entering the hidden doors could pass unseen by his pursuers. In both capitals, the principal rites consisted in anchoring the new settlement into the supernatural structure by placing the centres of sacred energy in the five nerve-centres of the traditional plan. Charms and talismen were buried at the four doors sited at the cardinal points and at the centre of these axes where the ruler's palace is located. These rites have not been practised in the Islamic layout of towns in Nigeria since the jihad, yet the present form of such settlements may hark back to this ancient tradition.

The Hausa market is a place of social importance, where people meet and crowds gather. In pre-Islamic tradition, to draw crowds is a magical operation which manifests the power and influence of the community. The market remains the preferred abode of the gods even when deserted by people: it is a place where blood, the exclusive nourishment of the *iskoki*, is constantly spilt by the butchers, therefore the founding of a market and abattoir cannot be effectively carried out without the blessing of the gods. The market is located outside the walls of the settlement and orientated to the cardinal points in similar fashion to the other main elements of the settlement.

Determining the extent to which Hausa cities in Nigeria have been influenced by earlier, non-Islamic traditions presents several difficulties. Since the jihad in the early nineteenth century, the Hausa in Nigeria have been more thoroughly Islamized than their northerly cousins in Niger, for one of the aims of the jihad was the purification of society, and former practices often no longer persist—at least overtly. The growth and influence of Islam has proceeded more quickly and thoroughly in urban centres, the forms of settlement now being considered. Since the early nineteenth century the Hausa settlements have been resited, replanned or extensively modified, outlines of the former settlements being difficult to trace accurately from earth remains. It should be remembered that it is unusual for model settlement forms to be implemented in their entirety. Practical considerations such as existing development, land ownership patterns, inaccuracies in survey techniques, and land form make the implementation of a model difficult; and the organic nature of the material from which the settlements are built lends itself to a constantly evolving and changing urban pattern. The model solution is likely to be a general aim, achieved in part and for limited periods only.

Pre-Islamic planning in Zaria

Urquhart has tried to apply the Habe–Hausa or pre-jihad urban model to the settlements in the area of *birnin* Zaria, and was particularly concerned with just one walled enclosure. He found that the Madarkaci enclosure, 'which is smaller than and roughly concentric with the present city wall, corresponds closely to the ideal plan for Hausa town foundations as described by Nicolas'.[21] However, any definitive conclusion about the structuring of the plan form of urban centres located in the Kufena region where *birnin* Zaria now stands must await evidence of the date of each of the great walls clearly shown on aerial photographs, some of which can be traced on the ground.

3.7 *Ancient Walls*, Birnin *Zaria (after Urquhart)*

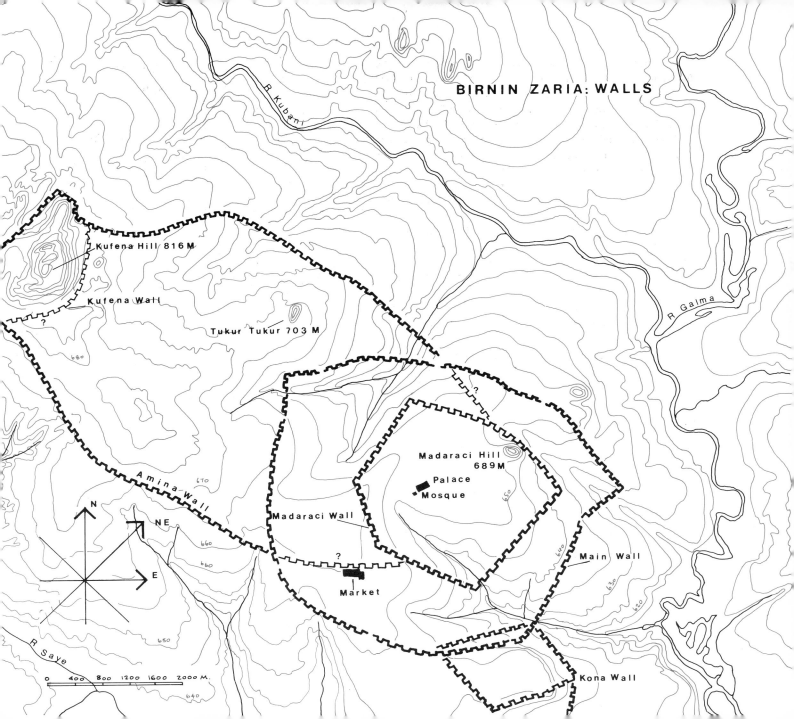

BIRNIN ZARIA: WALLS

Kufena Hill 816M

Kufena Wall

Tukur Tukur 703 M

Amina Wall

Madaraci Hill
689M

Palace
Mosque

Madaraci Wall

Main Wall

Market

Kona Wall

R Kubani

R Galma

R Saye

N
NE
E

0 400 800 1200 1600 2000 M.

Within the area between Kufena hill and the Rivers Galma, Saye and Kubani, several walled villages, towns and cities have existed for many generations. (See Figure 3.7.) Defensive structures have been built around the base of Kufena and around the hill at Tukur Tukur; another encircled the present emir's palace, and the Madarkaci wall encircled that hill. The Kona wall; the Amina wall around Kufena and Madarkaci hills, and the present Zaria main wall were all part of the defences. The 'Amina' wall and the present Zaria main wall are the two most easily seen on the ground, the present city wall having been maintained within living memory.

Making due allowance for practical considerations such as land form, drainage patterns and the difficulties of setting out large areas using primitive surveying techniques, the walls in the Kufena region approximate more closely to rectangular than curvilinear form. A further remarkable similarity between the group of enclosures is their general orientation, with an emphasis on the north-west–south-east and south-west–north-east axes. The Kona wall, which at first sight appears to vary from the other enclosures, has its diagonals along these axes.

According to Smith, 'Presently preserved traditions say that the oldest Islamic quarter in the city is the *unguwa* of Kona, lying outside Bakwa's citadel but inside the later wall'.[22] No buildings associated with the Kona enclosure exist, but he believes that this may have been a settlement of Kanuri immigrants from Bornu, for the Imam of the community is said to have been usually of Bornuan extraction. The early history of Islam in Zazzau is obscure; from the fifteenth century the *sarki* may have been muslim, but the first effective teaching of Islam in the area could well have been pursued by the Imams of Kona. Kona town, outside the walls of the main citadel, may have been a Muslim settlement established in the eighteenth century under the growing influence in Zazzau of the Islamic state of Bornu. This could account in some measure for the difference in the outline of Kona from the native settlements of the region.

Urquhart has shown that lines connecting the probable positions of the most northerly and the most southerly gateways and the eastern and western gateways of the

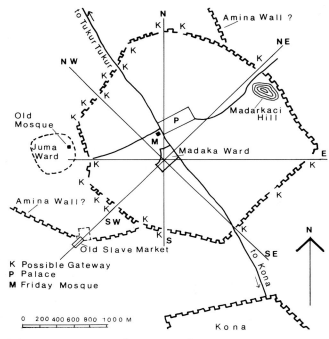

3.8 *Axial Planning: Zaria (after Urquhart)*

Madarkaci wall intersect in Madaka ward where the presumed family who founded the settlement lived. (See Figure 3.8.) Furthermore, the north-west–south-east and the south-west–north-east axes through this central point also cross the perimeter wall at points of probable gateways. The remains of the walls of a former palace and the present emir's compound face on to the road from Kona to Tukur Tukur, passing through the south-east gateway and crossing the rocky outcrop in front of the emir's palace which is still the site of traditional dances. Another interesting point of similarity between development patterns within Madarkaci wall and the findings of Nicolas is the orientation in a northeast–southwest or southeast–northwest direction of many of the pathways and boundary walls in the Madaka ward.[23]

3.9 *Aerial photograph, Palace area Zaria*

There is no evidence about the date of the building of the Madarkaci wall, nor of its builder. But it is possible it was built by Bakwa, the *sarki* who defeated the Kufena and moved his capital from Turunku to Zaria in about 1536. Later, as Zaria's importance and power grew, the 'Amina' wall was constructed to contain Kufena, Tukur Tukur and the Madarkaci walls. This wall is associated locally with Amina, daughter of Turunku Bakwa and famed as a great lover, warrior and wall-builder. Her sister, Zaria, is said to be the namesake of the Habe capital of Zazzau, Zaria. This story of the two queens may be a legendary account of the consolidation of several settlements and groups into one major city state, the predecessor of present-day Zaria.[24] If it is an accurate representation of events then it is easy to imagine the difficulty of integrating the diverse elements, built by different groups at different times, into a unified, idealized cosmic model: the result was more likely to be the compromise which is the fate of most exercises in planning and development.

Sometime in the seventeenth or eighteenth century the commercial centre of the city moved from Madaka ward to a point just outside the walls by the south-west gateway, on the north-east-south-west axis. Here, as Nicolas's research would suggest, a slave market and execution point were established. The market has grown in influence and importance and is now the main market in the old city. It has been absorbed within the latest city wall.

The present city walls of Zaria were probably built before the jihad and reinforced by Malam Musa the first Muslim sarki installed by the Shehu after the jihad. (See Figure 3.7.) Malam Musa moved the administrative quarter from the Juma ward to its present location, granting lands to Fulani jihadist families and settling slaves on land adjacent to the palace. Many compounds built in this period are orientated in the same direction as the palace. (See Figure 3.9.)

Pre-Islamic City planning: Conclusion

An examination of other Nigerian Hausa cities indicates that they are more irregular than Nicolas suggests. (See Figure 3.10.) This may result from a free interpretation of the ideal cosmic pattern which has been adapted to suit individual sites, and also from the techniques used for setting out boundaries as described by Nicolas:

This ceremony is called 'The opening of the bush'. When it is completed the cultivators get started. For example, a villager from Bakawa leaves his village early in the morning reciting the following prayer: "Kure, you go before me, Lead me to a place where I can find nourishment so that I may eat and feed other men." He goes to an uncultivated place. He then turns towards the southeast and says: "I thank the gods, I came to the bush for food . . . Here is a sacrifice from our stock for clearing the field." He kills a red bull, an offering to the god of millet (*kure*). He then plants a dry tree in the place he is standing, goes from there towards the southeast and plants a green tree wherever he thinks appropriate. He comes back towards a point in the northwest and begins clearing the site to be cultivated, beginning his work from the right, that is, towards the southwest until he reaches the little tree planted in the southeast. From there he returns in a straight line towards the *magarya* (Jubejube tree, also utmost extension) of the northwest and renews his clearance operation in the opposite direction. From the southeast finally, he comes back towards the northwest by way of the northeast. The cleared area forms a quadrilateral, the northwest–southeast forming a diagonal.[25]

Houses, markets and towns were no doubt laid out in a similar manner, although greater care may have been taken in some cases. Zaria is the traditional home of the great builders of Hausaland, and techniques in that city state may have reached greater perfection.

However, it must be remembered that the application of axes and regulating lines to a city layout after the event and without accompanying documentary evidence can only be speculation. Yet the little, planned slave settlement (*rinji*) of Bassawa follows the idealized model very closely. Perhaps on virgin territory such as this, where the Mallawa family settled slaves to farm their land, it was possible to approximate more closely to the traditional geometry. Even here, however, the river and important *fadama* land significantly modified the rectangular layout. (See Figure 2.5.)

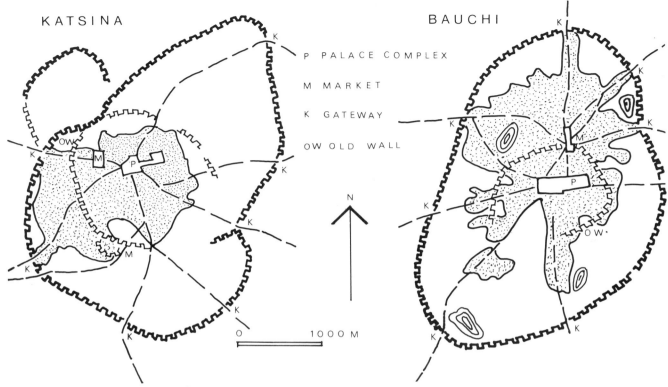

KATSINA   BAUCHI

P PALACE COMPLEX

M MARKET

K GATEWAY

OW OLD WALL

N

O _____ 1000 M

3.10 *Katsina and Bauchi (after Urquhart)*

Islamic influence on City structure

The major cause of change to the physical structure of the city, since the early nineteenth century and until recent times, has undoubtedly been the growth of Islam. Islamization has given rise to another concept of space which, fortunately, coincides to some extent with the traditional Hausa perspective. The important orientation for Hausa Muslims is east, towards Mecca the Holy City. This coincides with one of the major traditional axes used for structuring the Hausa physical world. But Islam has introduced other concepts of space and its use, including purdah, family privacy, public gatherings for prayer and processions associated with Islamic festivals. These later spatial concepts overlay the traditional geometry, in some cases concealing it.

The people of Hausaland are predominantly Muslim, but as Trimingham has shown, Islam is in effect a veneer overlaying a basic animism.[26] The culture of the people has been further modified through contact with the West, but although these three cultural heritages can and do fuse in various ways to affect different aspects of the physical environment to a greater or a lesser extent, the urban populations of the emirate cities in particular, tend to practice the purer forms of Islam. It is in these emirate cities, particularly those caliphate cities founded after the jihad, that we would expect to find the greatest influence of Islam on built form.

To the Muslim, religion means law and community, and governs all facets of his life and relationships. The five daily prayers are important features of the Muslim day, and although private prayers are acceptable, community worship at the local or neighbourhood mosques is favoured. The day is structured for worship and local community gatherings; the week is ordered around the Friday prayers at the Friday Mosque (*Masallacin Jumma'a*), when the larger community of the city is gathered together. The enthusiasm for Friday prayers may be due in part to the fact that they are based on a direct command in the Koran, but they are also seen as a symbol of Muslim solidarity and an important state occasion. At the times of the greater and lesser *sallas* (*Id-El Fitr* and Ramadan), all the active male members of the community gather for celebrations outside the emir's palace. The ultimate show of community solidarity is at the time of *haji*, the pilgrimage to Mecca, centre of the Muslim world.

This religious structuring of time, emphasizing as it does community solidarity, is clearly reflected in the spatial organization of the Hausa city. In the emirate cities there is a hierarchy of spaces for worship and community gatherings. Womenfolk and menfolk unable to attend a mosque carry out their devotions in the privacy of the home. Men sit, meet and talk to neighbours and passers-by outside the entrances to their homes: sometimes a group of such entrances defines a communal gathering place. At important locations in the city structure, perhaps outside the entrance to the home of the ward or district head, are outdoor praying areas and the neighbourhood mosque where the menfolk from the neighbour-hood gather for daily prayers. At a higher level in this spatial hierarchy is the Friday Mosque (*Masallacin Juma'a*) and its surrounding walled space which is entered through screened ablution chambers. The main city mosque is usually placed near the emir's palace and is the gathering place for the whole community on a weekly basis. (See Figure 3.5.)

Finally, at the head of the spatial sequence in the city structure is the *dendal*, a vast area in front of the emir's palace and adjacent to the Friday Mosque, which together with the prayerground outside the walls of the city acts as a gathering

place during important festivals. At times of the annual Muslim festivals the menfolk from the city and surrounding dependent towns and villages gather at the *dendal* in a show of allegiance to the emir. In Zaria, for example, on the day of the *salla* the emir and his followers process on horseback to his family (*katsinawa*) prayerground outside the walls to the north of the city. The procession continues from the northern gate around the walls to the *kofa kuyambana*, the southwesterly gate, and from there back along a northeasterly route to the *dendal* and the palace. Two days after *salla* there is a further procession: this time along the north–south axis to the main gate of the city in the south, *kofa gayan*, the old slave gate. From this gate the procession proceeds outside the walls to *kofa kuyambana*, then on to the market and back to the *dendal* and the palace. The routes of these processions follow the pre-Islamic pattern for setting out areas for farming or settlement and may be the remnants of Habe tradition. It is interesting to note that the *dendal* in Zaria itself lies between the outcrop of rock used for traditional dancing and the Friday Mosque.

At the top of this Islamic spatial scale in Hausaland is Sokoto, birthplace of the jihad and one of the twin capitals established by Uthman Dan Fodio and his son Bello. It is the

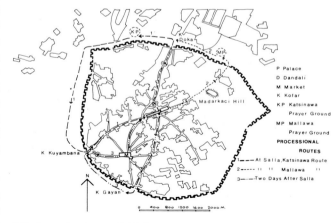

3.11 *Processional routes in Zaria*

present religious centre of the Caliphate to which emirs and officials from the city states journey to show allegiance to the *saradauna* of Sokoto, the spiritual head of the caliphate. Finally, pilgrimage to Mecca, to which all Muslims aspire at least once in a lifetime, is the final rung in this spatial ladder, symbolizing a religious life based upon community and ritual.

Commercial Structure of the Hausa City

In addition to satisfying spiritual and symbolic needs, the Hausa city developed at the centre of a vast commercial web connecting its rural hinterland to other emirate cities and to far-off commercial centres across the Sahara. Important factors in the growth of the *birni* were the industrial wealth of the black hills around which many such cities grew; the agricultural wealth of the hinterland, and the exploitation of the slave trade. To those who controlled the local community which produced it, this wealth gave the ability to prevent the emergence of rival centres of power; thus boosting the further centralization of wealth and power. Riches, and consequently power, depend to a certain degree upon the control of external trade. The function of the main walls around the city was mainly defensive, but they were also a means of controlling trade. As Smith points out, 'the greatest of kings of Kano, Muhammad Rumfa, was not only a wall-builder but also the founder of the great city market—*Kasuwa Kurmi*.[27]

The city walls were probably as important in peacetime as in war for they allowed the control of trade and collection of taxes by the *sarkin kofa* (chief of the gate) at each of the city gates, which were closed at night.[28] Under the protection of both the wall and the *sarki*, Zaria, for example, became 'a huge market of local inter-gari and town-countryside trade . . . fitting into the network of markets by which goods were distributed'.[29] This control of commercial activities in that city is no doubt the reason for the description of Zaria people as '*Kiffin Rijia*'— fish contained in a well.[30] The dominance of the present market in Zaria old city is documented by Davies: it is one of the three main markets of greater Zaria which between them bring to the Local Authority a total fee over one hundred times larger than any other market within about 65km. of the city.[31]

At some stage the market in Zaria moved from the Madaka ward within the old Madarkaci wall to a point south-west of the city and outside the walls. Sometime in the seventeenth or eighteenth century the town was doubled in area and new walls built to include sufficient land for the growing population. The town may have been extended to include the new and thriving market, bringing it under the closer control of the *sarki*. The symbolic significance of his control is still recognized in the processional route through this market taken by the *sarkin* Zazzau at times of *salla*. The extension of the city in this southerly direction has given Zaria city its present dual focus of market, palace and mosque: a city of two centres, one commercial, the other spiritual, with the *sarki* as the administrator and leader of both.

Superimposed on the ancient Habe axial order relating the community to the cosmos, which itself was subject to change and development over time, particularly in its adaptation to Islam, is the commercial life of the city which follows its own dictates of spatial organization. Close to the market, population densities tend to be much higher than in the rest of the city. At this point in the city structure all roads radiate from the market; here too are the wards associated with trading— dyeing, weaving and so on. The distinction between the commercial and the spiritual centres is most marked in Zaria, but the city with a dual nucleus is common throughout Hausaland.

Detailed Morphology of the Residential Areas

The palace, the Friday Mosque and the market are deeply embedded within the total structure of the city. There are no sharp distinctions between functions in the built-up areas of the settlements, a fact emphasized by the visual unity of the total urban scene, which, even in the recent past, was due to the almost total reliance on one material, mud, for building purposes, and to the repetition in all buildings of similar shapes, details and components. The introduction of the ubiquitous tin roof has not destroyed the unity, although in the last twenty years this has been the innovation which has

3.12 *Kano from the Minaret*

most changed the appearance of the emirate cities. The general appearance of greenness associated with Zaria, for example, has been further emphasized by the building of schools with large playing-fields within the walled settlements.

Within the apparently formless complex of buildings inside the city walls (see Figure 3.12), there is a definite pattern of development based upon the social, administrative and economic organization of the Hausa people. The Hausa city is broken down into wards (*unguwoyi*, pl. *unguwa*, s.), often associated with a particular city gateway. (See Figure 3.13.)

The people living in each ward usually have something in common: they may belong to a particular guild and have the same occupation, such as dyeing, weaving or smithing; or they may have ties of class, such as membership of one of the ruling Fulani families. (See Figure 3.5.) In Zaria, for example, the city's ruling families from which the emirs are selected are grouped closed to the palace in Kwarbai ward; the houses were founded at the same time as the new palace was built.[32] (See Figure 3.9.) Each ward is further subdivided into units of three or four compounds, all members of which are descended from

3.13 *Market and dye pits*

a recent common ancestor. At the centre of the ward is the home of the ward head who may be one of the emir's office bearers.

The Babban Gwani ward in Zaria city is typical of such wards. (See Figure 3.14.) It is occupied by the builders and takes its name, 'great expert', from *babban gwani* Mallam Mikaila, the builder of the Friday Mosque in Zaria. Mallam Mikaila is said to have had a dream in which he saw a great light in the north. He travelled north and met the Shehu, Uthman dan Fodio, going with him to Mecca several times. He is reputed to have brought back knowledge of Egyptian architecture. Being a loyal follower he was offered an emir's position by the Shehu, but declined the offer. Instead his profession, building, was honoured and he was appointed the chief builder in Hausaland.[33] All the chief builders of Hausaland are appointed from Sokoto and are descended from Mallam Mikaila. The post is therefore equivalent in some senses to that of an emir. The current owner of the title, Alhaji Haruna, still occupies the home built by *babban gwani*. The space in front of *babban gwani's* home is orientated approximately

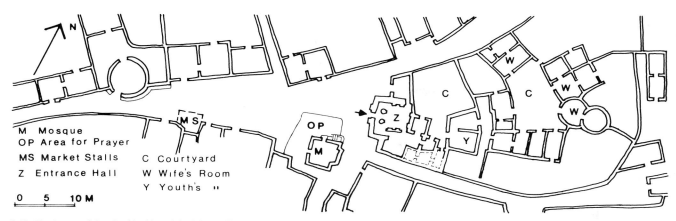

M Mosque
OP Area for Prayer
MS Market Stalls
Z Entrance Hall

C Courtyard
W Wife's Room
Y Youth's "

0 5 10 M

3.15 *The home of the chief builder of the Hausa, Zaria*

east-west, and although much smaller than the *dendal* it has a similar shape and function, with access to the home towards the east and a small mosque to the south of the space. (See Figure 3.15.)

Both the ward and the city are based on a pattern of street blocks. Each street block, irregular in shape, is enclosed by a high mud wall and contains the main social and economic units, either the extended family or the simple unit, based on marriage. Family compounds are linked by a complex system of pedestrian routes. The pathways connect the important elements in the city, the *dendal*, palace and Friday Mosque, the market place and the gateways. These routes are sequences of spaces and passages, some of which are barely wide enough to permit the passage of a fully-laden donkey. The passages widen into outdoor praying places, shaded sitting areas in front of the houses, Koranic teaching areas and the spaces left after the recent filling in of the one-time borrow pits.

Some areas in the old cities are undergoing change as pathways are widened to permit the circulation of the motor car. But the process of change is not in itself a new feature in the Hausa city: changes in street form take place with

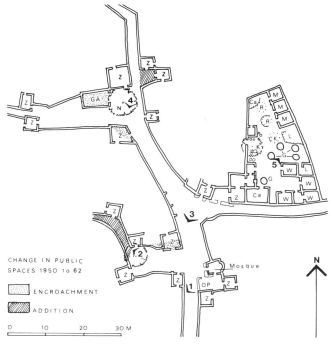

CHANGE IN PUBLIC
SPACES 1950 to 62

ENCROACHMENT

ADDITION

0 10 20 30 M

3.16 *Plan of spaces in the ward of the butchers in Daura*

3.14 *Babban Gwani Ward (Builders Ward), Zaria*

considerable rapidity, mainly due to the instability of the mud walls with which the major part of the city is still built. The diagram of part of Daura shows in a remarkable way the effect of the cycle of organic change on a small group of pedestrian spaces over a period of thirteen years. (See Figures 3.16 to 3.21.) These changes, occasioned by the impermanent nature of the building materials, have been made to accommodate the break up of extended families; new units requiring their own entrance (*zaure*) and sometimes an access route to it. In the right-hand corner of the diagram can be seen the formation of two cells, each with its own *zaure*, but with an internal connection between the compounds: perhaps the last family link before the separation into two independent socio-economic units.[34]

3.18 *View 2)*

Perspective views of the butchers' ward, Daura
3.17 *View 1)*

3.19 *View 3)*

3.20 *View 4)*

3.21 *View 5)*

Such changes in the fabric occur quite naturally and automatically, partly as a consequence of the traditional attitude to the alienation of land which has user rights attached to it, but is not a commodity to be owned. Any land and boundary disputes are decided by the emir, but good neighbourliness, close family relationships between adjoining compounds and a common interest in the use and maintenance of public spaces probably prevent the complete alienation of public space to private users. As long ago as 1964, Blair noted a change in attitude to land ownership in Kano, and found land being exchanged for money in the city.[35] No doubt this sort of land transaction will increase in areas where there is pressure for development, despite the Nigerian Federal Government's attempt to nationalize land. In developmental backwaters of some of the cities, the traditional system will probably be maintained.

Hausa families fall into three categories: individual families and composite units, composed of either a married man, his married sons and their dependents, or a group of collateral agnates and their dependents. With the exception of the ruling families, large, localized co-residential kin-groups are unusual in Hausa communities: although brothers are expected to live in the same compound, the Hausa attach no blame to cousins separating. The varieties of Hausa co-residential kin groups are not formal alternatives, but manifestations of the same rhythmic and dynamic cycle. (See Figure 3.22.) The effect of the household cycle is most evident in the organic nature of the settlement pattern. New family units are continually being formed, maturing, then breaking up. Consequently, new family compounds are constantly being formed, as illustrated in Daura (See Figure 3.16), and the movement of families within cities creates new housing areas on the periphery of old settlements and new suburbs.

Evidence of this continuous process of growth and decay can be seen in the old cities: during the dry season, the time for building, new compounds are built: in each rainy season, vacant huts and compounds are rendered first to rubble and then to mounds of laterite. The organic process of growth and decay is assisted by the nature of the building materials, for

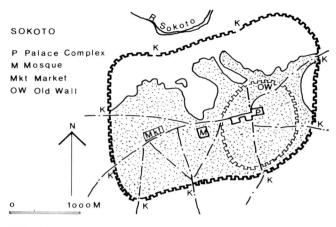

Nuclear Family

Growth of Marital Family

Extended Family

Change of Household Head

Change of Household Head

Formation of 2 Households

3.22 *Hausa Family organisation*

once vacated a building soon disappears, if not naturally, it is demolished, its material re-used for another building and its site added to the farmland. The growing use of concrete blocks and tin roofs may, together with the possible demise of the extended family system, signal the end of this way of life, where building technology, urban form and social systems appear to be in congruence.

The Caliphate Cities

The caliphate settlements of Sokoto, Wurno, Bauchi and Yola were nineteenth-century foundations, the result of the successful jihad of Uthman dan Fodio. Until 1902, as was mentioned above, Sokoto and Wurno alternated as the capital of the caliphate; Bauchi and Yola were founded by flag-bearers of the

SOKOTO

P   Palace Complex
M   Mosque
Mkt   Market
OW   Old Wall

N

o   1000 M

3.23 *Sokoto*

Shehu. It is in these cities that the full impact of Islam on city planning is most evident. None of the settlements had connections with the main communication network during the British occupation. Sokoto was linked by paved road to Zaria and Bauchi connected to the Nigerian Railway system since independence. Wurno remains a pleasant backwater, known only for the tomb of Muhammad Bello the famous son of the Shehu.

Sokoto was founded in the first decade of the nineteenth century as a walled encampment, one of the many *ribats* acting as armed bases and rallying points along the frontier of the empire. (See Figure 3.23.) It was modelled by Bello on the strongholds established by the Arabs in the conquest of Syria and North Africa, and was considerably extended later in the nineteenth century. The older walls were circular with strong north-south and east-west axes. At the centre of the city is the palace, facing west towards the Friday Mosque. The compounds of both the Shehu and Bello, in the tradition of the pastoral Fulani, face west, with the private quarters on the east wall, garden in the north and reception halls and courts in the west; entrances to the palace and the houses are eastwards.[36]

The markets in Sokoto, Wurno and Bauchi were originally located· outside the walls of the settlement. In Sokoto, however, as Clapperton points out, the market was already incorporated within the walled area by 1823:

> Unlike most other towns in Hausa, where the houses are thinly scattered, it is laid out in regular well-built streets. The houses approach the walls . . . (which are) between twenty and thirty feet, high, and (have) twelve gates . . . There are two mosques . . . a spacious market place in the centre of the city, and another large square in front of the Sultan's residence. The dwellings of the principal people are surrounded by high walls, which enclose numerous coozies . . . and flat roofed houses, built in the Moorish style.[37]

The city walls built by Bello for Sokoto are almost rectangular, perhaps built under the influence of the Zaria builder, *babban gwani* Mallam Mikaila, a devoted follower of the Shehu whom Clapperton found building a mosque in Sokoto in 1828.[38]

From the early nineteenth century onwards, the Fulani rulers certainly adopted many of the building forms of the conquered Habe, but they brought to city planning the primacy of the east-west axis, although it was not always possible to implant this schema on to existing settlements. In new settlements it was applied more vigorously.

Pre-Colonial City Planning: Conclusion

Interstate warfare and extensive slave-raiding prevalent in Hausaland resulted, as Barth noted, in the depopulation of large areas. Defence was a vital factor determining both the distribution of population in dense groupings and the siting of settlements to withstand long sieges. The internal structure of the settlements still shows evidence of this earlier need for defence, the walls of each major city encircling large areas of agricultural land, the built-up area developed at high densities. The internal structures of the settlements are at first glance formless and haphazardly laid out. But close inspection reveals two important nodes, the palace, Friday Mosque, *dendal* complex, and the market place. It is to these two nodes that the important routes lead, routes in some settlements being related to former axial compositions associated with pre-Islamic schemata adopted or adapted to suit later Islamic

practices. The main residential areas are broken down into elements which have their origin in the social, economic and administrative organization of society.

Development of Hausa Cities since 1900

Since the British occupation of Northern Nigeria in the first decade of this century most development in the great Hausa cities has occurred outside the walls. Surrounding the traditional core of the old city are a number of well-defined 'strangers' quarters inhabited by Nigerians from other parts of the country and people of other nationalities. Most of these suburbs and the new commercial centres date from this century.

Development in Zaria since 1900

Zaria is typical of such colonial and post-colonial development. After surrendering to the British in 1900, it was declared a Province in 1902 at which time a government station was established there.[39] As part of his policy of 'indirect rule', Lugard, the High Commissioner, created in Zaria, as in other cities, a dual system of government consisting of a township under direct colonial administration, separated by the River Kubani from an area of native administration consisting of *bimin* Zaria (the old city) and Tudun Wada (hill of wealth).[40] A key concept of colonial planning was segregation of groups of people and different activities in the urban area. Within the native administration Tudun Wada was separated from the old city by the wall and the area controlled by the native administration was separated by the River Kubani from the colonial township. The main elements were also physically separated within the township.[41] (See Figure 3.1.)

The main physical elements of the Zaria township were a residential area for Europeans, a commercial zone and Sabon Gari, a new town for Nigerians and other Africans working for the colonial administration and commercial concerns. Lugard's plan for Zaria township in 1914 incorporated all the areas under direct rule into one single composition which has largely determined the structure of the present city. His plan was orientated towards the railway line which reached Zaria in

1911, connecting the city with the colonial trade routes. An important feature of the plan, repeated in colonial extensions to other Hausa cities, was an area reserved for Europeans surrounded by a 400m. building-free zone separating it from Sabon Gari, the native location within the township. Within the European quarter, the residential area, the 'Government Residential Area' (G.R.A.), was separated from the commercial zone by the railway line.

The Government Residential Area, the largest part of the former European location, is planned in the style of the then fashionable garden suburb in Britain. The broad, tree-lined roads give access to large compounds (often between 0.5 and 1ha.) with spacious colonial style houses surrounded by ornamental trees and shrubs. The area also contains public offices on large, well-landscaped plots. At the centre of the European area is the Zaria Club, with its polo ground, race course and golf course separating the G.R.A. from the residential compounds of the senior railway officials and completing the picture of the British 'Sylvan' suburbs.

The commercial area to the south of the G.R.A. and between it and the River Kubani was laid out on a grid plan, with wide streets intersecting at right angles. The plots are large, and used for both commercial and residential purposes. Many of the colonial style buildings remain, the streets being as well landscaped as the G.R.A.; the numerous *madaci* trees and colonial style building groups retain the flavour of former times. The commercial area was originally occupied by British, French and German trading companies, later by Syrians, Lebanese and Asian commercial establishments and currently by Nigerian-controlled concerns. But although parts of the commercial area still maintain the rural quiet and spaciousness of colonial Nigeria, the recent oil wealth of the country and the boom in car ownership has broken the slumbers of this part of Zaria; its appearance has been transformed to fit more properly its function as the city's centre of gravity for economic affairs.

The older part of Sabon Gari, between the Kano-Baro railway line, the Bauchi light railway line and the army barracks, was also designed and laid out by British colonial administrators as a garden suburb. The plan adopted was a grid of tree-lined streets; plot sizes were 15.25 x 30.5m., meant originally for single families but converted to occupation by many families, each family renting one or more rooms in the plot and sharing kitchen and bathroom facilities.

Sabon Gari, originally meant for non-native Nigerians working for colonial establishments, was part of the township, but by the mid 1920s it had become a home for many Northern Nigerians escaping from the traditional restrictions of the Native Authority. In the 1930s the colonial government gave more authority in Sabon Gari to the Native Authority, until finally in 1940 this suburb was placed under the control of the Zaria Native Authority. It now forms the headquarters of the district of Sabon Gari under the local authority, the successor to the Native Authority since independence.

Sabon Gari expanded to the north across the light railway line when it was closed after the Second World War. The later phases of Sabon Gari contain more single-family dwellings and larger open areas for schools and churches; streets follow the fashions of post-war planning in Britain, being curved rather than rigidly rectangular. The major focal point of Sabon Gari and possibly the whole of the city is the market. Streets leading to the market are lined with hotels, bars and offices; everywhere there are heaps of rusting cars and bicycle spares: it is a shanty town, full of brash character, noise and colour.

Tudun Wada, occupied largely by Muslim strangers, is outside the walls of the old city on land which in 1904 was part of the emir's farm. On the death of the emir in 1906, the farm was divided for settlers from the old city. In 1914 it was laid out by British surveyors in a grid iron pattern, and four years later it was specifically allocated by the High Commissioner, Lord Lugard, for 'all natives of Nigeria not being in the employ of Europeans'. The grid iron village of Tudun Wada grew from about 250 people engaged in farming in 1908 to 8,417 in 1952 and 37,359 in 1962. The principal focal points are the Kaduna and Jos roads, particularly their junction where the market, slaughter slab and places of work are located. The General Hospital and the Pharmacy School between the old city and Tudun Wada were major employers in the late 1920s and stimulated the growth of the village. Since the Second World War employment prospects in the area have grown with the establishment of the Clerical Training Centre which later became the Institute of Administration, the Gaskiya Corporation, Government College and other educational institutions. The area is also one of small industries and thriving commerce.

The Agricultural Research Station founded in Samaru in 1924 was the original stimulus for the growth of the most northern suburb of Zaria. The Station was laid out with its own European Residential Area, surrounded by a building-free zone. In 1945, the School of Agriculture was founded in Samaru, followed by the Zaria branch of the Nigerian College of Arts, Science and Technology which later became Ahmadu Bello University. Other major employers are the Leather Institute, the Industrial Development Centre, the Building Research Unit and the Civil Aviation Training Centre.

The elements of Samaru are separated by considerable distances, designed and laid out with the car in mind. Each institution has its own residential area consisting of large plots well landscaped with ornamental trees and shrubs. Samaru village itself is similar to Sabon Gari in character, having unpaved streets, open drains and high density housing. It is an active place and the residence of workers, students and traders. The focus of the village is the daily market, the shops, churches and cinema which are strung out along the Zaria-Funtua highway.

The morphology of the twentieth-century additions to the emirate cities can be seen to be due in part to the application of Lugard's policy of indirect rule, the natives of the country being permitted to continue to follow a traditional way of life. Colonial developments were parallel to, but outside this stream of life; the colonial city reflected views about zoning and urban form current in Britain at the time. There were attempts at social engineering, different sectors of the city being earmarked for different ethnic groups and social classes. A strict zoning of the city according to race and tribal group was never completely successful, however.

The policy which allocated Sabon Gari, Zaria to non-native Africans proved unsuccessful and eventually the area had to be transferred to the Native Authority. In 1958 the traditional area of Tudun Wada, Zaria, consisted of 2,267 Hausa, 1,896 Fulani, 1,406 Nupe, 997 Yoruba and 185 Igbo, while in the same year even in *birnin* Zaria, the Hausa heartland of the city, there were 731 Nupe and 779 Yoruba. With the exception of the European quarter, the sectors of Zaria were probably never quite as homogeneous as the colonial planners would have wished. Since independence the blurring of the distinct social groupings has continued. The G.R.A. is no longer the home of the privileged European, and with the growth in car ownership and reliance upon the mini bus and taxi for movement in the city the process of social integration is accelerating.

Conclusion

Lugard's policy of indirect rule, which emphasized the maintenance of established traditions and non-interference with Muslim settlements, was an important contributory factor in establishing the structure of Hausa settlements as they are today. Yet the physical interpretation of that policy represents the natural or normal method of integrating strangers into most city structures from New York to Singapore. It is in tune with African traditions in particular. If colonial planning can be regarded as sensitive in any way, certainly Lugard's attempt to work within the traditions of Northern Nigeria was so.

Western influence and Nigeria's new wealth are most in evidence outside the walls of the traditional cities. There are changes within the old cities too, where modernization includes the use of new building materials, improved social, educational and engineering services, and the widening of streets to permit the penetration of the motor car. But these changes are being accommodated within a traditional, stable Islamic culture which retains its essential social and religious structures. Physical changes occur, too, but within an architectural spatial composition derived and developed over many generations, which in essence consists of a hierarchical series of spaces linking the privacy of the home to the street, local meeting place, market, Friday Mosque and *dendal*.

4. The Architectural Programme

Introduction

Buildings result from an implicit or explicit programme. This may be simply a schedule of accommodation listing the rooms to be built, and perhaps an indication of their physical and functonal relationship,[1] or it may be imbued with symbolic or spiritual meaning. When man identifies himself with what he builds, using it as a means of expression, then he engages in the activity of architecture. The distinction between shelter and architecture, as Labelle Prussin argues, 'rests precisely on differentiating between real, concrete space and philosophic, existential space. Ultimately, it is the changing pattern of their interrelationship over time which constitutes the fabric of architectural history.'[2]

The study of African architecture has been retarded by the ethnocentric attitudes of Western scholars, particularly in the search for a Darwinian evolutionary explanation of architectural developments.[3] This, combined with the myth of darkest Africa, prevalent even today, demotes the glory of African cultures to the bottom rung of the ladder, labelling them primitive. It leads to a limited view of African architecture and a narrow functional evaluation of buildings beneath titles such as 'shelter' or 'housing', which neither describe nor analyse the process of giving meaning to form.[4] Furthermore, the materials used in construction are described as 'mud'; the construction itself as 'hut', and its life expectancy as 'temporary'. Such terms are denigratory and reduce the significance of the objects of study.

In so reducing the architectural experience of African peoples, these ethnocentric studies render it worthless in the view of those responsible for planning and development in third and fourth world countries. The position is exacerbated by glossy books and journals illustrating the latest fashionable architecture of the developing world, for such fashions become a goal of society, influencing clients in government and schools of architecture and legitimizing the lucrative position of the foreign consultant.[5] Rapidly growing African cities are being built to standards of design imported from centres higher on the imaginary scale of architectural evolution. The result is plain for all to see: a host of expensive and often inappropriate public buidings in one of the 'international' styles, public housing that the poor cannot afford and vast squatter areas denuded of architectural meaning—the ultimate in environmental degradation.

There is, however, a growing interest in the architectural traditions of Africa and the developing world,[6] which in part may be explained by changes in architectural theory. Theoretical interest has moved away from the monumental edifice to the broader framework of the anthropologist, who sees the built environment as a facet of man's material and spiritual culture with form and meaning.[7] Denyer and Prussin go some way to re-evaluating African architectural traditions, but there is a great need for the sort of detailed architectural survey carried out in Nigeria by the late Professor Dmochowski before a more thorough analysis is possible.[8]

Building Types

Unlike the complex cities of the West or the great capitals of the third world where many building types have been developed to house a wide range of highly specialized activities and institutions, the Hausa city comprises few such elements. The main constructions of the Hausa city are the defensive wall

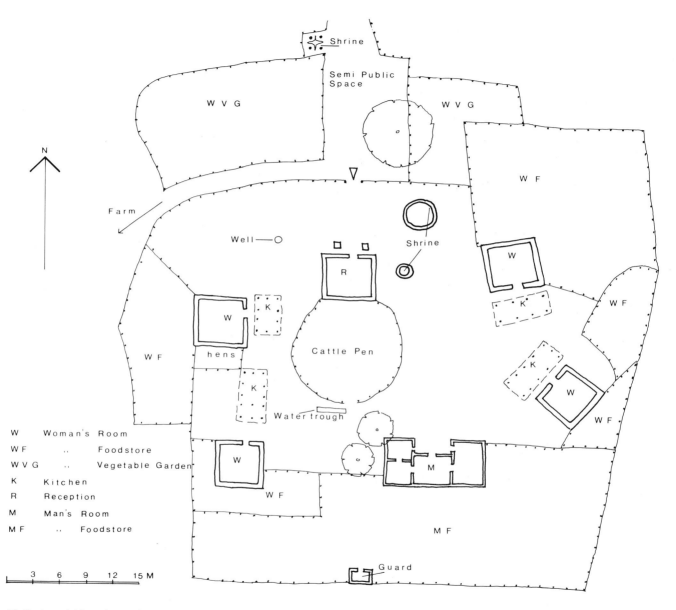

Shrine

Semi Public
Space

W V G

W V G

N

W F

Farm

Well —○

Shrine

R

W

hens

K

W F

Cattle Pen

K

K

W

W F

K

W F

Water trough

W   Woman's Room

W F   ,,   Foodstore

W V G   ,,   Vegetable Garden

K   Kitchen

R   Reception

M   Man's Room

M F   ,,   Foodstore

W

W F

M

M F

3   6   9   12   15 M

Guard

4.1 *Traditional African house plan*

56   HAUSA ARCHITECTURE

encircling the settlement, the palace, the central and neighbourhood mosques, the market and the domestic buildings. Education at Koranic schools is largely outdoors and an extension of the household function of the *mallam* or teacher; industry and local retailing have no specialized buildings, again being a function of particular households and carried out in an extension or adaptation of the domestic premises. Modern buildings, usually of a low standard of design, have been built in the old centres, first during British colonial occupation and later since independence. Such buildings are necessary for new and expanding activities like Western-style education and local administration, yet are often out of scale and character with the traditional landscape.

Generally speaking, no matter what function they serve, traditional buildings are variations on a theme employing three main elements: the room or primary cell, the courtyard and the wall. With these three basic elements the Hausa builder creates an amazing variety of compositions to solve the main architectural programme set for him by society. It is unfortunate, to say the least, that the modern extensions to the old city have ignored or rejected this basic pattern language which is capable of moulding together many disparate elements into a unified architectural composition extending over the whole area of the traditional city.

Domestic architecture

The Hausa house plan for both Muslim and non-Muslim families follows the traditional African pattern (See Figure 4.1), having rooms arranged within or surrounding a courtyard. In common with other types of African housing, the compound wall is an important feature of the Hausa house. It may have been developed initially as a wind-break or for reasons of defence and to a certain extent it still fulfils these functions, but whatever its original purpose, there are now other very good reasons to justify the cost of its construction. The wall demarcates an area within which members of the family may withdraw from society and remain in privacy. It also serves the same defensive function for the family as does the city wall for the community as a whole, providing security for the family,

preventing the escape of small farm animals and discouraging thieves from entering the compound.

The compound contains the main economic unit, the extended family (*gandu* s., *gandaye* pl.), which works the same fields, shares the same grain store and eats from the same pot.[9] The marital units which make up the extended family occupy separate areas within the compound which are called *sassa* (pl.), *sashe* (s.). *Sassa* are separated from each other by walls, generally lower than the compound walls and sometimes little more than a light screen of guinea corn stalks. Security and privacy for the marital unit within the extended family group is not of great importance and the walls between *sassa* seem to function purely as spatial dividers demarcating areas of a more personal nature.

The structure of the family is in a process of constant change leading to growth, subdivision or decline. In Hausa society it is unusual for the family to remain as a single socio-economic unit once the sons of the founder of the family have died. At this stage, or perhaps earlier, the family breaks up into a set of smaller units, some of which may be simple families based on marriage (*iyalai*) and potential extended families of the next two generations. (See Figure 3.22.) The cyclic and organic nature of the family structure affects house planning in several ways.[10] When an extended family changes structure, the original compound, if it is big enough, may be sub-divided and apportioned between the new compound heads (*maigida*, s.; *masugidaje*, pl.), the male inheritors of the estate. If this happens the divisions between the *sassa* become harder and each newly-formed compound has its own perimeter wall and external gateway. (See Figure 3.16.) Alternatively, the family group may break up completely and new cells be built on family land, on unused and therefore 'unowned' land, or on land rented from the traditional user.

The effect of the formation of new cells on the structure of the settlement has been described already, but even within the compounds of the extended families there is evidence of constant adaptation to changing family circumstances. From field studies it would appear that a man setting up a compound of his own first builds a perimeter wall, an entrance hut (*zaure*)

4.2 *Main Entrance to the home of Babban Gwani, Zaria*

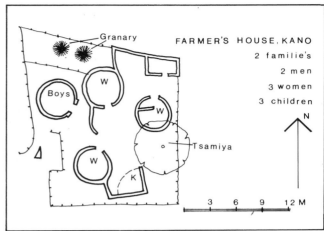

4.3 *Farmer's House, Kano*

and sleeping huts for himself and his wife. As the family grows, huts are added where and when they become necessary; later, screen walls are built to sub-divide the house into *sassa* for married sons. When the family shrinks through death or the loss of a breakaway family group, the land soon returns to agricultural use. Land within the compound has a high agricultural potential and since the maintenance cost for repairs to buildings is high, the tendency is for unused huts to be demolished, the site put to other uses and the building materials recycled. Such huts may remain for a while as stores or animal stalls, but neglect of maintenance soon renders them unstable even for this purpose and the process of demolition is completed during the heavy rains. It has been the custom for the dead occupant to be buried beneath the floor of his hut and the building permitted to decay, eventually forming a mound over the grave. Like the settlement itself, the house is not an accumulation of accommodation which remains static for long periods, for even during a man's lifetime the house is constantly adapted to suit changing family needs. This process of growth and decay is facilitated by the short life of the building materials, but is given form and continuity through the cellular nature of the architecture

where the unit of growth and decay is the hut: an organic architectural form in perfect harmony with its purpose.

Pre-Islamic influence on house form

According to Nicolas the schema for the non-Muslim house form of the Hausa is similar to that of the town or settlement:[11]

> The head of the household (*maigida*) buries five pots containing ointments and charms in the east, west, south, north and centre of the site; he then surrounds the area by a boundary wall. Within the area each adult member of the household is allocated a hut of thatch or earth. For those respecting tradition the entrances of the huts should be sited to face west so that those entering it face east. The rooms of the wives of the same man are always placed on a north south orientation with the first wife having the room in the north and the last wife the one in the south. The physical order of the rooms reflects the hierarchy of the womenfolk: the first spouse (*matar jari*) whose rank is mistress of the house (*uwal gida*) is often called "the woman of the north" (*matar arewa*) and the last one woman of the south (*matar gusum*).[12]

From a study of aerial photographs and the present survey of Hausa homes it would seem that they do not conform strictly to this schema of house planning: but it would be surprising if they did so. Idealized plan types are rarely implemented in strict accordance with a geometry dictated by a set of rules: such regulations are more often amended or compromised to suit more pressing practical problems of cost, existing development and exigencies of site. In addition, the growing influence of Islam has diluted the traditions and practice of former building customs. Nevertheless, the Hausa still follow the pre-Islamic order of building operations, the boundary wall taking priority over the other elements of the building. It is interesting to note, too, that the entrances to the emir's palace in Zaria and to the home of the chief builder of Hausaland (*sarkin gini*), again in Zaria, are in the west facade of the building. (See Figures 4.2 and 3.15.) It is possible to find examples of extended family compound houses where the wives' huts are orientated on a north-south axis, but such haphazard findings are insufficient evidence to support the idea of continuing traditions dating back to pre-jihadic times.

Islamic influence on house form

Important to an understanding of the form of the Hausa dwelling is the influence of Islam, in particular the institution of marriage. Where Islamic culture has taken deep roots in society the African compound house has been further developed to provide the degrees of privacy necessary for the segregation of the sexes (*auren kulle*). Various degrees of wife seclusion are practised by the Muslim Hausa, as Smith points out:

> Hausa classify their various modes of marriage in the following ways: The "religious" classification distinguishes *auren kulle* = purdah-type marriage with complete seclusion of the wife: *auren tsare* = partial seclusion of the wife, and *auren jahilai* = "marriage of the ignorant", with no seclusion of the wife.[13]

The homes of families who practise *auren jahilai*, 'marriage of the ignorant', are similar in structure to those of non-Islamic people. (Compare Figures 4.1 and 4.3.) Figure 4.3 is the home of the farmer dependent upon his wife working on the farm: purdah is impossible to practise in such a household economy. In this case the home is surrounded by a guinea

Family Structure 1962

1. Maigida, 2 wives, 2 children
2. Brother, 1 ,,
3. ,, , 1 ,, , 1 ,,
4. ,, , 1 ,, , 2 ,,
5. ,, , 1 ,, , 4 ,,
6. 2 Widows

Total 7 adults, 9 children

First Floor

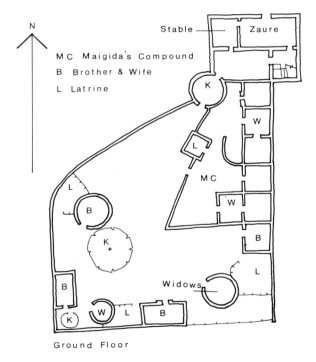

N

MC Maigida's Compound
B Brother & Wife
L Latrine

Ground Floor

0 3 6 9 12 15 18 21 24 27 30 33 36

4.4 *House of Mohamadu Mazawachi, Kazaure*

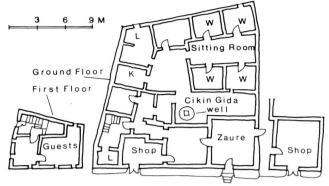

4.5 *Home of Prosperous Trader, Zaria (Taken from Schwerdtfeger, F.W., Traditional Housing in African cities (Wiley, Chichester, 1982), p.31.*

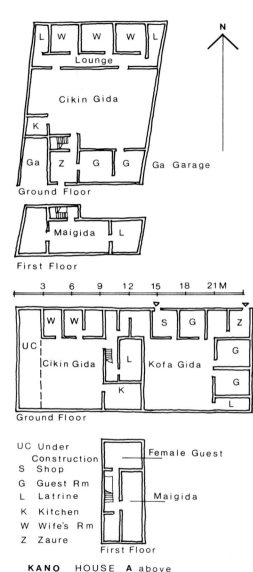

4.6 *Homes of the emerging middle class, Kano*

corn stalk fence with no special provision for entertaining male visitors.

The family house governed by the practice of *auren kulle* (wife seclusion) is surrounded by a mud wall 3 to 4m. high. It is entered through an entrance hut (*zaure*) which may be round with a conical thatched roof, or if the family is wealthy, an elaborate two-storeyed building with an upper floor of guest rooms (*bene*, s., *benaye*, pl.). Circulation from the *zaure* to the family part of the house (*cikin gida*) is through one or more courtyards (*kofar gida*). In the entrance courtyards (*kofar gida*) are built the huts for unmarried young men and male guests. Most entrance courtyards have a pit latrine and a wash place and if the compound head (*maigida*) possesses a horse, it may be tethered here. At the perimeter are located secondary entrance huts (*shigifa*, s., *shigifu*, pl.) which lead to the quarters of the individual families (*sassa*) making up the extended family. In the smaller houses there is usually only one *shigifa*; however, in those homes where there are many *shigifu*, one is usually more important than the others and is used for entertaining great friends of the family (*aboki*, s., *abokai*, pl.) and trusted male visitors.

The interior of the home (*cikin gida*) is sub-divided into quarters (*sassa*) for the individual families where only close male relatives, girls and boys under the age of puberty are permitted. Within the *sassa* each wife has one or two huts—in some cases two round huts are combined to form a most beautifully shaped room (*adada*, s., *adadai*, pl.). The wife decorates the room with her dowry and other belongings and in it she sleeps with her children. The family head (*maigida*) and each married male in the group have their own rooms (*turaka*) located within their individual *sassa*. If the man has no room of his own then he sleeps in turn in his wives' rooms, usually for two days at a time when it is that particular wife's turn to cook the family meals. Also within the *cikin gida* may be found huts of other dependent womenfolk such as widowed mother or divorced sister.

A latrine and a well, together with the granaries and kitchens, are placed in the inner courtyards of the house: an arrangement which is particularly important if the family practices *auren kulle*. In some of the more wealthy homes piped water has been installed, which reduces the health hazard when well and pit latrine are located in close proximity, a normal Hausa procedure. In most compound houses there are at least two kitchens, one for use during the rainy season (*dakin dafuwa*) and the other for the dry season (*dakin girki*). The dry season kitchen is simply a space in the inner courtyard set aside for cooking purposes, but during the rainy season a special hut is used. Other outdoor rooms are built in the inner courtyards from a series of poles supporting thatched roofs: such structures are used as shaded rest areas.

The general structure of the house throughout Hausaland is surprisingly uniform. It is governed by the need for privacy, but as Schwerdtfeger suggests, 'it may derive with little change from a very early compound'.[14] Within this very general thematic plan form, however, are many variations depending upon the size of the family, its occupation, status and location in the settlement.

Figure 3.16 is the house of a butcher in the small town of Daura: his is a single marital unit in the process of breaking away from the main part of the extended family. Because he has to be close to the slaughter yard and the land in the neighbourhood is fully occupied, the *maigida* of this compound

has to be satisfied with a small space. The tight site has resulted in the combination of *zaure* and *shigifa* into a single unit comprising a series of complicated visual locks giving the privacy normally achieved by separating an outer and an inner courtyard. Since butchery is an occupation of low status a plan form of this type is quite acceptable.

Figure 4.4 was recorded in 1960. At that time it was the home of Mohamadu Mazawachi, the *maigida*, a descendant of the first emir of Kazaure whose main occupation was farming. In this house plan the *maigida* had his own private area (*sassa*), while his four married brothers and two elderly female relatives share the remaining private space. This is an important family in Kazaure and although the compound is small for the size of the family, status demands a two-storey *zaure* which in this case is used by visiting *mallams*. In order to achieve this status symbol, the four brothers of the *maigida* live in cramped conditions sharing a room with their wives and children.

Figure 3.15 is the house built by Babban Gwani Mallam Mikaila in the middle of the last century. In this house plan an inner and an outer courtyard have been retained, despite being situated close to the market in Zaria where densities are high and land at a premium. The original *zaure* built by Mallam Mikaila is retained and well maintained by the family. This and the two courtyards are necessary symbols of the status of this important family.

The next example, taken from Schwerdtfeger, is the house of a prosperous trader in Zaria city and Sabon Gari markets (see Figure 4.5). It is situated in a densely built up area of Zaria, so there is no space for the usual double courtyard system for securing privacy. The functions of the *shigifa* and *zaure* are combined in an intricate system of winding passageways, in similar fashion to the home of the butcher in Daura (see Figure 3.16). In this case, however, the *maigida* is a wealthy man and gives expression to his status by building a two-storey *zaure* with guest rooms on the first floor.[15]

Figure 4.6 shows the homes of two mallams, administrators in the local authority of Kano, which were surveyed late in 1962. At that time the household heads were members of the

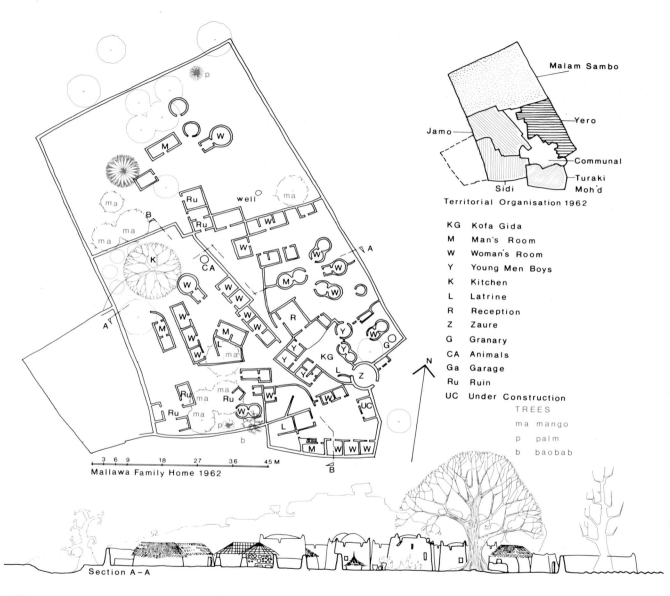

Malam Sambo

Yero

Jamo

Communal

Turaki Moh'd

Sidi

Territorial Organisation 1962

KG   Kofa Gida
M   Man's Room
W   Woman's Room
Y   Young Men Boys
K   Kitchen
L   Latrine
R   Reception
Z   Zaure
G   Granary
CA   Animals
Ga   Garage
Ru   Ruin
UC   Under Construction

TREES
ma   mango
p   palm
b   baobab

well

Mallawa Family Home 1962

3 6 9   18   27   36   45 M

Section A–A

4.7   *Home of the Mallawa family, Zaria in 1962*

emerging middle class, with formal 'European' education up to secondary school standard. The house shown in Figure 4.6a, built in the old city, follows Hausa tradition closely, having two courtyards: one is semi-public and is surrounded by guest and reception rooms; the other is an inner, private family courtyard (*cikin gida*) surrounded by rooms for the wives.

Mallam Lawal Sulaiman, then of the Social Welfare Department, Kano (see Figure 4.6b), built his house outside the walls of old Kano city and introduced many new ideas into the planning of his home. The most important innovation in this house is the grouping of the wives' rooms into a simple rectangular block connected by and sharing a communal lounge leading directly to covered latrines and bathroom: a similar feature to the arrangement in the merchant's house in Zaria (see Figure 4.5). Mallam Lawal Sulaiman explained that he was unable to plan for two courtyards because of site restrictions, but had maintained privacy as far as possible by an arrangement of screened doors between the street and the inner house. The master's reception suite was planned at first-floor level above the *zaure* and is connected to it by a staircase, a common feature of Hausa planning either for a restricted site or as an expression of status. An interesting innovation in the master suite (for that time) is a first-floor latrine, shown to me by Mallam Sulaiman with justifiable pride. It consisted of a modern porcelain pan connected by a 15cm. diameter pipe to the traditional pit latrine below.

As was mentioned above, it is unusual for the family to remain a single socio-economic unit once the sons of the founder have died. While the Hausa expect brothers to live together in the same compound no blame is attached to cousins separating.[16] This social norm is expressed in the physical structure of the city, the majority of dwellings taking a form similar to those so far illustrated in this chapter. There are exceptions to this norm: for example, Polly Hill has described the large rural households in the region surrounding Kano, while the royal lineages, the families from whom the emirs are chosen, remain as a large socio-political unit occupying extensive compounds.[17]

Figure 4.7 is the plan of a large extended family compound belonging to the Mallawa royal lineage of Zaria. As one of the families competing for the position of emir it is in the political, and therefore the economic interests of the group to remain together, loyal to the member or members of the group with the greatest possibility of being selected as the next emir. As M.G. Smith explains: 'The basic units in the system of political competition were four dynasties. Of these the Suleibawa were the last to acquire the throne (1860), and they were also the weakest. The three powerful dynasties were the Mallawa, Bornawa and Katsinawa; and of these, the first two were the more important. Membership in these dynasties were based on patrilineal descent. . .'[18]

The branch of the Mallawa family occupying the house shown in Figure 4.7 is descended directly from Mallam Musa, the first Fulani emir of Zaria appointed by Uthman dan Fodio after the successful jihad of the early nineteenth century. Being members of one of the two main political groups in Zaria they are encouraged to remain together as a cohesive group maintaining a strong power base of communally owned property and an extensive network of clients and supporters. Successful manipulation of the family fortunes holds the prospect of achieving the principal objective of the dynastic competition—the position of emir, still in the 1980s a goal worth pursuing. The position gives temporary control over the subordinate offices of state normally distributed among kinsmen and clients of the emir. By rewarding his supporters, the emir simultaneously discharges his obligations of patronage and kinship, increases his followers and ensures the future power of the lineage.

Intra-dynastic rivalry is restricted by limiting succession to the throne to the sons of former emirs and to only those princes who hold or have held territorial office. Members of dynasties not descended from past rulers, but from former officials, are not eligible, but because of lineage ties are valuable allies in the competition for emirship and are themselves competitors for lesser administrative offices. Figure 4.8 shows the family tree of the section of the Mallawa family under the headship of Miagida Sambo, occupying the house in Figure 4.7. Although still an important group, they are

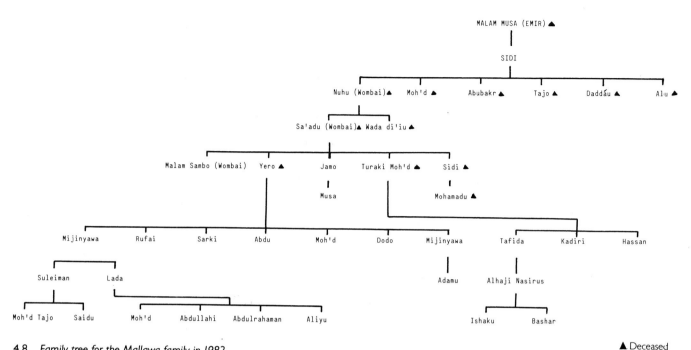

```
                                              MALAM MUSA (EMIR) ▲
                                                      │
                                                    SIDI
                                                      │
            ┌──────────────┬───────────┬─────────────┼──────────┬──────────────┐
       Nuhu (Wombai)▲   Moh'd ▲     Abubakr ▲       Tajo ▲    Daddáu ▲         Alu ▲
            │
      Sa'adu (Wombai)▲ Wada di'iu ▲
            │
    ┌───────────────┬───────────┼──────────────┬──────────────┐
Malam Sambo (Wombai) Yero ▲   Jamo   Turaki Moh'd ▲         Sidi ▲
                      │         │                              │
                    Musa                                  Mohamadu ▲
```

4.8   *Family tree for the Mallawa family in 1982*   ▲ Deceased

receding from the centre of competition for emirship. Nevertheless the family has grown in the past twenty years. Figure 4.9 is the plan of the same house surveyed in 1982. It illustrates not only the changes in architectural forms, but more importantly the increase in the density of the development.[19]

Within the family itself the fortunes and positions of individual section heads can be traced by the movements of groups within the family house. For example, Yero's descendants, the largest group, have moved into the section once occupied by Sidi, the dead brother of the present *maigida* whose particular line has disappeared. Even in 1962 this part of the house was falling into ruin, being occupied by a few old people. Mallam Sambo, the *maigida*, is himself an extremely old man in his late eighties and is without children; Jambo, the brother has few descendants. The real competition within the family group is therefore between the descendants of Yero and Turaki Mohammad, both deceased, and in particular between Mijinyawa (son of Yero), currently away from the compound but occupying an important government post, and Tafida (son of Turuki Mohammad).

The least changes in this compound are to be found in the areas occupied by the older generation of brothers Sambo and Jambo and in the quarter occupied by Turaki and his family. Mijinyawa and his descendants, some of whom also hold administrative posts, show the greatest changes with the introduction of new building technologies and styles. In the rivalry between Mijinyawa and Tafida, with the family of Mijinyawa appearing to the outsider to be in ascendancy, is

Malam Sambo

Yero

Jamo

Shared

Turaki
Moh'd

Territorial Organisation 1981

N

well

3 6 9   18   27   36   45M

Mallawa Family Home 1981

Section B–B

4.9   *Home of the Mallawa family in 1982*

4.10 *Mallawa home 1962*

4.11 *Mallawa home 1962 (Turaki Mohamed's section)*

4.12 *Mallawa home 1962 (Jamo's section)*

4.13 *Mallawa home 1962 (Jamo's section)*

4.14 *Sambo (1982)*   4.15 *Jamo (1982)*

the internal trigger which may herald the future sub-division of a family moving away from the centre of the political stage. The point of crisis and decision-making will come with the deaths of Sambo and Jamo, the last surviving sons of Wambin Sa'adu, the great-grandson of Mallam Musa.

Despite the changes that have occurred in the Mallawa family house over the last twenty years, it still conforms to the fundamental scheme or programme for a Muslim family in Hausaland. For example, the main method of achieving privacy in a house of this type is by building a high perimeter wall which completely surrounds the house. Womenfolk who are friends of the family can wander anywhere within the inner household (*cikin gida*), but it is usual for such visits to be confined to the evening when the sun has set. Adult male visitors must wait outside the entrance hut (*zaure*) while a young boy is sent to bring the head of the compound (*maigida*). The visitor, if he is a stranger, will probably be taken no further than the *zaure* where he and the *maigida* will transact their business. If the visitor is well known to the family he may be taken into the outer courtyard where discussions take place in some convenient shade. In the case of the Mallawa family, friends are conducted into the main *shigifa* or reception room of the *maigida* where they formally meet all the male members of the family. The *shigifa* is designed to maintain the privacy of the family part of the compound, having a system of staggered doors which prevent a direct view from the outer courtyard to the more private areas of the house. The *shigifa* may consist of two rooms, the second one being used by the womenfolk to listen to the male conversation while remaining out of view. It is unusual for an adult male to be taken further than the *shigifa* unless he is the very great friend (*babban aboki*) of the *maigida*.

The form and layout of the Muslim compound reflects the preoccupation of the Hausa with privacy. The stranger's view of a Hausa settlement is of large mud walls enclosing the public spaces, each of which has its own particular function. The people one meets on the streets during daylight are men, old women and children. The only indications of family life are the many entrance doors in the spaces outside which may sit groups of menfolk deep in conversation. Each entrance door from the street leads through a series of spaces which become increasingly more private, starting with the semi-public space outside the entrance where neighbours gossip but where the stranger is an intruder, through the semi-public-semi-private *zaure*, to the semi-private entrance courtyard (*kofar gida*), then on to the private *shigifa* which leads to the *cikin gida* and complete seclusion. The *cikin gida* itself is divided into quarters (*sassa*) demarcating territory for marital units within the extended family, with personal space taking the form of a hut (*daki*, s, *dakuna*, pl.).

Moving through such a family home is a delightful aesthetic experience involving the appreciation of open and covered spaces, a succession of light and shade evoking a deepening sense of privacy. For the visitor, entrance into a home, starts with the long wait at the door, followed by an equally long greeting from the *maigida* in his *zaure* until finally one is conducted through the *kofar gida* and into the *shigifa*. This emphasizes the deepening sanctity of the place. Being permitted to sit with the *maigida* and his friends in the cool of the *shigifa*, listening to the long and extremely courteous greetings

to newcomers and to the farewells of departing guests, emphasizes the formality of Hausa customs. At this point even the highly privileged visitor has still seen only a small fraction of the whole house; and merely walking around the perimeter wall does not reveal the full extent of development within. This complex form of Hausa home and its relationship to the settlement is a beautiful physical expression of the highly developed nature of the society and the formality of its customs.

Housing and the process of change

All cities are in a continuous process of change, but at certain stages of development the process may take on a new dimension. In the Hausa cities it is possible to see the effects of accelerated development since 1960, caused partly by the forces of urbanization unleashed at independence. Traditional house form is evolving in response to growing pressures; the agents of change being the group of middle-class *mallams* with formal education who now hold administrative or teaching positions. The changes introduced by such people show clearly in the house of Mallam Lawal Sulaiman built in Kano in 1960 (see Figure 4.6b), and in the alterations to the Mallawa house by Mijinyawa and his sons, all of whom have received formal education.

Although they are the agents of change, the new middle class have retained deep religious and cultural roots, and the alterations they have introduced into domestic architecture are only those necessary for an improvement in the physical rather than the social or spiritual quality of life. The loss of a fine traditional building form and an inept use of new materials may be regrettable, yet there are solid gains: such features as a safe water supply, a solid concrete floor and a garage for the essential car are the requisites of modern life. These facilities have been incorporated into the general scheme of the house without obscuring the essential programme: the development of a compatible expression of building structure using modern technology may come later.

The direct influence of British occupation is not as apparent as the changes introduced from within society. For

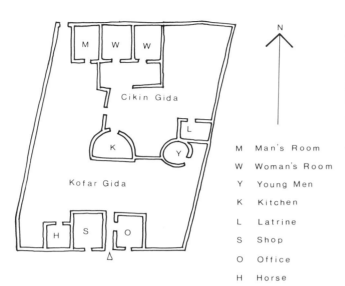

4.18 *Tudun Wada, Zaria*

Cikin Gida

Kofar Gida

M	Man's Room
W	Woman's Room
Y	Young Men
K	Kitchen
L	Latrine
S	Shop
O	Office
H	Horse

HOME OF DISTRICT HEAD
TUDAN WADA KANO

3   6   9   12   15   18   21M

4.16 *House in Tudun Wada, Kano*

4.19 *Tudun Wada, Decorated House, 1962*

4.17 *Local mosque, Tudun Wada, Zaria*

example, the houses in the Muslim strangers' quarters like Tudun Wada, Zaria and Fagge, Kano are built on rectangular plots laid out according to the by-laws introduced during British occupation: in general they follow the usual Hausa pattern, traditional elements being adjusted to fit into the regular site (see Figure 4.16). The harsh lines established by the engineer in places like Tudun Wada, Zaria are softened by the humanity of the Hausa builder working in mud, a material unimpressed by the rigid disciplines of the surveyor's instruments (see Figures 4.17 to 4.19). Such Hausa buildings are in

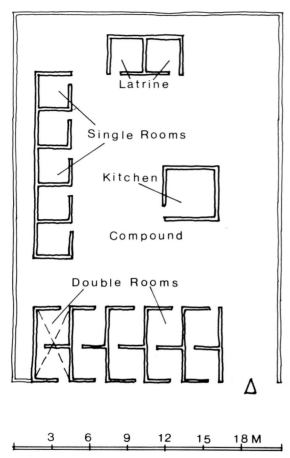

4.20 *House in Sabon Gari, Zaria*

marked contrast to those areas such as Sabon Gari occupied by non-Hausa people who, having been uprooted from home and culture, live in serried ranks of rooms neatly stacked within the rectangular plots of the gridiron plan. (See Figure 4.20.)

The Western concept of home – a villa standing in its own landscaped garden – though built with great regularity in the suburbs surrounding the Hausa cities, appears to have had

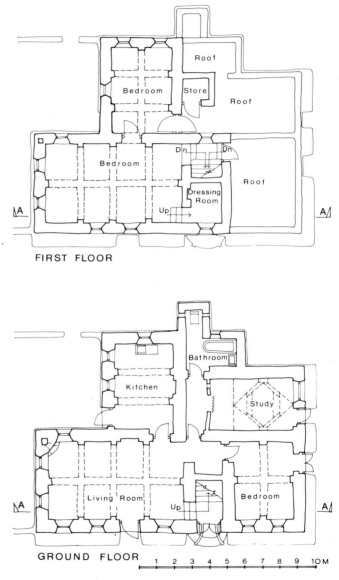

4.21 *House at Wusasa, Zaria Plan*

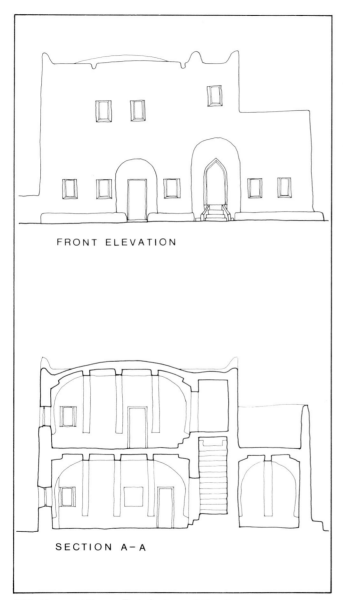

FRONT ELEVATION

SECTION A–A

4.22 *House at Wusasa, Zaria Section and Elevation*

4.23 *House at Wusasa, Zaria*

little if any effect on traditional building forms. An interesting example of this house type is the one developed for British administrative and technical staff who went to Nigeria at the beginning of this century. The Northern Nigerian version of this house form is shown in Figures 4.21 to 4.23, these particular examples being built for the Christian mission at Wusasa, Zaria in the early 1930s. These houses are built of mud by Hausa builders using traditional techniques to form spaces, the size and disposition of which are decided according to 'Western' ideas of comfort and to suit the life-style of the nuclear family. They usually consist of a living room, dining room, study/bedroom, kitchen and bathroom downstairs and two bedrooms and a dressing-room upstairs. The rooms have the usual delightful Hausa proportions with high ceilings supported by arches, and when whitewashed and simply furnished they are pleasant houses in which to live.[20]

Hausa society is not, nor can it or should it be insulated from the changes affecting the life of great cities in Nigeria; but if those changes are kept to manageable proportions then it is possible for society to adapt its architectural language to absorb the new ideas essential to healthy development.[21] The greatest danger facing Hausa society – and indeed people throughout the developing world – is from the scale and rapidity of the process of urbanization: cities are being

4.24 *Mathare Valley, Nairobi, Kenya*

4.25 *Mathare Valley, Nairobi, Kenya*

swamped by masses of rootless migrants (see Figures 4.24 and 4.25). Alternative methods of planning for population expansion and rural migration are a matter of urgency if environmental squalor and degradation are not to swamp the fine urban traditions of the Hausa.

The homes of the Hausa people who have moved south to Ibadan and Lagos as part of the process of urbanization illustrate the deterioration of design standards, harbingers of a possible future of the great Northern caravan cities. In Lagos and Ibadan, for instance, land is so expensive that the space requirements of the fully-developed Muslim house make it an impractical proposition. Other reasons for change in the house form of the Hausa in these cities may be a 'Western' approach to marriage and the breakdown of the extended family as a social institution or, quite simply, the removal of distant cultural controls.[22]

One official answer to the problems of rural-urban migration, overcrowding and poor housing conditions has been the implementation of low-cost housing schemes often designed by foreign 'experts'. Figures 4.26 to 4.28 illustrate such a housing project on Zaria Road in Kano which was designed and constructed by the Metropolitan Kano Planning and Development Board. While it represents a brave attempt to solve the housing problem by using a design based loosely on traditional house forms, it fails in many respects. The estate is laid out in a grid pattern with road access to all dwellings and with large open spaces between the blocks. There are one- and two-storey patio houses and a few three-storey blocks of flats. The buildings are solidly built with all the necessary basic services, including kitchen, bathroom and toilet. Table 1 shows the costs of the dwelling units in this estate; they are in excess of costs for dwellings in a similar estate in Ibadan which Onibokun analysed and found to be well beyond the means of the population most in need of such housing. As one of the local people interviewed by Onibokun said, 'the buildings are very good, but can a person like me, a messenger, earning N900 per annum build or buy such a house?[23]

Table 1. Housing costs in the Kundila Housing Estate on the Zaria Road, Kano (1977)	
2-room type	N 6082.80*
3-room type	7658.30
4-room type	10918.90
dwelling in block of flats	11987.50

*Nigerian Niara; 1.18N = £1 sterling

Source: The Metropolitan Kano Planning and Development Board.

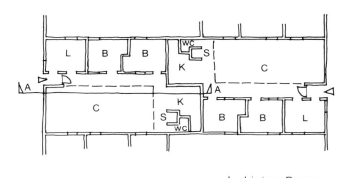

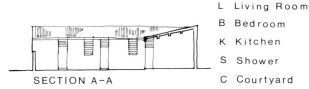

SECTION A-A

L   Living Room
B   Bedroom
K   Kitchen
S   Shower
C   Courtyard

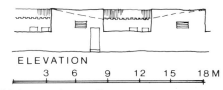

ELEVATION

3   6   9   12   15   18 M

4.26 *Low cost housing, Kano*

4.27 *Low cost housing, Kano*

4.28 *Low cost housing, Kano*

In terms of the detailed design of the project, the space surrounding buildings is excessive, particularly when compared with the provisions of private space within each house. In the traditional Hausa compound, large areas are devoted to private and semi-private space; external space outside the compound wall is limited to useful areas such as agricultural land, borrow pits, small praying and gossiping areas. This project contrasts sharply with traditional architectural forms, having only a 5.0m. × 7.5m. courtyard for each house while lavishly providing for the motor car and public garden space.[24]

With so much land devoted to external open space, it is difficult to understand the rationale for introducing into this project such an alien form as the three-storey block of flats, a particularly strange decision since the cost of each unit is far greater than that of the single- and two-storey houses. Also, precious hard currency has to be used to import foreign materials for the reinforced concrete frame. At great public expense a series of culturally unacceptable structures have been built which even in terms of climatic control leave much to be desired; some rooms face the morning and evening sun with little thought given to the direction of the prevailing winds.

The Hausa palace (gidan sarki)

At one level of analysis the palace may be regarded, quite simply, as the normal Hausa compound house on a much larger and grander scale. For example, the palace in Kano, *Gidan Rumfa* (the house of Rumfa) extends over approximately 13.5 hectares, has grazing land within its high boundary walls and houses about 1,000 occupants, besides containing the apartments of the ruler and the semi public rooms for court purposes. Leary describes the palace in Kano as follows:

> It resembles in macrocosm the traditional walled compound with entrance *zaure* leading first to a semi-private courtyard, the *kofa gida*, then to the senior man's reception hut, *shigifa*. Beyond this is his sleeping hut, *turaka*, and a private courtyard, the *cikin gida*, occupied by wives and children.[25]

Such a description fits neatly within the architectural programme, outlined here and elsewhere, for the fully developed Hausa compound where the family practises wife seclusion.[26]

In addition to being the home of the Emir and his family, the palace is the symbol of political power, community solidarity and religious authority: for this purpose location at the centre of the city is of paramount importance. A central location for the palace certainly pre-dates Islamic influence but is still significant now the Hausa are Moslems. The entrance to the palace, usually in the west wall, faces onto the *dendal*, a long, wide public space whose axis runs east-west. It is here that the whole community gathers for the greater and lesser *sallah*, and the Emir's subjects express loyalty to him in front of his palace entrance. Clapperton vividly describes the ceremony in front

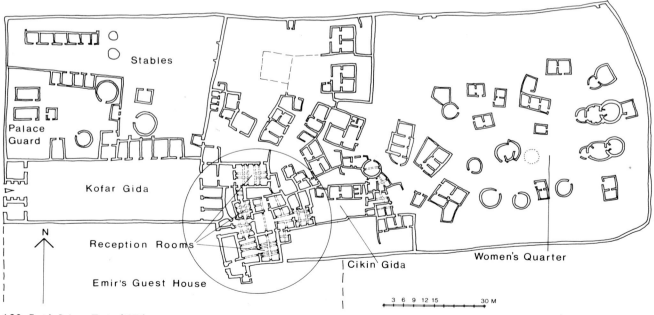

Stables

Palace Guard

Kofar Gida

N

Reception Rooms

Emir's Guest House

Cikin Gida

Women's Quarter

3 6 9 12 15   30 M

4.29 *Emir's Palace, Zaria (1971)*

74 HAUSA ARCHITECTURE

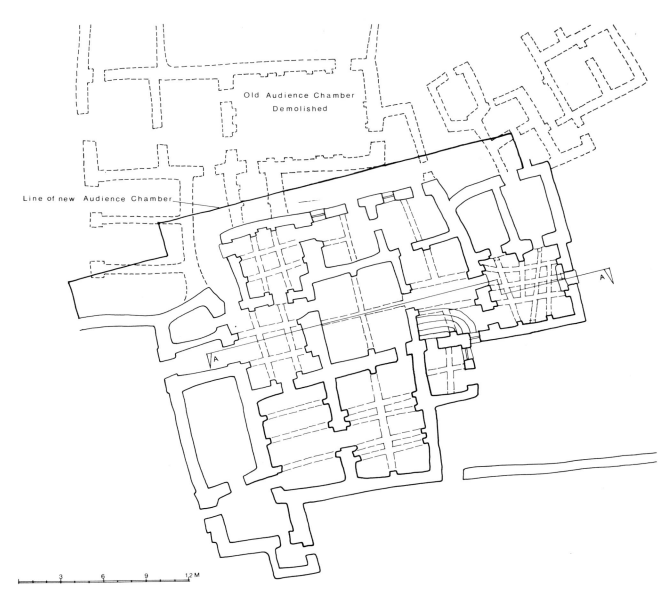

Old Audience Chamber
Demolished

Line of new Audience Chamber

A

A

3   6   9   12 M

4.30 Emir's Palace, Zaria, Reception rooms, 1977

SECTION A–A

4.31 *Emir's Palace, Zaria, Reception rooms, 1977*

of the palace of the Emir of Kano at the end of Rhamadan in 1824:

> May 30 – . . . The evening turning out cloudy, all were in low spirits, but at midnight a horseman arrived express to acquaint the Governor that the new moon had been visible.

> May 31 – After the arrival of the horseman, nothing was heard but the firing of musketry and shouts of rejoicing. – Paying and receiving visits now became a serious occupation. In the morning accompanied by Hat Salah, I went on horseback to pay my respects to the Governor. I accepted his invitation to ride out with him, according to their annual custom; and we proceeded to an open space within the city walls, amid skirmishing and firing of muskets, attended by his people on horseback, and the Arabs and principal townsfolk dressed in their gayest rainments . . .[27]

The main Friday Mosque (*Masallacin Jumma'a*) is sited on the southern boundary of the *dendal* close to the palace entrance from where the Emir processes to the mosque to lead the community in Friday prayer. It is this formal relationship of *dendal*, *Masallacin Jumma'a* and *Gidan Sarki* which symbolizes the unity of the community under the political and religious leadership of the Emir.

In Zaria, where the position of Emir has rotated among the four ruling families, the palace is the temporary home of the Emir while he holds office; each royal lineage has other homes within the city. The palace is a temporary home and an official residence of the Emir, but more important, it is an institution of state. The plan of the palace of Zaria (see Figure 4.29) shows clearly the under-developed nature of the family part of the compound which consists of a small group of rooms scattered randomly in a large open space (*cikin gida*). The important elements of the plan are the public or state rooms facing on to the semi-public courtyard (*kofar gida*). (See Figure 4.30.)

As Leary points out, 'The palace reception area is therefore equivalent to the *shigifa* of an ideal Hausa compound and with its offset entrances and asymetrical plan remains, despite indirect influences from the Mediterranean littoral, essentially an African building.'[28] However, the concept of the *shigifa* has taken on a totally new dimension: not only has the scale of the building complex been dramatically increased, but the function here is one of government. The *shigifa* is no longer a single room with staggered entrances where the master of the house (*maigida*) meets his male friends and kinsfolk, but a suite of rooms where the Emir can meet visiting

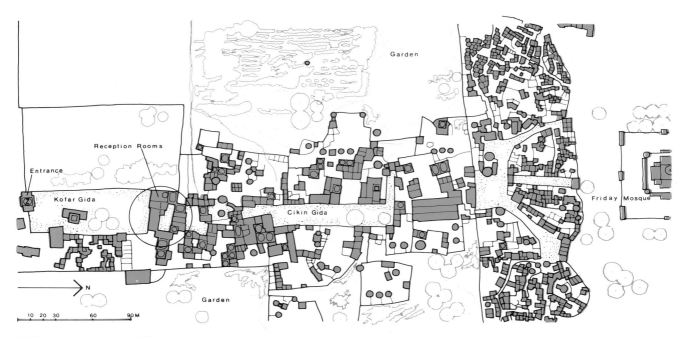

4.32 *Emir's Palace, Kano, 1970*

dignitaries and hold audiences with his ministers of state. (See Figures 4.32 and 4.33.)

Entrance to the inner courtyard (*cikin gida*) of the palace is not via a *zaure*, *kofa gida* and *shigifa*, but along a tortuous system of passageways as described by Barth on his visit to Kano palace in 1851:

> a real labyrinth of courtways provided with spacious round huts of audience, built of clay, with a door on each side and connected together by narrow intricate passageways.[29]

The plan of the entrance to the palace at Kazaure (see Figure 4.34), dating from the mid-nineteenth century, illustrates the tortuous progression through the outer palace.[30] Entrance to the palace from the courtyard in front of the Friday Mosque is through a dimly-lit *zaure*, with trabeated roof supported by two large square pillars. From there the visitor proceeds up two steps and out into a small, irregularly shaped courtyard to a round, thatched throne room with decorated mud throne. This turns the axis beautifully to the right into a further irregularly shaped courtyard and on to a two-storey mud building, on the ground floor of which is a niche with mud bed, a flight of steps to a first-floor balcony and further bed chamber.

The extent and complexity of the semi-public quarters in the palace are best illustrated by Clapperton's description of successive visits to Bello's palace in Sokoto in 1824, when on each occasion he was taken further into the palace:

> March 17 – . . . . We passed through three coozes, as guardhouses, without the least detention, and were immediately ushered into the presence of Bello, the second sultan of the Felatahs. He was seated on a small carpet, between two pillars supporting the roof of a thatched house, not unlike one of our cottages . . .

4.33 *Emir's Palace, Kano, Reception rooms, 1977 based on a drawing in Leary, A.H., A Decorated Palace in Kano*

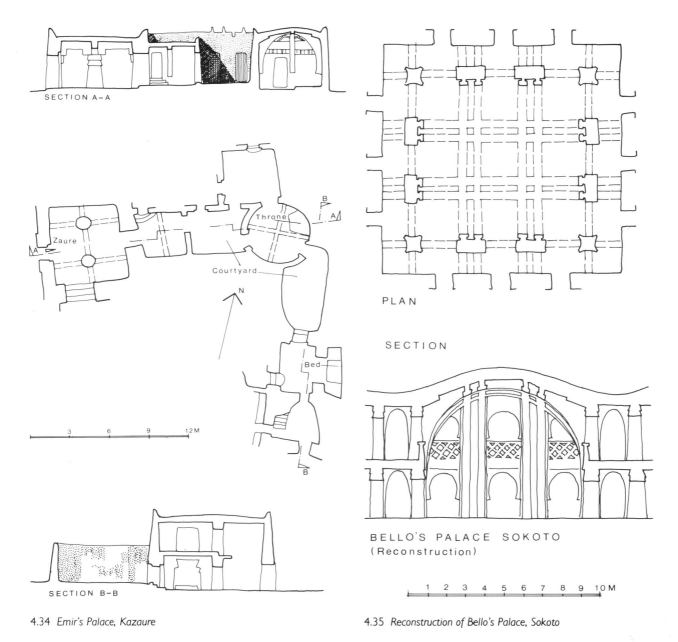

SECTION A-A

Zaure

Throne

Courtyard

B

A

A

N

Bed

B

3   6   9   12 M

SECTION B-B

PLAN

SECTION

BELLO'S PALACE SOKOTO
(Reconstruction)

1 2 3 4 5 6 7 8 9 10 M

4.34 *Emir's Palace, Kazaure*

4.35 *Reconstruction of Bello's Palace, Sokoto*

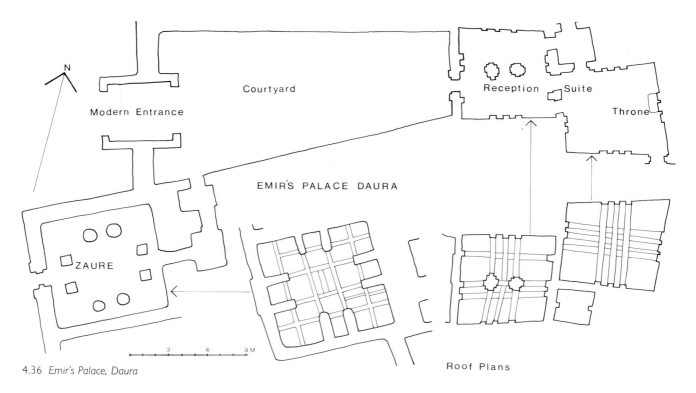

Modern Entrance

Courtyard

Reception ⊐Suite

Throne

N

EMIR'S PALACE DAURA

ZAURE

4.36 *Emir's Palace, Daura*

3   6   9 M

Roof Plans

March 10 – . . . I was conducted farther into the interior of his residence than on my two former visits. This part consisted of coozies, pretty far apart from each other . . .

March 27 – . . . We were conducted farther into the interior of his residence than I had ever been before: the Sultan was sitting reading in one corner of a square tower . . .

April 30 – . . . I was taken to a part of his residence I had never before seen: it was a handsome apartment, within a square tower, the ceiling of which was a dome, supported by eight ornamental arches, with a bright plate of brass in its centre. Between the arches and the outer wall of the tower, the dome was encircled by a neat balustrade in front of a gallery which led to an upper suite of rooms.[31]

Figure 4.35 is a possible reconstruction of this last room, which according to the account must indeed have been a splendid audience chamber.

For stranger and citizen alike the awesome symbolic significance of the palace is achieved through its central location, the area of its ground plan and the fortress-like qualities of its wall and towers:

> The Governor's residence covers a large space, and resembles a walled village. It even contains a Mosque, and several towers three or four storeys high, with windows in the European style, but without glass or frame-work. It is necessary to pass through two of these towers in order to gain the suite of inner apartments occupied by the Governor.[32]

The visitor entering the palace is further impressed by the splendour of the chambers which reinforces the image of the palace as the most significant building in the city and its seat

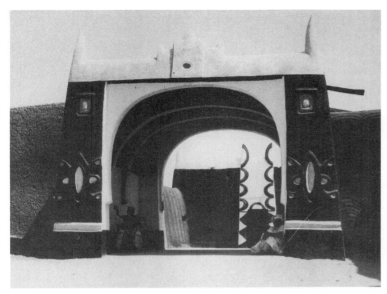

4.37 *Emir's Palace, Daura, main entrance*

4.38 *Emir's Palace, Daura, Zaure*

4.39 *Emir's Palace, Daura, Interior of Zaure*

of political power. Some impression of the splendour of the public and semi-public reception rooms in the Hausa palace can be gained from Figures 4.36 to 4.43 which illustrate the eighteenth-century *zaure* and nineteenth-century public chambers.

The changes in the planning and construction of palaces during the latter part of this century are similar to those of the homes of ordinary citizens. For example, in Zaria the palace

4.40 *Emir's Palace, Daura, Interior of Zaure*

4.41 *Emir's Palace, Daura, Interior of Zaure*

has a new entrance which permits the emir's official car to penetrate the outer wall and enter a garage, a feature which is now as important, if not more so, than the stables for his horses. A large new reception hall of modern construction and materials has also been built there. Despite these and other changes the old suite of reception rooms remains in the Zaria palace; similar rooms in the Kano palace appear to be actively preserved, for they are in excellent condition.

4.42 *Emir's Palace Daura, Reception Room*

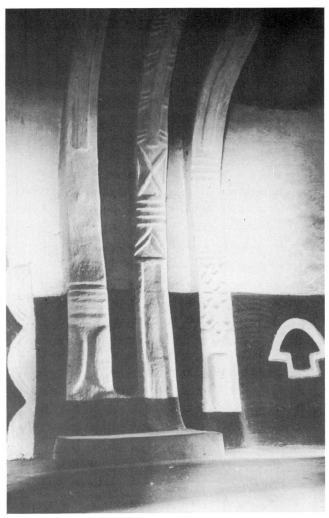

4.43 *Emir's Palace, Daura, Throne*

The Mosque

Islam is essentially a religion for laymen. Prayer can be performed anywhere provided the correct procedure is observed. In most settlements, therefore, there are small public spaces enclosed by low walls which act as outdoor praying spaces for the local community. Here male members of the neighbourhood gather at the specified times to recite prayers under the leadership of the local *liman*. (See Figure 4.45.) A wealthy member of the community may donate enough money to build a small mosque (*masallaci*, s., *masallatai*, pl.), which usually consists of a single room whose east wall (*quibla* wall) is emphasized by a small niche (*mihrab*). The mosque may be roofed with mud or thatch, or more recently with tin; it may also have a small platform, reached by steps, from which prayer-time is called. (See Figures 4.44 to 4.47.)

Whenever possible, all male members of the community are expected to attend every Friday at the main mosque in the settlement (*Masallacin Jumma'a*). Since Friday prayer is a community occasion, an essential requirement of the Friday Mosque is that it is capable of holding a large congregation. One method of building large spaces in mud is by the use of many reinforced columns about 2.0 to 2.5 metres apart to support reinforced beams on which the heavy roof rests. The other method of constructing a mud roof spanning large spaces is to use reinforced arches in complex interlacing patterns. The mosque is orientated so that one wall (*quibla*) faces Mecca, which to the Hausa is symbolic of the east. The *mihrab* niche is placed in the *quibla* to indicate to the

4.44 *Local Mosque, Daura*

4.45 *Call to Prayer, Zaria, 1962*

congregation the correct direction to face when praying.

The trabeated form of mosque is illustrated in Figures 4.48, the Shehu's mosque in Sokoto; 4.50, the mosque in Kazaure, and 4.51, the mosque in Bauchi, all probably dating from the early nineteenth century. The roofs of all three mosques are supported on a forest of pillars (see Figures 4.53 to 4.54), the pillars at Bauchi being particularly monumental in proportions. Using this structural solution, light from the small doorways barely penetrates to the innermost parts of the space, making it impossible to see the *mihrab* from most parts of the hall.

A large congregation is accommodated more successfully within the larger spaces created by arched construction. The Friday Mosque, Zaria, built sometime in the late 1830s or early 1840s is designed in this way used arched construction.[33] (See Figures 4.57 to 4.64.) It was built by Babban Gwani, Mallam Mikaila the first chief builder of Hausaland appointed by Shehu Uthman Dan Fodio.[34] The Friday Mosque, Zaria is probably the high point of Hausa architecture, built during a period of puritanical fervour which followed the jihad. Part of the old mosque has been demolished, and the remainder enclosed within the shell of its modern successor. The beautifully modelled walls have been coated with cement

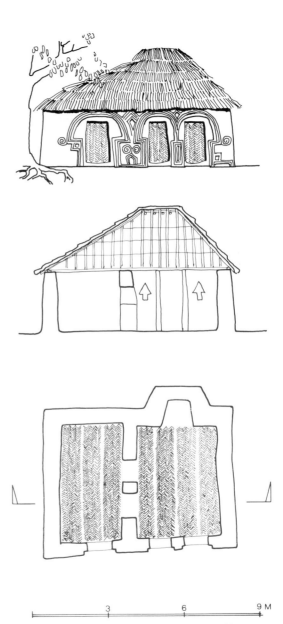

4.46 *Local Mosque, Babban Gwani Ward, Zaria, 1980*

4.47 *Local Mosque, Zaria, 1962 designed by Mallam Haruna*

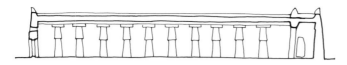

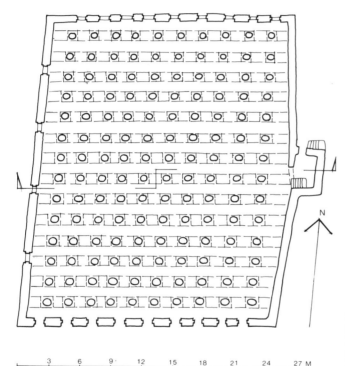

4.48 *Shehu Mosque, Sokoto, 1962*

chevrons typical of Hausaland for much of this century.

The first impression on entering the mosque is of big sculptural forms. Decoration is restrained and in the background, such as there is consists of deeply incised verticals, triangles and circles on the piers, and horizontals on the undersides of the arches emphasizing and complementing the main forms. The plan of the building is such that only one to two decorations could be seen at any moment; because of the contrast of light and shadow they blended into the total architectural effect. The more complex designs, such as the decorated architrave surrounding the *mihrab* niche on an otherwise undecorated wall, together with the bold designs on the adjacent pier faces, were purposely placed to emphasize and enrich the *mihrab* area.[35]

The mosque is usually placed within a rectangular, or nearly rectangular walled courtyard, the sides of the walls facing the cardinal points. Entrance to the courtyard is through ablution chambers in each wall, built in the form of the *zaure* or *shigifa*, with staggered doorways to obscure the view. The mosque may have a tower (*hasumiya*) attached to it. In the Friday Mosque, Zaria there was, until it was demolished, a most beautiful *shari'a* court (see Figure 4.57) through which the Emir made his formal procession to the Mosque for prayers.

4.49 *Shehu Mosque, Sokoto, 1962*

plaster, reducing the sensitive decoration to a crude mechanical copy. Yet much of the mosque remains for the visitor to imagine the building in its true splendour. The relief patterns in the interior were before 'improvement': sober and formal, the dignified work of an age of religious reformers, the very antithesis of the arabesque-like spirals, interlacing knots and

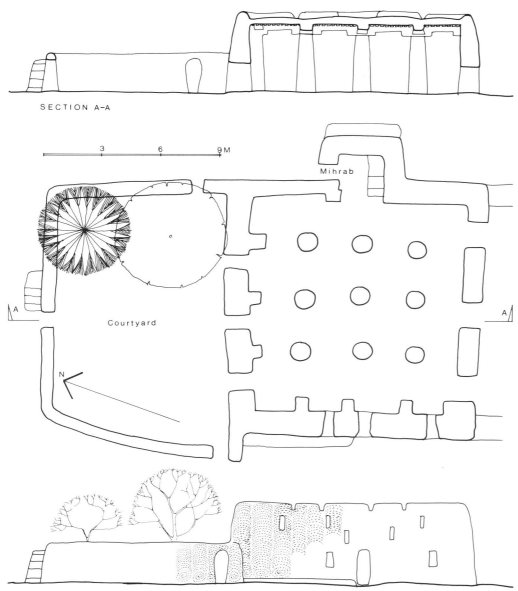

SECTION A-A

3   6   9M

Mihrab

A

Courtyard

N

A

4.50 *Mosque at Kazaure, 1962*

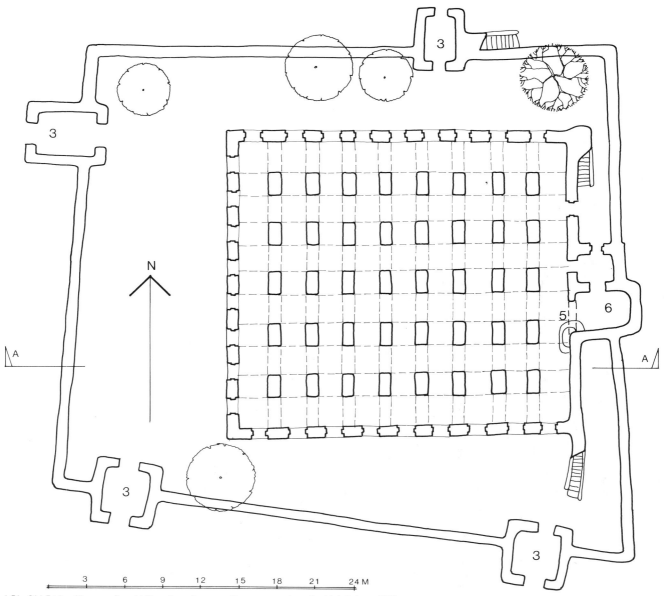

3

3

3

N

A

A

5

6

3

3 6 9 12 15 18 21 24 M

4.51 *Old Friday Mosque, Bauchi Plan, based upon a Survey carried out by Abdullahi in 1981*

SECTION A–A

4.52 *Old Friday Mosque, Bauchi Section*

4.53 *Shehu Mosque, Sokoto (Interior) 1962*

4.54 *Old Friday Mosque, Bauchi (Interior 1962)*

4.55 *Old Friday Mosque, Bauchi (Mihrab 1962)*

4.56 *Old Friday Mosque, Bauchi (Interior 1962)*

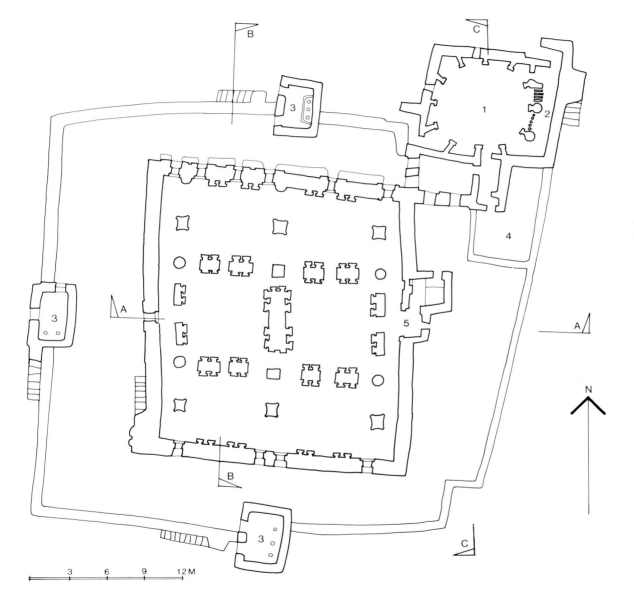

4.57 Friday Mosque, Zaria (Plan 1962)

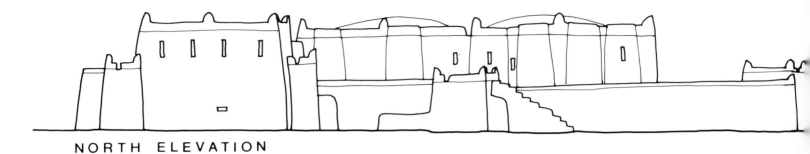

NORTH ELEVATION

4.58 *Friday Mosque, Zaria (Elevation)*

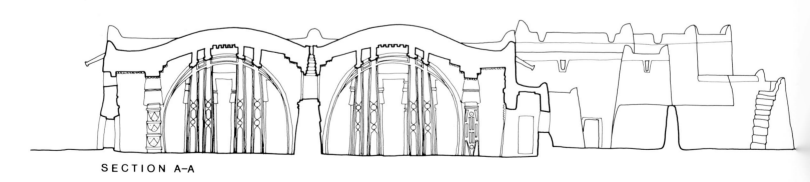

SECTION A–A

4.60 *Friday Mosque, Zaria (Section AA)*

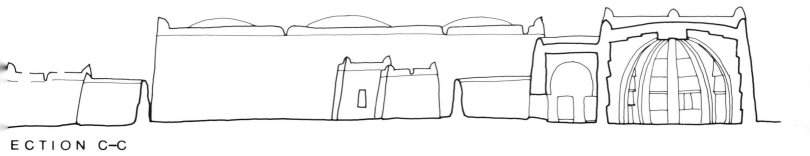

ECTION C–C

4.59 *Friday Mosque, Zaria (Section CC)*

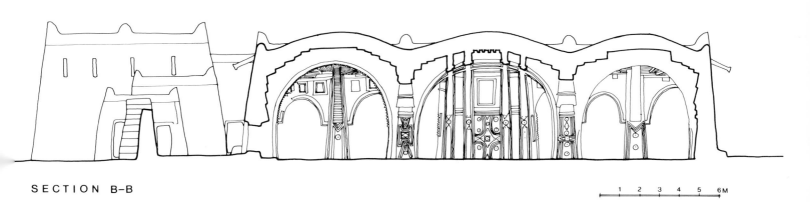

SECTION B–B

4.61 *Friday Mosque, Zaria (Section BB)*

1 2 3 4 5 6M

4.62 *Friday Mosque, Zaria (Interior) Photographed by A.H. Leary*

94   HAUSA ARCHITECTURE

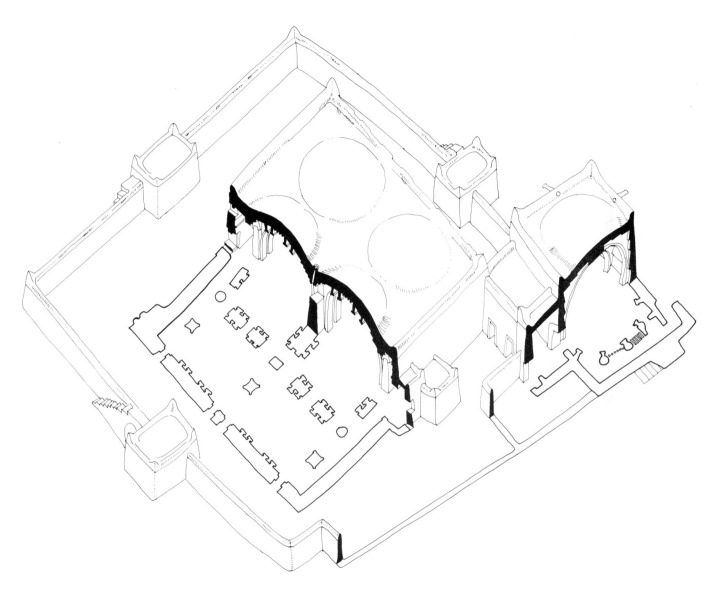

4.63 *Friday Mosque, Zaria (Axonometric)*

4.64 *Friday Mosque, Zaria (Interior) Photographed by A.H. Leary*

4.65 *Habe Tower at Katsina*

4.66 *Habe Tower at Katsina*

4.67 *Tower Bauchi Mosque*

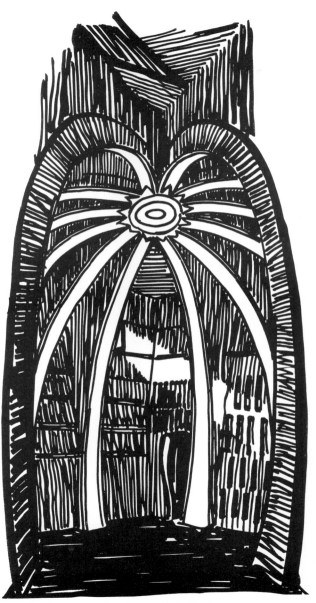

4.68 *Shari'a Court, Friday Mosque, Zaria 1962*

Conclusion

The Friday Mosque, *shari'a* court, palace and *dendal* are sited at the centre of the city and together symbolize the power of Allah, Islamic law and government, state and community solidarity. The city is subdivided into wards, each of which has at its centre the ward head's house, a meeting space and neighbourhood mosque. At the hub of the extended family house is the *shigifa, kofa gida* and prayer mat, which complete the city structure binding citizen and state into a cohesive society with Islam as the governing discipline. The implicit architectural programme of this society, disciplined as it is by Islam, results in a unified and highly organized spatial structure which expresses in built form the significant features of Hausa culture.

5. Architectural Construction

Introduction

The elements of Hausa material culture have been developed from the natural products in the local environment, until quite recently, supplemented in a limited way only with imported goods. But under the growing influence of industrialized nations, the number and variety of materials and techniques for constructional purposes has increased dramatically. The changes in building technology caused by external contacts are most apparent in the work of government agencies and commercial concerns, but have been introduced into the traditional structure of the old cities by the growing middle class: those who can afford to now build in concrete blocks, and the tin roof is preferred to thatch or the mud dome. Yet despite these rapidly accelerating changes, which may bring about the demise of a once great architectural tradition, Hausa builders are still only marginally affected by the new technology. Most constructional work outside the scope of the formal building industry is still of materials found in the local environment.

Laterite, used with various additives for walls, roofs and finishes, is still the most important material used by the traditional Hausa builders. There is an abundance of stone in the many stark, black granite outcrops—those marvellous inselbergs that contrast so sharply to the flat savanna landscape of the Hausa plains—yet its use, as a traditional building material is confined to a few of the smaller ethnic groups of the Jos plateau. The primitive stone walls of these peoples are a reminder of earlier great builders responsible for the abandoned and enigmatic dry stone walls of the plateau. Evidence of earlier great periods of building is to be found in travellers' descriptions of traces of ancient burnt brick buildings in areas adjacent to Hausaland.[1] Such archaeological remains may indeed be the last vestiges of a building technique introduced by Islamic scholars such as al Saheli

many centuries before.[2] Rejection of diverse forms of structural techniques, and concentration on the development of one system of construction and the almost universal use of one building material has produced a unified architectural composition for complete cities. The uncompromising nature of the architectural pattern derived from constantly repeated structural forms expresses the social and spiritual needs of the Hausa through the symbolic use of those forms and the spaces they create. It is because of this unity of form and the meaning attached to it that Hausa building can be classified and studied as architecture.

The main structural types

There are three main traditional structural building types: the circular room made entirely from vegetable material (*dakuna*); the circular, figure-of-eight or rectangular room with mud walls, thatched roof and sometimes a verandah (*adada*), and the building constructed entirely of mud (*soro*) reinforced with beams split from the *deleb* palm (*azara*, s., *azarori*, pl.). Mud buildings (*soro*) take a number of forms: they may be circular or rectangular and have a roof supported on corbels, pillars and beams or arches; some are elaborate, two-storey structures (*bene*). In addition to these traditional building types others have been introduced over the last thirty years which are made of more permanent materials. For example, the tin roof may be used with any combination of the former structures, replacing the mud or thatched roof and sometimes in addition to an existing mud roof to increase its weather resistance. The latest and most desirable structure, to which many Hausa people aspire, consists of concrete-block walls, tin roof and verandah. These are the principal building units which now make up the city; in this study, however, only those of mud will be discussed in detail.

5.1 *Mud wall construction I*

5.2 *Mud wall construction 2*

The structural process

The constructional process for a mud building is a long one: too little time spent in preparing the materials or in the construction of the building results in repeated and costly maintenance. Preparation of the building takes two to three weeks; the minimum period for building the walls of a small room from foundation to wall-plate is ten days. Since there is no way of speeding up the process, building starts at the beginning of the dry season and ends just before the rains; a period of three months is necessary to build the normal house.

The mud walls are made from regular courses of unbaked bricks (*tubali* s., *tubala*, pl.) laid in mud mortar. (See Figure 5.1.) The mud brick is made from earth (*kasa*), preferably red laterite which is thoroughly soaked in water, left for twenty-four hours, again soaked, trampled and kneaded. This process is repeated a number of times before the earth is rolled into bricks, usually circular cones varying from 5cm. to 15cm. in diameter, depending on the district in which they are made. Making the building mud is graphically described in *Labarun Al'Adun Hausawa Da Zantatukansu*:

> Then they started work and dug up the earth on the surface. It was soaked with the water which they brought in water-pots, from morning till about three p.m. – their time for leaving off work.

They left the earth to soak for twenty-four hours. On their arrival at daybreak they turn it over with all their might, mixing it thoroughly with water till it is properly mixed. When it has been properly mixed they leave it for another twenty-four hours . . . This is the work they will go on doing every day without interruption for about fifteen days.[3]

Before they can be used structurally, the bricks are allowed to dry out thoroughly, which takes about ten days. Old bricks taken from ruins are sometimes re-used in the top courses of new buildings, but better practice dictates breaking them down into earth and repeating the process of soaking and trampling.

The method of making mortar is similar to that used for bricks: after soaking and trampling the earth it is covered with horse manure and continually soaked with water for several days. The mixture is then trampled to get a thorough mixing of earth and dung; and the process is repeated using a fresh layer of dung. This material is mixed three or four times and is ready for use in two to three weeks.

The first step in erecting a building is to clear the ground (*schema*) of stones, vegetable matter and topsoil. Then the building is set out using pegs, ropes and hoes. The plan (*sura*, s., *surori*, pl.) of the house is drawn on the ground by the chief builder (*sarkin gini*) with his foot:

5.3   *Mud wall construction 3*

5.4   *Maintenance of wall*

They came in the morning, and Tanko gave them a rope, hoe and 'pegs'; they marked out the house exactly rectangular, with its entrance facing south; they marked out four huts, a square house, a mud-roofed house, and an entrance-hut.[4]

Shallow trenches (0.45m.) are dug along the line of the plan just beneath the loose topsoil: mud foundations without footings are constructed in the trenches, the load of the roof and wall being distributed over a large area of subsoil because of the large batter given to the wall. Foundations of important buildings are protected from erosion by the construction of a wide external plinth at the base.

Wall construction

When constructing a wall only two or three courses of mud bricks are laid in one day, and on reaching the height of the door lintel the work is suspended for twenty-four hours so that the walls are thoroughly dry before completing the top courses. The normal method of building is for the builder to sit astride the top of the unfinished wall; mud bricks and pats of mortar are thrown up to him. (See Figure 5.3.) On finishing the day's courses within his reach, the builder moves backwards, away from this new work, and sits on that part of the wall built the previous day. So scaffolding and ladders are used in the construction of large buildings only, such as the emir's palace and important mosques, but ladders are sometimes used for repairs, maintenance and decoration.

Hausa builders have learned, through the accumulated experience of many generations, that the stability of a clay wall is increased by decreasing its thickness towards the top.

Consequently, the battered wall is a universal and very beautiful feature of Hausa architecture. The use of the vertical line and plumbob is unknown to traditional builders: they achieve structural stability by the mass of the wall acting vertically downwards. Buttresses are not important elements and are used only to prop failing walls.

5.5 *Construction of building with thatched roof I*

Because mud roofs are heavy, walls supporting them must be extremely thick. Then they are often strengthened by timber reinforcement taken from the *deleb* palm (*giginya*, s., *giginyoyi*, pl.) (*Borassus flabellifer*), the *dumi* palm (*Hyphaene thebaica*), or *kurna* (*Zyzyphus spina-christi*), none of which is attacked or destroyed by the white ant, a termite found in large numbers in many parts of West Africa including Hausaland. Timber taken from the *deleb* palm for building purposes is called *azara* (*azarori*, pl, *azaru*, pl.).[5] It is placed in walls about half to one metre above the ground and again at a level just above the height of the door head. This reinforcement consists of *azarori* laid transversely across the width of the wall, on top of which are placed additional *azarori* running longtitudinally. Walls vary in thickness from 15cm. for a small partition to 1.20m. for two-storey buildings (see Table 2). Piers and columns are also reinforced using groups of bonded *azarori* bound together with mud mortar and surrounded by a thick coating of mud: their size varies from 0.9m. square to 1.8m. square.

Roof construction

There are three main types of traditional roofing. The cheapest and most common is conical and thatched; then comes the flat, mud roof and finally, until very recently, the most

---

Table 2. Wall thickness at ground level[6]

1.2m. thick	for two-storey buildings
0.9m. thick	for rooms 4.5 × 4.5m. and over
0.75m. thick	for rooms 3.9 × 3.9m. — 4.5 × 4.5m.
0.6m. thick	for rooms less than 3.9 × 3.9m.
0.45m. thick	for partition walls
0.3m. thick	for low partition walls and small grass-roofed huts
0.15m. thick	for partition walls less than 1.8m. high

5.6 *Construction of building with thatched roof 2*

5.7 *Construction of building with thatched roof 3*

expensive and most prestigious, the domed mud roof supported on mud arches. Corrugated iron is now becoming the most popular roofing material and the most prestigious.

Whenever possible, the conical thatched roof is made from the fronds of the raphia palm (*gwangwala* or *tukurwa*, s., *tukware*, pl.) *Raphia vinifera*. But this is expensive and it is more usual for raphia palm fronds to be used for the main rafters, with sticks *kara* or guinea-corn stalks (*karan dawa*) between them. for small huts, the whole roof is generally constructed on the ground then lifted into place on the mud walls; roofs of huts with a diameter greater than 4m. are constructed *in situ*.

The wall plate (*jiniya*, s., *jiniyoyi*, pl.) for the roof is made first and to it the thickest ends of the palm stalks are fixed; their thin ends meet at the top where they are securely bound with rope. Bands of corn stalks are tied around the sloping rafters at centres of between 0.2m. and 0.3m. Thatch is brought up to the site in bundles of about 8m. long and up to 1.5m. wide, depending on the length of grass available. The grass is held together near the thick ends with one row of sewing, and is unrolled from the bottom of the roof towards the apex. The thick ends of the grass are at the bottom, each layer of grass overlapping the one below by a few centimetres less than its total length. All the layers of grass are sewn to the framework and the whole roof is held down by a net which is made by tying rope over the thatch at about 0.6m. to 0.9m. centres. (See Figures 5.5 to 5.9.)

5.8   *Construction of building with thatched roof 4*

5.9   *Construction of building with thatched roof 5*

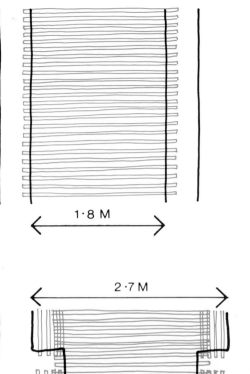

1·8 M

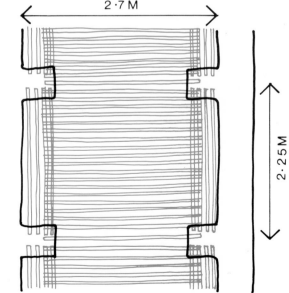

2·7 M

2·25 M

The simplest mud roof is formed by spanning a space with *azara* joists. The economic span of *azara* is about 1.8 metres; in other words, the weight of the usual thickness of mud required to weatherproof the roof can be held up by closely spaced *azara* joists without an intermediate support over a space of just under 2 metres. It is usual to place the *azara* beams less than 2.5 centimetres apart, but for the sake of economy they may be at intervals of 15 to 30 centimetres, with sticks placed over them at right angles to the main span. The whole structure is covered with grass matting (*zana*, s., *zanaku*, *zanaki* and

5.10 *Spanning a space of 1.8m*
5.11 *Spanning a space of 2.7m*

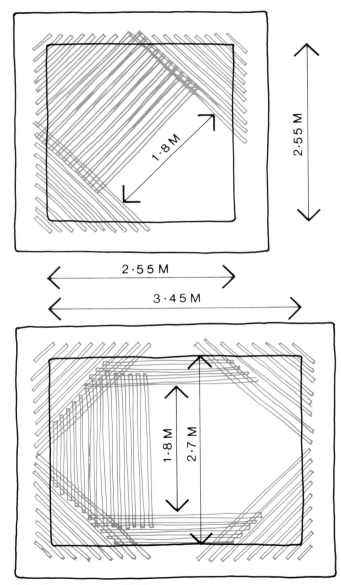

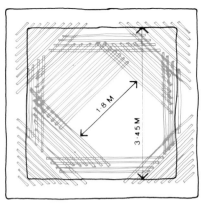

5.14 *Spanning a space of 3.45m square*

5.12 *Spanning a space of 2.55m square*
5.13 *Spanning a space of 2.7m x 3.45m*

zanaiku, pl.) on which the mud roof rests. An understanding of the structural limitations of this simple roof form is the key to analyzing and interpreting the form of Hausa architecture from the simplest mud cell to the most complex roof patterning adopted by Mallam Mikaila in the Friday Mosque, Zaria.[7] (See Figure 5.10.) Spaces larger than the economic span for *azara* may be roofed by a complex system of corbelling and coffering; the division of the space by pillars, or the use of arches. Sometimes a combination of such devices is employed.

When corbels are used they are reinforced with several layers of *azara* projecting 0.45m. from the face of the wall at about 2.1m. centres. The space between the corbels is spanned by a beam made of several layers of *azara* from which *azara* joists span across to the other wall in the usual way. This extension of the constructional system allows a room to be increased in width from 1.8m. to 2.7m. (See Figure 5.11.)

Roofing a rectangular room larger than 1.8m. square requires the use of *azara* placed diagonally across the corners of the space. From these triangular platforms (*tanyi*) at the corners of the room additional beams span parallel to the walls. By repeating this process a shallow reinforced dome (*tuluwa*) is formed covering a room about 3.4m. square: the free space to be bridged by the joists is gradually reduced to 1.8m. by the clever system of corbelling shown in Figure 5.14.

For very large rooms, the roof may be supported on a series of columns (*al'amudi*, s., *al'amudai*, pl.) connected by beams. The column is usually surmounted by a simple capital, consisting of two or four *azara* corbels which make it possible to increase the spacing between columns from 1.8m. to 2.7m. The spaces between the columns are spanned by beams reinforced in the usual way with *azara*, the roof joists spanning between the beams. Figure 5.15 is the drawing of the roof plan and Figure 5.16 is a detail of the column of the Friday Mosque at Kazaure, a simple trabeated structure in which some of the corbelling techniques have been used.

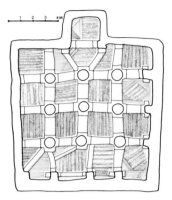

5.15 *Roof plan of the Mosque at Kazaure*

5.16 *Column and capital, Mosque at Kazaure*

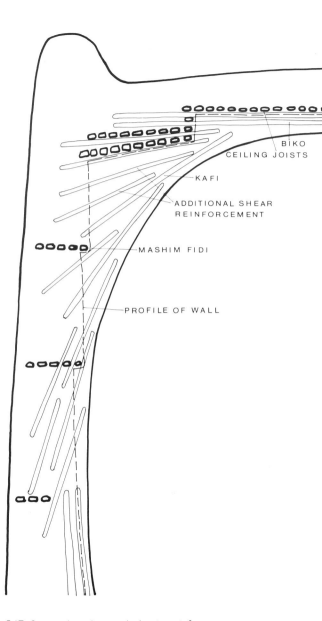

5.17 *Section through an arch showing reinforcement*

Labels in figure:
BIKO
CEILING JOISTS
KAFI
ADDITIONAL SHEAR REINFORCEMENT
MASHIM FIDI
PROFILE OF WALL

5.18 *Arch: structural failure*

Arch construction

Forming spaces larger than 3.5m. square requires the use of the mud arch (*baka*): with this structural system it is possible to construct rooms 8m. square. The 'mud arch' as used by the Hausa builders is not a true arch in the structural sense of the word, but simply a series of reinforced mud corbels placed one on top of the other until they meet at the centre. They are coated with mud to take on the shape and outward appearance of the arch.

Figure 5.17 is a section through such an arch showing a typical arrangement of *azara* reinforcement. In good construction, the layers of *azara* (*Kafi*) should not project more than about 0.7m., nor should the change in angle between succeeding *kafi* be too great. For these reasons the arch should start quite low down as in the Friday Mosque, Zaria.

Arches are normally constructed in the following manner: each layer of reinforcement (*kafi*) is tied back to the preceding one, beginning from both walls and working upwards and outwards towards the centre of the room. When the gap between the two halves of the arch is small enough, horizontal *azara* called *biko* are used to complete the arch. Each corbel is allowed to dry overnight before the next one is constructed: in this way the arch can be built without centring or scaffolding.

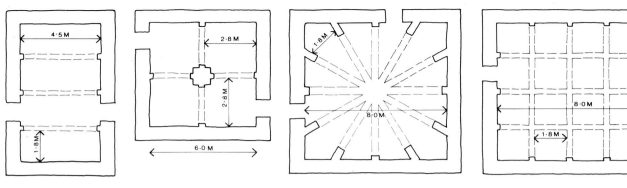

5.19 *Arch construction: room 4.5m wide*

5.20 *Arch construction: room with central pillar*

5.21 *Arch construction: Kafin laima construction*

5.22 *Arch construction: daurin guga construction*

Additional *azara* for sheer reinforcement, (*guntun azara*) are placed at right angles to the wall and project into the body of the arch. Lengths of *azara* called *mashinfidi* put in the wall at the back of the arch at right angles to it distribute thrusts through a large area of wall and prevent cracking.[8] In a rectangular room where the shortest side is less than about 4.5m., the room is usually divided into bays of 2.1m. and simple arches span across the room parallel to the shortest side. *Azara* covers the area between the arches which usually conforms to the standard 1.8m. (See Figure 5.19.)

A room having all walls longer than 4.5m. may be roofed using arches in three ways: internal pillars with arches spanning from them to the walls (see Figure 5.20); arches spanning from wall to wall, all passing through one central point (*kafin laima*) like a tent construction (see Figure 5.21); arches spanning from wall to wall, but all being parallel to one or other wall called *tulluwa*, or *daurin guga* (see Figure 5.22):[9] a variation of this latter type of roof consists of three half arches meeting at mid span, and is called *kafar kaza* or *takalnin kaza*.

Figure 5.23 illustrates the process of building a simple, domed roof supported on four half arches of *tulluwa* construction. The arches are built out from the walls until they meet at the summit as previously described. Then diagonal lengths of *azara* are laid across the corners of the room,

forming triangular platforms (*tanyi*). From these platforms *azara* beams are carried over the backs of the arches. Similar but lighter beams are formed near the apex of the vault from which the *azara* joists span to the wall beam. Using this form of construction most of the weight of the roof is placed directly on the wall, reducing the loading on the centre of the arches which is the most vulnerable part of the structure.

The Friday Mosque, Zaria

The six domes (*tulluwa*) of the Friday Mosque, Zaria (see Figures 4.57 to 4.64) show all the subtleties of structural technique available to the Hausa architect. Here Mallam Mikaila has exhibited his greatest skill as a builder. Compare the size of the main hall (20m. × 23m.) with that of the *Shari's* court (7m. × 7m.) which pushes *kafin laima* structure to its limits. Using arches springing from all four walls in the *daurin guga* style produces a space of about 5.5m. × 12.5m., far too small for the purposes of Mallam Mikaila. Instead, he created six main spaces, each approximately 7.0m. square, using two main structural walls, twenty-one piers and one isolated wall at the centre of the composition. At first sight the pattern of the coffering on the ceiling may look arbitrary, but it represents the culmination of many generations of structural experiment. The domes and the arches that support them are bound

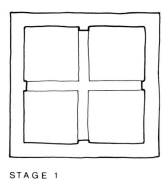 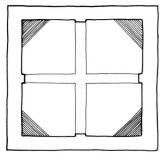 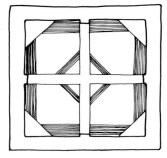 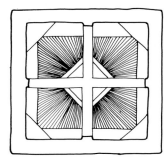

STAGE 1　　　　　STAGE 2　　　　　STAGE 3　　　　　STAGE 4

5.23 *Process of arch construction*

together into a rigid and monolithic structure by a series of rising beams along the haunches of the arches so that the great mass of the clay domes is transferred to pillar and wall with the least possible eccentric loading.

An important visual feature of the mosque, which perhaps gives it much of its character, is the repetitive use of the double arch supported on twin piers. This device is a simple effort to increase both the free space between the piers and the stability of the structure. But the twin arch was an important structural innovation: it was for mud buildings as important a development as was the flying buttress for medieval European architecture. Look at the roof plan of the mosque and imagine the two main spaces constructed using three arches in both directions. (See Figures 5.24 and 5.25.) This roofing solution is the obvious one conforming to the modular discipline of *azara* construction, but it leads to the use of more piers, one of which is badly placed in relation to the *mihrab*. Following this system each dome is supported by only six instead of eight arches. By doubling up the arches it is possible to create voids in the centre of each face of the space, which most architectural critics would consider aesthetically desirable. Mallam Mikaila therefore designed a stronger solution and one that is visually more pleasing, while maintaining a distance between arches within the limits of the economic span of *azara*.[10]

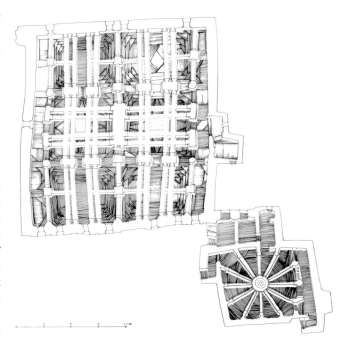

5.24 *Friday Mosque, Zaria, Roof Plan*

Modular design

The structural technology employed by Hausa builders is one important factor in determining the architectural form of buildings. Heights and plan sizes, while not rigidly conforming to a strict set of rules, nevertheless provide the designer with an almost modular discipline based upon a set of preferred dimensions determined largely by the constructional process. Heights, to a large degree, are decided by simple reference to the human body. According to the account in *Larbarun Al'Adun Hausawa*, the arches spring from about shoulder or head height: 'When the building of the mud-roofed room reaches the height of a man's shoulder, or his full height, short *azaras* are put in to form the base of the arch'.[11] The height of a simple flat-roofed domestic building is about that of a man with upraised hand; the height of a room with a roof supported on arches is entirely dependent on the span, which in turn determines the height of the arch.

Strictly speaking the 'mud arch' is a curved beam made from a series of cantilevered corbels reinforced with *azara*: it is not a true arch, which is an arrangement of wedge-shaped blocks mutually supporting each other. The shape of the Hausa arch is decorative: it takes on an approximately semicircular form, with the base of the semicircle at the level where the first layer of reinforcement cuts the face of the wall. The usual practice is to continue the arch shape downwards for some distance, giving it the appearance of a semi-eclipse; sometimes it is narrowed into the 'horse shoe' shape so common in the medieval Islamic architecture of North Africa. In yet other examples, including the Friday Mosque, Zaria, the arches spring from the ground. This is stronger not only visually, but structurally, particularly if *azara* is carried down this extra length of arch.[12] Despite its structural ambiguity in visual terms, the preferred shape of the arch determines the height of the building. For a room of maximum size using *daurin guga* construction—5.4m. × 12m.—the height of the ceiling is approximately 4.8m; while for a room of maximum size using *kafin laima* construction—7.8m. × 7.8m.—the height of the ceiling is 6.0m. Other room sizes are calculated in a similar manner; but in all cases there is a direct relationship between the plan shape and the height.

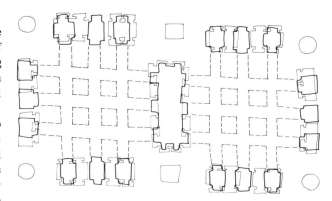

5.25 *Friday Mosque, Zaria, alternative planning solution*

There is no rigid system by which building heights are determined; this is done empirically, where necessary making reference to the height of a person, or simply working within the structural limits of the building material and the preferred constructional technology. The building technique is such that ladders and scaffolding are used only on important edifices and mainly for maintenance. So the maximum height of a single-storey wall in those buildings which comprise most of the settlement is determined by the height to which a clay brick (*tubali*, s., *tubala*, pl.) can be thrown to the builder who sits astride the top of the wall.[12] The height of the wall plate in a circular thatched room is also standardized at approximately the height of a man.

Although in Hausa settlements buildings vary in height, the variations are all within close limits of the standard norm for the particular structural type and its plan form. The account of the building process in *Labarun Al'Adun Hausawa* shows clearly that the Hausa are interested in the appearance of their buildings and conscious of the fact that height has an effect on appearance:

> One must take care about the height, lest one hut be higher than another. It is better to arrange it so that they are all of the same height.[14]

The diameter of the round hut with a thatched conical roof is determined largely by the lengths of available rafters; most round huts are between 3 and 4m. in diameter. Sizes outside this range do occur, but it is more usual to join two round huts together to increase the living area. In such cases, each hut has an independent conical frame; the frames are joined together at the points with a ridge pole and the whole frame, so formed, is thatched as one roof.

Plan dimensions of mud buildings are governed by the system of dimensions that results from the use of economically sized balks of *azara* as both joists and reinforcement. (See Figures 5.10 to 5.14.) The maximum room size using this construction is about 3.5m. square at roof level, which after allowing for the batter on the walls gives a floor space of approximately 3m. square. Increasing room sizes further requires the use of columns or piers whose spacing is again determined by the effective span of *azara* beams which, including two mud corbels, gives a clear space between columns at the capital of about 2.7m. Based on these dimensions the ideal arrangement of columns is at approximately 3m. centres, after allowing for a column size of 1m. square with a batter on each face. The form of the building resulting from such a structural system is very similar to the hypostyle hall of Pharaonic Egypt, the product of a similar trabeated constructional system but in stone. In both cases the roof is supported on a forest of columns which in Hausaland vary in size from the huge polished clay pillars of the Bauchi Mosque (about 2.7m. × 2.1m. at the base) to the slender cylindrical columns of the Shehu's Mosque in Sokoto which are only about 1m. in diameter at the base.

Arch construction is also based on the set of dimensions which determines bay sizes in flat roof construction. Rooms where one dimension is less than 4.5m. can be formed using arches spanning in the shorter direction only. The arches are built at centres of 2.1m. so that the roof is divided into bays of 1.8m., making the length of room 1.8 + 0.3 + 1.8 = 3.9m., or 1.8 + 0.3 + 1.8 + 0.3 + 1.8 = 6m., and so on to a maximum size of 12.3m.

Rooms greater than 4.5m. wide require arches spanning in two directions. The limit of the structural system using either *kafin laima* or *daurin guga* appears to be the construction of a space 8.0m. square. At this size great care must be taken with the construction and first class supervision is required. As shown earlier, the Friday Mosque in Zaria is particularly interesting in its layout of the main spaces where the architect has extended the system to its limits by the technique of twinning the structural arches. Using normal methods, with two single arches in both directions, a floor plan of approximately 5.4m. is created. However, by using sets of twin arches the architect has been able to increase the free floor area to 7.2m. square while maintaining the discipline of spaces between main structural members conforming to the requirements of *azara*.

Room sizes may be increased further by detaching from the wall the piers which support the arches. The *zaure* in the Emir's palace at Daura has been designed in this way: here the maximum free space created by the *daurin guga* construction has been increased from 7.2m. square to 10m. square. (See Figure 4.36.) Similar treatment can be seen in the Friday Mosque, Zaria, and in the *zaure* of the house built by Mallam Mikaila in Zaria. (See Figures 4.57 and 3.15).

Protecting the building from the weather

A steeply sloping thatched roof with large overhang protects the walls of the Hausa peasant building from rain. But protection from rain of the mud roofed building (*soro*) is a much more complicated process of design.

It is important that rainwater is removed from the building as quickly and efficiently as possible. For this purpose all roofs are designed with a minimum fall of 1 in 15, which is achieved by laying the *azara* joists at this angle and not building up the thickness of clay at one side of the roof. The roof, as was mentioned above, consists of *zana* mats placed on the joists followed by 15cm. of mud then 5cm. of waterproofing compound. The rainwater is conducted from the roof by spouts (*indararo*, s., *indararai*, pl.) projecting from 0.6m. to 0.9m. from the face of the wall. At one time the spouts were made of pottery, but now they are entirely of beaten tin. At the foot of the wall is a protective plinth which prevents the rain-water damaging the main wall and its foundations.

In addition to these design precautions, the external surfaces of the building are protected with various waterproof finishes. The finish used on a particular building depends upon its type and purpose and the prestige of its owner; on how much is to be spent upon this element of the building and the orientation and exposure of the surface to be treated. *Laso* is the most important waterproof cement in use; its main ingredient is *katsi*, a by-product of the dyeing trade. The slurry at the bottom of a worn out dye pit is removed, partially dried, then moulded into lumps (*kunku*). These lumps are put between layers of wood in an open-air kiln and thoroughly baked. After baking, the lumps are beaten into powder: it is this powder which is known as *katsi*. The description of the manufacture of *laso* is given in *Labarun Al'Adun Hausawa* and is as follows:

> Cement cannot be prepared quickly. A hole is dug first, about four feet [1.21m.] deep. Then *katsi* is taken and poured into the hole together with old indigo liquid. It is stirred in the hole. When it has been properly stirred, it is covered and left for two or three days. Then hair is got from a tannery, and the roots of the wild vine, as well as horse manure without any straw in it. These vine roots are thoroughly beaten with a stone till they are soft. They are poured into large earthen pots which are filled to their brims with water. The horse manure is thoroughly broken up until it becomes powder. Then sticks, such as pestles, are obtained and the *katsi* is pounded in the hole. It is taken out, then put back in again, and so on until it is ready. Then it is left for two days.
>
> One continues to treat the mortar in this way until it is ready, i.e. it begins to smell, and becomes sticky and soft; then the cement is quite ready for use.[15]

Laso has a life expectancy of five or six years when used as a finishing coat for external walls and roofs. Before it is applied to the roof, the roof is twice plastered with good building clay: during the last plastering the parapet walls and pinnacles (*zanki*, s., *zankwaye*, pl.) are built. On top of the mud is sprinkled powdered *katsi*, or a mixture of *katsi* and old *laso* from a demolished building. The *katsi* is watered, and for two days is stamped upon until it becomes very hard. The *laso* is

5.26 *Makuba*

taken to the site where it is mixed with water until it becomes the correct consistency, after which it is applied to the roof in two coats. On flatter surfaces it is covered with a protective layer of red earth mixed with dung which is washed off during the rains, by which time the *laso* has hardened. *Laso* is the best finish for roofs and parapets and if used on walls produces a lovely silvery white building weathering to darker greys.

5.27 *Finger patterning in mortar*

5.28 *Finger patterning in mortar*

The most expensive and by far the best finish for external walls is *cafe* which is reputed to last for many years without maintenance. This wall finish varies from place to place in Hausaland, but usually consists of black earth collected from a borrow pit, which is mixed with a solution of the pounded seeds of the *bagaruwa* tree (*bagari*, pl.).[16] The black mud is then plastered on to the wall and allowed to partly dry. Pebbles, sifted to remove fine particles, are pressed then beaten into the wall surface. This hardens for two days, then on successive days it is twice wetted with *bagaruwa* fluid and twice with *makuba* solution. *Cafe* is a dark earthen colour with a rough texture which is extremely durable.

The most beautiful wall finish is perhaps *makuba* itself. It is a deep purple brown applied with bold circular sweeps of the arm which gives it a distinctive patterning. (See Figure 5.26.) *Makuba* is made from the fruit pod of the locust bean tree, *dorowa* (*doroyi*, pl.), *Parkia filicoidea*. The husk of the fruit is ground to a powder which is then mixed with water before it is added to red earth. Unfortunately, the waterproofing effects of *makuba* last for only about two years and the plaster is prone to attack by white ants.[17]

The most expensive and best wall finishes are normally reserved for entrance huts or for important buildings such as the palace or the Friday mosque. Usually the bricks are simply covered with mortar as the wall is built and then given a further finishing coat of ordinary building mortar. This is often delicately decorated with trailing finger patterns, the colour changing from wall to wall, from silver brown to dark earth orange depending on the age of the structure. (See Figures 5.27 and 5.28.) It is the finish which predominates in the old cities.

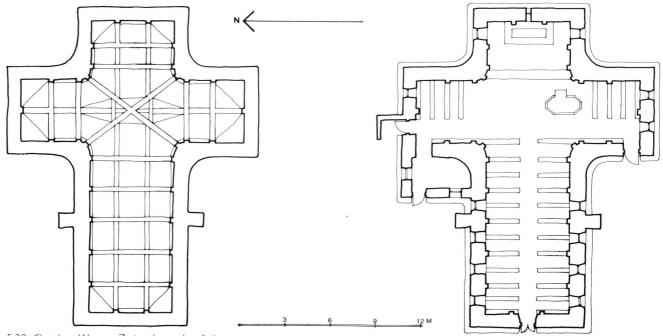

5.29 *Church at Wusasa, Zaria, plan and roof plan*

Internal surface finish

Internal plastering consists of two coats applied over rough mortar covering the *tubali*. First a coat of mud mortar is applied, followed by a finishing coat of red earth and sand which can be brought to a smooth finish on which to whitewash. For ceilings, a special plaster is used which has greater adhesive properties than normal plasters: the undercoat is made from black earth and grass; the final coat is the usual finishing plaster. There are special plasters too, such as the one used occasionally in emirs' palaces, which consists of small fragments of quartz set in gum arabic, or the one used in Wusasa church, Zaria, which contains mica flakes and makes the whole church glisten with a golden or silver sheen dependng upon the quality of light which filters through the narrow slit windows. (See Figures 5.29 to 5.32.)

5.30 *Church at Wusasa, Zaria, Interior*

5.31 *Church at Wusasa, Zaria, Interior*

5.32 *Church at Wasasa, Zaria Interior*

Floors are made from a mixture of laterite and gravel. The following is a Hausaman's description of the process of floor making:

> Then some other earth called *birji* is dug and put on top of the floor. Then they bring gravel and enough water for their needs. When they have put the gravel on to the laterite, scattered all over the place and not left in a heap, they then start to do the work with the proper sticks; they go on beating until all the gravel has become embedded in the *birji* and it is strong. Pods of the acacia tree are got and pounded up, or the husks of the locust-bean tree are soaked. This liquid is sprinkled all over the floor, which is again beaten, but lightly, till it penetrates the whole floor. It becomes black when it dries. If this is done, it will prevent the floor from cracking.[18]

Conclusion

Although the climate of Hausaland is not particularly suitable for buildings made entirely from mud, an essentially alien style of architecture has been cleverly adapted to the environment through the development and use of special external finishes. However, despite the ingenuity of the Hausa builder the soft lines of the final building forms are as much the product of nature as of man. When newly built, the Hausa building is crisp, neat, efficient in appearance and based upon a rigorous structural discipline. It is the erosive effect of the rain which produces those softened moulded forms and incidental charm associated with mud buildings. The Hausa builder has learned to accept this outside interference with his designs: each dry season he repairs parts of walls, and even whole buildings when necessary.

The profiles of the buildings vary with great rapidity: a whole street changes from season to season and from year to year, producing what is essentially an organic architecture in which static form is unknown. Such changes take place within a highly disciplined architectural context, where elements added, removed or changed are part of a unified system of design based upon a set of preferred dimensions which maintain continuity and coherence within a continually evolving built environment.

6.1   *Termite mound*

6. Climate and built form

Introduction

Shelter from the climate is usually regarded as an important function of a building. It could be said that Hausa buildings are designed to control the climate in such a way that interiors are dry and occupants remain comfortable during periods of intense heat or cold, when humidity is high and during the rains. This concept of a building sees it simply as a filter between the external and internal environments, mitigating the harsher features of the climate to maintain the comfort of its users. This view of the building as a climatic filter may be extended to include large areas of the built environment, so that building groups may be analysed in terms of the shelter provided for outdoor activities. At a simplistic level traditional Hausa buildings and building groups conform to this general-ized model: buildings for man's use are designed so that interiors are dry and comfortable. Externally, buildings, walls and trees are arranged to provide areas of shade in hot dry periods, while maintaining ample space for breezes to circulate during the hot humid times of the year.

The idea that a building is designed to control climate has to be modified to take account of the psychological interpreta-tions of climate, the level of understanding of the problem and the cultural preferences of the group using and constructing the building. Although there is evidence that man has adapted physiologically and psychologically to some environmental conditions, he generally attempts to change environment to suit cultural and physiological needs.[1] For example, in the north of Hausaland during the cool evenings of the harmattan when a European, not yet acclimatized, is comfortable, local people require a fire for warmth: a common feature of the home in this part of the world is a mud bed built like an oven over a hearth. Design for comfort in the context of traditional architectural forms should not be confused with the overt application of scientific methods to the problems of building design in order to achieve prescribed internal environmental conditions. The phrase 'designed for comfort', in the sense it is used here, refers to the builder's skill in using well tried and trusted traditional forms of structure, developed over many generations for a particular group of people. This is true of Hausa culture, therefore climatic control must be considered an essential part of the architectural programme imposed upon the Hausa builder by his society.

How far society is willing to pursue the goal of environ-mental comfort depends upon its priorities, which in turn depend upon cultural norms. For example, the two-storey entrance hut with mud roof is probably a form of architecture most suited to the hot dry conditions on the margins of the desert, yet it became a common feature throughout Hausaland. It penetrated the more humid outlying regions to the south and was a status symbol required by all families with aspirations of prestige. Similarly, the building with concrete block walls and tin roof is now the symbol of wealth and position despite its obvious failings in terms of climatic control. Presumably Hausa society rates status more highly than comfort. Despite these reservations, the Hausa have developed a built form which has by and large mitigated the effects of local climatic conditions. Even the latest buildings which incorporate modern materials are often built with a verandah, illustrating a perceived need of comfort.

With the possible exceptions of nomadic herdsmen and agriculturalists who practise shifting cultivation, all societies attempt to build as permanently as levels of technology permit. In this matter the Hausa are no different from any other settled society. Traditional Hausa buildings, however, are constructed from the all-pervasive and readily available laterite, a material quickly eroded in this area where rainfall is heavy during the wet season. Permanent shelter built using this material requires the invention and use of a range of waterproof finishes described in the last chapter. Prolonging the life of a building made from laterite is dependent upon constant maintenance. The annual chore of wholesale re-plastering means that building profiles are in a constant state of flux. The everchanging outline of the Hausa building takes the 'line of least resistance', battered walls curve sinuously in two planes, roof lines sweep upwards into pinnacles and roof water is channelled down deeply incised vertical grooves. The resulting form has some of the quality and appearance of the natural shapes used by those other great mud builders, the termites, whose mounds compete with man's structures in this landscape. (See Figure 6.1.)

Climate

As was mentioned above, the climate of Hausaland varies from north to south, but in all areas there are two main seasons. From November to April the hot, dusty, north-easterly harmattan blows from the Sahara, bringing high temperatures during the day, low ones at night and low humidity throughout the day and night. For the rest of the year the south-western winds blow, bringing moist, warm air. Rainfall and humidity and both high, with even, high temperatures throughout the day and night.[2]

Buildings must therefore meet the requirements of both climatic conditions. In general terms the hot dry climate is more severe in the northern part of the region and the warm humid climate is more extreme in the south. Without taking into account cultural factors, one would expect the northern settlements in Hausaland to exhibit features in common with arid regions of the world, and those in the south to approximate more closely to the settlements of the humid regions of southern Nigeria.

Shelter for hot, dry climates

In areas having a hot dry climate it is advisable to trap the cool night air within the house and retain it there for as long as possible, so preventing the interior from being warmed by the sun or the external air. Physical comfort in hot dry climates (from November to April in Hausaland) depends primarily upon the reduction of intense radiation from the sun, ground and surrounding buildings. Interiors of buildings can be protected if the heat flow characteristics of the building materials used for walls and roofs are such that their inner temperature can be maintained at a level considerably lower than that of the outer skin.

Walls and roofs made from laterite are exceptionally good for this purpose and when used at the thickness common in Hausaland the interiors of buildings during daytime, even at the height of the dry season, remain deliciously cool, well within the range of comfort. At night air temperatures become uncomfortably cold. The heat stored in the thick mud structure is emitted, raising internal temperatures above those outside. Hence the structure acts as a filter between external and internal environmental conditions, modifying them so that they are more comfortable.[3]

In hot dry climates humidity is low, and evaporation greater than in any other climatic type. Special arrangements for cross ventilation or air conditioning are unnecessary. Breezes are hot, dry and dusty during the day and air movements through the building, unless artificially cooled and the dust removed, create uncomfortable internal conditions. Small, easily controlled openings are the most efficient form of window: they permit the penetration of some light with little air movement. The mud building (*soro*) with small, high-level windows and small doors, the traditional style throughout Hausaland, is ideally suited to the control of climate during the hot dry period of the year.

Outdoor conditions at the height of the harmattan are hostile, and external living spaces must be protected, as far as possible, from intense solar radiation and the hot dusty winds. For this purpose an enclosed, compact inward-looking plan is the most suitable. For in such a plan, distances are short to facilities such as water points, fuel and grain stores, thereby reducing the need for movement. The traditional Hausa house is built in this fashion around a courtyard, and the majority of building types are single-storey, so avoiding the need to climb stairs. An exception to this general rule is the two-storey entrance hut so popular in the recent past, which emphasizes once again the Hausa need to express status.

The courtyard, which is such a common feature of Hausa architecture, in addition to being an ideal planning system for the circulation of air, is also an excellent thermal regulator. High walls cut off the sun, so that large areas of the inner wall surfaces and courtyard floor are shaded during the day. The cooler air in the courtyard, the cooler wall surfaces and courtyard floor draw off heat from any overheated parts of the surrounding buildings, re-emitting it to the open sky at night.

In hot, dry areas, placing as much accommodation as possible under one roof, so minimizing the amount of external wall, reduces the thermal loading from the sun and hot air. The vast complex of reception rooms associated with the Hausa palace is ideal from this point of view, the dusky coolness providing a remarkable shelter from the hot, dazzling external world. Preferably, long elevations for such building complexes should face north and south since these aspects of the building receive less heat loading. However, this principle of layout is not consistently applied in Hausaland, other design criteria being obviously more important. Shading roofs, walls and outdoor spaces is important in this type of climate. This is often achieved by tree planting, the verandah and projecting roofs, features common in Hausa architecture. A traditional method devised to achieve maximum shade in hot dry climates is the arrangement of building close together in compact groups with narrow streets. This results in a high degree of overshadowing. Traditional Hausa settlements consist of close groups of buildings, narrow footpaths, small enclosed courtyards, high courtyard walls and groups of shade trees: such a townscape gives maximum climatic protection for the buildings and the people moving about the settlement during the hot dry days of the harmattan.[4]

Shelter for warm, humid climates

When the humid, south-westerly wind blows (from April to November), air temperature is close to skin temperature both at night and in the daytime. Physical comfort at this time of year depends upon the dissipation of heat from the body to the surrounding environment: the heat dissipated must be at least as great as its metabolic production. In an atmosphere of high humidity, evaporation of a small quantity of moisture from the body forms a saturated envelope of air which prevents further evaporation. Without the ability to cool through sweating, conditions become uncomfortable. Comfort can be restored by removing the saturated envelope of air by ventilation through the building passing across the occupants.

Heavy cloud and water vapour in the air act as a filter, preventing re-radiation of heat from the earth at night. Without significant cooling at night wall and roof surface temperatures tend to settle down to those of the air. Radiant heat loss from the body to outside surfaces is negligible, since skin and surface temperatures are similar. Apart from mechanical air conditioning, air movement is the only available relief from uncomfortable conditions during the rainy season in Northern Nigeria. So it is important to design buildings facing the breezes, and the walls of the buildings at right angles to those breezes as large, opening areas. In warm, humid climates, elongated plans are often used, consisting of a single row of rooms which permits cross-ventilation. Buildings may be arranged in extended plans in a line across the prevailing wind direction, permitting the penetration of breezes through the whole site. Large, overhanging roofs giving shelter from the sun and verandah access to rooms commonly mitigate the worst effects of warm, humid climates. Shade and a free passage for air movement are the two basic requirements of external spaces. Trees and other plants, pergolas and lightly-roofed spaces are often used to shade external spaces while permitting maximum air circulation.

There are two basic types of traditional shelter in warm, humid climates. In regions favoured with a plentiful supply of timber the usual structure is a light-weight timber frame supporting a pitched, thatched roof which extends over wide verandahs. Sometimes—the Malay house, for instance (see Figure 6.3)—it is raised on stilts, permitting the breeze to circulate beneath the ground floor. Where other building materials are more plentiful, the single-storey, earth-walled house with thatched roof and large overhangs is typical. This is the most common type of traditional building in many parts of Nigeria, including Hausaland.

Shelter for composite climates

Hausaland's composite climate of hot, dry and warm, humid seasons sets a difficult task for the designer of buildings: solutions suitable for one season may be unsatisfactory for the other. As has been seen, the ideal structure for the hot, humid season is a large roof giving protection against the rain but permitting maximum air flow through the building; the most suitable for the hot, dry season is a solid building with few openings, constructed from materials with good properties of thermal insulation and having highly reflective surfaces. The design requirements for achieving comfort in both seasons in Northern Nigeria using traditional building techniques are incompatible. The complete solution to the problem in the form of a single building can be achieved by using modern structural techniques and modern mechanical plant, but then only at great expense.

Traditional house styles in regions of composite climates are usually compromise solutions in terms of climatic control. The nature of the compromise varies from place to place depending upon the relative extremes of the climate, the perceptions of those extremes and the value attached to the mitigation of harsh conditions. A familiar urban solution in the type of mixed climate is a ground floor of massive walls and large, shuttered windows, with the accommodation laid out in the form of a courtyard. The first floor of this sort of dwelling is a light-weight timber structure for use in the humid parts of the year. Similarly, where the climate varies between extremes of heat and cold, as in the highlands of the Karakoram range in Pakistan, houses consist of a heavy ground-floor building with a light-weight superstructure. In composite homes of this type the occupants move from one part of the building to the other according to season.

Climate and Hausa architecture

The architectural solution to climatic control adopted by the Hausa is inevitably a compromise and consists of a combination of different building types for use at different times of the year. A house normally consists of structures having

6.2   *The Malay House*

different thermal properties. The hut built entirely of mud is ideal for the dry season, and the family compound may also contain simple structures of posts and grass roof for use during humid periods. Compounds have both indoor and outdoor kitchens and many trees which form useful shaded areas. The verandah is not unknown in Hausa architecture (see Figures 6.3 to 6.6): the external wall is usually made up of a grille whose mullions and transomes are made from *azara* coated with mud. The verandah has become more common with the introduction of new building technology. Many rooms built from concrete blocks with an iron roof have a verandah attached to the bedroom as an extra living area during the rains. When considering the Hausas' adaptation of built form, it is important to look at the complete range of buildings and spaces in the family compound, then it becomes clear that their system of house planning provides comfortable living conditions at all times of the year.

The two types of climate in Hausaland require quite different systems for the layout of buildings. As we have seen, the ideal layout in the humid tropics consists of narrow buildings set out with their long axis running approximately east-west, and at right angles to the direction of the main wind flows. Building densities in such circumstances should be low

6.3 *House in Swat, Pakistan*

6.4 *Verandah*

so that large areas of the site remain open and permit an adequate flow of air around and through the structures. In contrast the ideal building layout in hot, dry climates is one where the external surfaces of buildings are as small as possible so that the amount of heat radiated or absorbed by the buildings is reduced to a minimum. Such a condition can be achieved by spacing buildings closely together so that each has many surfaces in shadow at all times of the day. Hausa settlements are composed of both layout types, or rather they exhibit some of the properties of both. Large family compounds contain widely spaced groups of buildings and shade trees, while close to public streets, buildings and compound walls huddle together for mutual protection from the sun, providing shaded spaces.

Unlike, for example, the people of the Gezira in the Sudan, the Hausa do not orientate on an east-west axis. Such an orientation would maximize the cooling effect of local breezes and would present the least area of external wall surface to the direct rays of the sun when at its lowest angles. This apparent lack of consideration for mitigating some climatic effects may be due in part to the shape of Hausa buildings which are cubic or cylinderical: when used singly they have no long axis. However, when grouping rooms in one unit for wives, Hausa

6.5 *Verandah*

cultural traditions dictate a north-south axis with west entrances to each room, a preference diametrically opposed to a sensible climatic solution.[5] The Hausa also seem to favour a system of climatic control based upon the insulative property of mud used in great thickness and an arrangement of cells in clusters, so that inner compartments remain cool by the day and retain their heat during the cool nights; outdoor spaces associated with such clusters remain in shadow for long

6.6   *Room with grille*

periods of the day. Whatever the reason, orientation in house planning for climatic reasons has less significance for the Hausa builder than cultural norms: good internal environmental conditions are achieved at least in the hot, dry season using other methods.

The traditional Hausa solution to the problem of climatic control has tended to stress design for the Saharan climatic type. Until quite recently the Hausa built in mud as much of the compound as they could afford. There are perhaps three reasons for this tendency to prefer mud buildings. First, and purely cultural, mud buildings were fashionable and prestigious; secondly, they are more permanent and cheaper to maintain than other traditional structures; and finally, the Hausa may be physiologically and psychologically better equipped to live in humid tropical conditions than Saharan conditions. So the incompatible elements of climatic control in the building programme may have a fundamentally different significance for the indigenous Hausa than, for instance, the visiting European.

Today, most Hausa aspire to the rectangular building constructed from concrete blocks with a corrugated iron roof. From a climatic point of view it is less suitable than the all-mud house during the dry season, and less suitable than the light timber structure with thatch roof for the humid season. It is difficult to determine precisely the reasons for this latest preference. The cost of mud construction has increased with the closure of borrow pits in the cities, making it less economical in terms of capital costs. The concrete block structure is more permanent and has lower maintenance costs than any traditional building. The architectural model and the building standards to which the people of Hausa cities now aspire are set by those responsible for public buildings. The new schools, offices, mosques and additions to palace buildings are all built in the new, permanent materials. These large and prestigious projects, although often badly designed, dictate the fashion. The changes in building style are introduced into the vernacular by the new élite who work in national or local government service, educational establishments and business. The changes in building preference seem to indicate that the Hausa rate style of building and permanence of structure more highly than climatic control as factors determining form.

The new building technology has not penetrated all parts of Hausa settlements. Even in compounds where the new building type has been introduced there is a mixture of old and new structures (see Figures 4.9 and 4.13), and in much of the region traditional building technology is still dominant. Indeed, most Hausa people still live within the shell of the traditional architectural form.

The problem of building to achieve internal environmentally controlled conditions in an area with two such divergent climatic types is extremely difficult to solve even using modern design techniques. The Hausa compromise solution involving the use of a range of covered and open spaces is a thoroughly practical answer evolved over many generations. It is only now that the complex changes associated with rapid urbanisation make evident its inadequacies.

The Hausa way of life and use of the house is thought to be a contributing factor in the spread of epidemics such as meningitis. For part of the dry season the harmattan blows from the desert bringing with it fine particles of suffocating dust. Then the Hausa retire into closed, stuffy rooms and it is at this time that dust-born epidemics occur, increasing the chances of contact with infected people. The spread of epidemics is doubtless partly due to the growth in population and its concentration in large urban complexes such as Kano. It may also be indicative of a fundamental limitation to the traditional building system.

Mud is an extremely unstable building material in a climate like Northern Nigeria's with high rainfall and repeated rainstorms. Yet the Hausa have developed ingenious methods of adapting mud construction to the climate. The most common building type in Hausaland is still the circular hut with mud walls and a steep, conical thatched roof with eaves that direct the rainwater away from the mud wall. It is the hut type used by the non-Muslim peoples of the Jos plateau and has probably been in use in the Western Sudan for some two thousand years or more, at least since the Nok culture.

The shapes and forms used in fully developed Hausa mud architecture have been imported comparatively recently from drier climates in North Africa. It could be argued that they are not as well adapted to the climate as indigenous structures. But great ingenuity is displayed in the design of the North African building type in Hausaland and it is only because of its detailing and finishing that it acquires any resistance to erosion. Rainwater is directed away from the roof either through long drainage spouts (a most attractive feature of Hausa architecture) which project about 0.6m. from the face of the wall, or through deeply incised vertical channels in the face of the wall which are lined with a waterproof finish such as *laso*. The base of most walls projects some 0.45m. to form a plinth which, in addition to providing a seat, prevents surface water from damaging the foundation.

As discussed in Chapter 5 above, the Hausa have developed many waterproof finishes to prolong the life of their buildings. Every year at the end of the rains buildings are examined and replastered where necessary, and walls are rebuilt if unsafe. Despite good maintenance a building which is several years old owes much of its charm to the effects of weathering. Forms are softened and shapes changed by the constant cycle of erosion and maintenance. Often the vertical rain-gulleys down the walls are nothing more than regularized versions of the natural paths worn by rain as it flows over the parapet.

Occasionally line squalls in Hausaland reach 145km. per hour, greatly damaging buildings. It is not known to what extent the huge mud walls around the compounds reduce the effects of such squalls, nor indeed if these walls have been developed to act as wind-breaks. But it is interesting to note that in 1963, for instance, the greatest damage to property in Zaria occurred in Sabon Gari where compound walls tend to be lower than in the old city. Of course this damage may have been due to poor construction of the corrugated iron roofs. The monolithic mud roof has a distinct advantage over both the iron and the thatched roof in its ability to withstand even gale force winds, and although it requires constant maintenance to retain its weatherproof properties, unlike the other roof types it is rarely destroyed by line squalls.

Conclusion

For centuries the Hausa have been subjected to constant invasion by peoples from further north, and they have had contact with North African cultures through trade links across the Sahara. Hausa architecture owes its form to an assimilation of many diverse elements. From a combination of foreign and indigenous building techniques, the Hausa created a synthesis of form, the result of which is a strict code of design.[6] However, Hausa building technology is in the process of change, for more alien elements based on modern building materials are being introduced and overlie the deeper traditions of Hausa architecture. It is too early to talk of a new synthesis of form, but it is interesting to note that while all the elements, indigenous, North African and 'modern', are used by the Hausa to create a built environment having tolerable climatic conditions, climatic control as a determinant of form takes second place to cultural, social and economic factors.

7. Architectural decoration

Introduction

Throughout Hausaland, highly modelled decorative patterns of different styles and varying degrees of boldness have long been used to enhance architectural form. The decoration of buildings reached a zenith in the city of Zaria in the work of Babban Gwani, Mallam Mikaila during the mid-nineteenth century (see Figures 7.1 to 7.6), and flowered again there from the 1930s to the 1960s (see Figures 7.7 to 7.11). Each emirate city has made its contribution to this art form, and buildings in the palace in Kano indicate a decorative style of colourful exuberance dating from the earlier part of this century[1] (Figures 7.36 to 7.42 illustrate decorated entrances in Kano and Figures 7.23 to 7.32 are examples from Daura).

Many fine examples of Hausa wall decoration have been lost forever, damaged or destroyed during annual repairs to the mud walls; by the replacement of traditional structures with modern concrete block buildings and simply by a change in fashion. Now position in society is emphasized in ways other than a decorated entrance hut. Traditional, modelled patterning is dying out, but it is good to see the emergence of a new style of murals depicting naturalistic forms, which may indicate that the Hausa need for colour and decoration is taking on a new form more suitable to the new methods of construction. (See Figures 7.22 to 7.24.)

Meaning and Pattern

Until quite recently, Hausa wall decoration was an integral part of the building process. It was usually the work of the general builder and was carried out during the last phase of construction when the final coat of plaster was applied. The simplest and probably the oldest sort of house decoration in Hausaland is made by repetitive mechanical hand movements on the newly-plastered surfaces of mud walls. This decoration is used on the least important walls which are usually finished with a mixture of dung and laterite. Before it is dry, the fingers of one hand are moved along it in long, sweeping gestures to create a pattern of parallel lines. (See Figures 5.27 and 5.28.)

A similar form of mechanical decoration is applied when *makuba* is used as a wall finish. This is also made by rhythmic movements of the arm, using the side of the hand to produce a series of shallow, semi-circular troughs. (See Figure 5.26.) Both methods give an overall pattern which in the strong sunlight enhances a building with a lovely pattern and texture. The extra work involved in producing vast areas of decorated wall surfaces, which must be renewed annually after the rains, suggests that the Hausa have a deep psychological need for such patterning.

It is interesting to note, in passing, that the repetitive Hausa wall patterns are reminiscent of the patterns found by Morris in drawings made by chimpanzees which he observed resulted from the same arm movements as the animal used to make a bed of straw.[2] Certainly, some Hausa decoration is the result of simple motor movements, and the reasons for such non-structural, non-functional pattern-making may be lost in the distant cultural development of mankind. Nevertheless, it is possible to assert that the Hausa—like many other peoples—need such decoration, since so much labour is spent producing it. It might also be argued that the perimeter wall of a compound, as the interface between the inside and outside worlds, the known and the unknown, private and public space, has particular meaning and communicates to the outsider ownership and protection by extensive patterning. However, this explanation does not account for the wealth of similar mechanical patterning inside the compound where the only viewers are the occupants.

For continuing structural stability, a mud building must have a sound surface finish, so its lifespan is dependent upon maintenance. Among the Hausa the annual resurfacing of the wall is something of a ritual, for the whole community is

7.1–6 *Decorated pillars, Friday Mosque, Zaria (1962)*

Left to right. 7.7–11 Decorated Entrances, Zaria

Left to right:

7.12 *Decorated Façade, Zaria*

7.13 *House of Mallam Yagwa, Tudun Wada, Zaria. Decorated by Ango Tukur-Tukur, 1950-55*

7.14–16 *Decorated Doorways, Zaria*

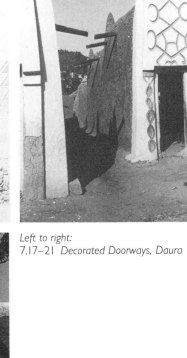

Left to right:
7.17–21 Decorated Doorways, Daura

7.22 House on the Kano Road, Zaria: Decoration by Musa Yola

7.23 Mosque on the Kano Road, Zaria: Decoration by Musa Yola

7.24 Mosque on the Kano Road, Zaria: Decoration by Musa Yola

involved. Patterning may therefore be a simple expression of this ritual. So it is not difficult to appreciate the special care that is put into the decoration of critical and weak points in the wall surface—openings, parapets, the crossing points of arches and where arches join the wall. Points such as these are guarded by the greatest use of protective symbols. Openings in walls, particularly the entrance, are most in need of protection, for as Labelle Prussin notes:

> Any enclosed space, whether physical or conceptual, requires an opening: the corollary of meaningful spatial definition of an 'enclosed' space is an entrance into it. The entrance is the mediator; it marks the point where man makes the transition between exterior and interior, between the unknown and known . . . Throughout West Africa, all rites and rituals relating to change or transition in man's existence occur at the entrance. 'Outdooring' or naming ceremonies announcing the birth of a child, hence its entrance into life, are performed at the entrance to the compound. Funerary rites take place at the compound entrance and strangers are received in the antechamber at the entrance to the compound.[3]

There is usually one entrance to the Hausa compound and it is here that until quite recently the Hausa have concentrated most decoration.

Pre-Islamic symbols

Some of the motifs used by the Hausa in wall decoration may have associations with pre-Islamic symbolism,[4] for the non-Islamic peoples developed their own wall decoration which was painted or modelled in low relief. The most common

7.25 *Animal representations*

decorative features of animism are natural objects, often connected with the group's totem.[5] Each family has its own particular animal from which the original founder was descended or to which he was indebted. The style of the drawings varies from people to people and may be naturalistic or highly conventionalized. (See Figures 7.25 and 7.27.)

Simple geometric shapes—triangles, circles and lozenges—are used in Hausa decorative work, but are common to other peoples in Nigeria including the Yoruba and Igbo and those in Gobir and on the Jos Plateau. Such widespread popularity makes it probable that they have been used for a considerable time and may therefore be regarded as indigenous features of decorative patterns in this part of Africa. Fitzgerald found that the indigenous designs of the Dakarkari people of Sokoto Province consist of some form of cross, usually made from bundles of grass tied at the point of intersection, or formed from two V's. According to Fitzgerald this form also occurs in the boat patterns of the Ga of Ghana and is typical of West African art.[6] The motif of the cross is a common feature of the mud grille used in verandah walls in Hausaland: it was also incorporated in the partition wall of the Shari'a court of the Friday Mosque, Zaria, which has been demolished. Such mud

7.26 *Mud grille, Shari'a Court, Friday Mosque, Zaria*

grilles are reinforced with *azara* or some other form of timber. (See Figure 7.26.) Leary, following Arkell, believes that some of the simple decorations in the older Hausa buildings resemble

7.27 *Motifs of pre-Islamic symbolism (After A.H. Leary)*

7.28 *The Palace at Daura*

Tuareg 'fertility charms' based on combinations of circle and triangle and known as *talhatana*.[7] (See Figures 7.27 and 7.28.) These are often placed beneath the arch at its point of junction with the wall, a particularly vulnerable structural point.

These indigenous symbols were incorporated in Hausa decoration throughout its lifespan, although after the jihad there may have been religious reforms which frowned on ostentatious decoration, particularly if it depicted living creatures. The latest mural art indicates a move to a more naturalistic approach in decoration. During the great period of mud architecture, until the mid 1960s, indigenous symbolism, although modified and given new expression by Islamic and later by Western influences, formed a basic element of the visual vocabulary of the Hausa. Later influences, like the different peoples who have come into the area, have been thoroughly assimilated. The resultant decorative style is a synthesis of all the varied influences and a reflection of the individuality of the culture from which it sprang.

Islamic symbolism

Labelle Prussin believes that with the introduction of Islam, Islamic symbolism replaced animistic symbolism: she sees the process as taking out a 'supernatural insurance policy with Islam'.[8] According to this view the new symbolism is based upon Arabic writing, which itself is believed to have sacred and magical powers. The power of the written word is further enhanced by combining it with a magic drawing or square, derived from Islamic mathematics and having divinatory powers. Many wall patterns in Hausaland are subdivided into rectangles, but such subdivisions may be derived from the structure of the building or from a simple need to organize and subdivide a large surface into more manageable units. In dealing with any aspect of the fusion of Islamic and pre-Islamic traditions in West Africa it is wise to bear in mind Trimingham's warning that:

> It is easy to exaggerate the influence of northern Hamites and of Islam. Without going to the other extreme and minimizing the efficacy of Hamitic influences preceeding Islam in modifying the original data, the broad fact remains that these were Negro civilizations with their own distinctive character . . . Nor do we want to minimize the effect of Islamic civilization. It is not enough to take the two ingredients, the pagan cultures and Islam, and consider change simply as a kind of quantitative transposition . . . for that would miss the creative and dynamic factor—the two forces reacting upon each other . . . the ultimate synthesis can only be apprehended dialectically.[9]

Tradition has it that Islam was introduced into Hausaland in the fifteenth century by merchants from Mali. Islamic law and culture were peripheral in the day to day affairs of the greater part of Hausa society until the jihad of the first decade of the nineteenth century. Thereafter Uthman dan Fodio and his Fulani followers assumed control throughout the Hausa settlements, especially during the early days of reforming zeal, Islam's prohibitions against imagery and idols were particularly effective. How seriously the orthodox tenets have been applied to decorative wall art since then is difficult to determine. As Bravmann points out:

In Songhay, Al-Maghili points to the many examples of syncretism between Islam and indigenous religion and to the way of life established by the Songhay rulers utilizing the two faiths. Even during periods of religious fervour and doctrinal rigour—for example, during the early nineteenth century jihads—orthodoxy was easily compromised . . . The correspondence between Al-Kanemi and Uthman dan Fodio lays bare the syncretism between Islam and animism in Bornu. Everywhere and at all times, Islam and its adherents concede to local traditions and make compromises.[10]

Social status and display

Alan Leary has tried to chart the path of Hausa wall decoration in the last two centuries. He found that in addition to the iconoclastic mood of the early nineteenth century, it was a time when display in terms of decorated buildings was confined to the rulers, their kinsmen and appointees. The Fulani rulers and office holders of this highly stratified society had privileges that included the right to wear rich apparel and to express rank through the building of elaborate homes.

The commoners (*talakawa*, pl., *talaka*, s.) linked to the rulers through clientship and patronage, were not permitted to express themselves in this way. They remained submissive partly because of the system of political and economic control, and through a sense of modesty or propriety (*kunya*) which compels all Hausa to conform to custom: a custom according to which, in its extreme legal interpretation, disobedience to a superior might occasion a sentence of death or imprisonment. Within the *talakawa* class prestige was also according to rank. The clerics and Koranic scholars came first, followed by successful merchants, craftsmen in cloth, then lesser traders, farmers and minor craftsmen. Musicians, butchers and blacksmiths formed the lowest rungs in the social hierarchy.

In Hausa society wealth (*wada*) is only a partial explanation of a man's prestige: *azziki*, prosperity or good fortune, is more greatly prized. *Azziki* may include wealth but its main component is respect which money alone cannot buy. Before this century the Hausa merchant's concept of *azziki* did not include the display of wealth in terms of house decoration, and this seems to be true of the last twenty years too. In contrast, and despite the puritanical fervour of the religious reformers, the Fulani rulers were expected to embrace the function of their Hausa office of state which required ostentatious display in terms of clothes and palace building.[11]

Kirk-Greene noted that 'one of the striking features in the development of urban Hausa architecture over the past decade (1950s) has been the growth in both frequency and fantasy of the art of house decoration'.[12] Leary suggests that such growth may be due to 'the gradual relaxation of the extreme sanctions against display by the indigenous merchant class; the example of Arab traders [and] increasing prosperity and buying power for both farmers and the merchant families.[13] Military conquest of Northern Nigeria in 1902–3 constrained the absolute power of the traditional rulers, and brought extreme measures such as capital punishment and imprisonment under the control of the colonial administration. The economy of the Hausa states began to change and expand, especially during two major periods of prosperity in West Africa: the first in the mid to late 1920s, the second after the Second World War.[14] The wealth created by this economic activity and the new-found freedom of the merchant classes resulted in the outpouring and profusion of house decoration this century.

Language of built form

For those who interpret the meaning of the built environment —the builders and users—it fulfils an important role of communication. The language used to express meaning in built form includes the size of the building or space, its position in relation to others, architectural form, materials and surface treatment. This chapter considers the last element, wall treatment, which is particularly important in a non-literate society such as the Hausa were until recently. The development of wall decoration is seen here as the changing physical record of social, economic and political forces within Hausa society at a time when the norms of communication were themselves undergoing change. The evidence for analyzing changes in decorative style during the nineteenth century is the writings of European travellers and the few remaining mud buildings from the period, two of the most important being the *zaure* in the palace in Daura and the Friday Mosque in Zaria.

Examples of 19th century decoration

An early example of decorated mud building in Hausaland is the *zaure* of the palace in Daura, which according to tradition was built by the Habe rulers before the jihad. The dominant features are the magnificent structure and the lofty space it encloses; decorative patterns are few and subdued, set in a background of whitewashed walls in deep shadow. The patterns in this *zaure* appear to be informative: they tell a story rather than simply decorate. (See Figures 7.29 to 7.33.) On the soffit of one arch is the snake which tradition says was killed at Daura by the founder of the Hausa states; beside it is the sword with which Bayejida killed it. On one of the columns is the crescent, symbol of Islam, on another a formalized lizard or some similar creature significant as a totem in pre-Islamic times. Beneath the springing of the arches are simple geometric shapes which may be fertility charms. Through this group of symbols it is possible to trace the two major changes in the structure of society. First, the change from a matriarchal to a patriarchal society, which is associated with the Bayejida invasions. Secondly, the gradual conversion of an animistic society to the monotheism of Islam.

The next major example of Hausa decoration, part of which has been preserved, is the Friday Mosque in Zaria, built by Babban Gwani Mallam Mikaila. (See Figures 7.1 to 7.6.) Mallam Mikaila decorated his mosque as magnificently as he conceived its structure and spatial composition. The mud relief patterns in the interior are sober and formal; the dignified work of an age of religious reformers, and the very antithesis of the arabesque-like spirals, interlacing knots and chevrons typical of later work. Although Mallam Mikaila was a follower of Uthman dan Fodio and received from him a flag and chieftaincy his decorative work seems more complex than any surviving contemporary examples in Hausaland and may represent the first step towards the greater freedom exhibited in later work.

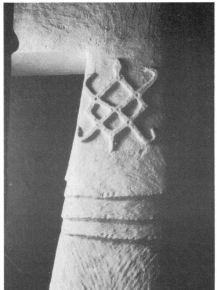

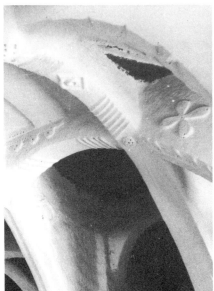

The Zaure: Palace at Daura

Left to right:

7.29 *The snake and sword*

7.30 *The lizard*

7.31 *Talhatana*

7.32 *The crossing of arches*

7.33 *The crossing of arches*

7.34 *Mihrab area, Friday Mosque: Zaria*

shadow they took their place easily in the total scheme. The more complex designs, such as the decorated architrave surrounding the mihrab niche or an otherwise undecorated quibla wall, together with the bold designs on the adjacent pier faces, were purposely placed to emphasize and enrich the mihrab area.[15] (See Figure 7.34.) This experience of the mosque in its original condition is unfortunately lost in the rehabilitation. The great mud mosque now stands within the shell of a modern building, sliced in half to reveal its section, brilliantly painted in gloss white with a glossy green metre-high dado, and brightly illuminated with artificial light. It is an impoverished aesthetic experience.

An important decoration still existing is on the rear wall of the central pier. (See Figure 7.35.) This is formed of curved lines and circular medallions and is very similar to a decoration on a column in Daura Palace. The meaning and purpose of this design is not clear, although it is a motif which appears quite often in later Hausa decoration. Its position suggests that its purpose is to indicate the direction of Mecca to those out of sight of the mihrab. It has been explained by a Hausa informant as a charm to ward off evil spirits: he described the lines and circles as swords and stars having some connection with Mohammed, but it is quite possible that the design acquired this magical significance long after it was executed, or it may be based upon pre-Islamic symbolism converted to the use of Islam. No representational designs appear in the mosque: the only motif which may be derived from natural forms is one which could be based on the snake, an important creature in Hausa mythology, for it is a symbol used in animistic decoration too.

Nineteenth-century travellers' descriptions of Hausaland indicate that wall decoration may have been of the bold geometric type found in the Zaria Mosque. Such decoration seems to have been confined to the interior of the most important buildings, palaces and mosques; certainly nine-teenth-century descriptions were confined to these buildings.

In 1824 Clapperton described Bello's palace in Sokoto as 'a handsome apartment, within a square tower, the ceiling of which was a dome supported by eight ornamental arches, with

The first impression on entering the Friday Mosque, before it was so tragically treated in redevelopment, was of big sculptural forms. Decoration was restrained and in the back-ground: deeply incised verticals, triangles and circles on the piers, and horizontals on the undersides of arches, empha-sized and complemented the main forms. The plan of the building was such that only one or two decorations could be seen at any moment, and because of the contrast of light and

7.35 *Central pillar, Friday Mosque: Zaria*

visited the palace in Kano and described a 'small hall . . . a room 25 feet square [2.32dm.], 18 feet high [4.5m.], decorated with quaint shapes and designs in black, white, pale green and yellow . . . the latter formed of micaceous sand which glistens like gold'.[19]

The only reference to wall decoration in mosques is given by Clapperton on his second visit to Hausaland in 1828 when he witnessed a builder from Zaria building a mosque which he described thus:

> Like all mosques, it was a quadrangular form, the sides facing the four cardinal points, and about 800 feet [244m.] in length. The roof of the mosque was perfectly flat, and formed of joists laid from wall to wall, the interstices being filled up with slender spars placed obliquely from joist to joist, and the whole covered outside with a thick stratum of indurated clay. The roof rested on arches, which were supported by seven rows of pillars, seven in each row. The pillars were of wood, plastered over with clay and highly ornamented.[20]

From the little evidence available it seems that external decorative murals in Hausa architecture may be a phenomena of this century. In nineteenth-century Hausa society social position was indicated by the possession of one or more large *soro*, earth buildings, of which the most important in each city were the palace and the Friday Mosque. Contemporary descriptions show that urban commoners (*talakawa*) lived mainly in round, thatched dwellings surrounded by high earth walls.

The influence of women

The older geometrical patterns first used by the Hausa on interior walls became common features of external decoration this century. The origin for this patterning is possibly indigenous to this part of Africa and may be the contribution of women. Conquering newcomers in the Sudan have always been in the minority, and any changes they instituted are likely to have been exotic features of the culture, soon to be absorbed within the total native scheme or lost forever. The newcomers practising polygamy and wholesale concubinage gradually accepted many of the features of indigenous

a bright plate of brass in its centre'.[16] Barth visited the palace in Kano in 1851 and described one hall as 'very handsome and even stately for this country . . . the more imposing as the rafters supporting the very elevated ceiling were concealed; two lofty arches of clay, very neatly polished and ornamented appearing to support the whole'.[17] Staudinger, visiting the same palace in 1885, noted a 'huge hall spanned by a mighty cupola . . . the ceiling coloured a deep blue'.[18] In 1903 Lugard

culture. Among such conservative traditions are probably the older and simpler geometric patterns of wall decoration of the last two centuries.

Although in Hausaland the building and decoration of houses is the work of men, each wife decorates the inside of her own rooms. The various pots, pans and dishes that form her dowry are used by the wife and her female relatives to decorate the new house. After the marriage has taken place the dowry is carried ceremoniously to the wife's new home where it is plastered piece by piece into the walls of the hut, the whole composition making colourful patterns of shining brass bowls mixed with modern, enamelled tin plates. Although the crafts of building and mud patterning are a man's task in Hausaland, the same is not true of other parts of West Africa. Among many peoples part of the building process and, in particular the final decorative treatment, may be carried out by the women. Thomas, for instance, in a study of the decorative art of the Edo-speaking people of southern Nigeria, came to the conclusion that inter-marriage between villages was probably the reason for the spread of certain patterns associated with the women of one particular ethnic group.[21]

Labelle Prussin also sees the tradition of Hausa decoration as owing its origin to the work of women: not to Hausa women, but to the traditions of tent hangings made by the women of the conquering Fulani. She argues that with the sedentarization of the Fulani nomadic tent, 'the mat walls are replaced by an earthern wall, . . . the tent armiture is enveloped in an earthern covering, and mobile interior furnishings are gradually replaced by earth-moulded ones'.[22] Among the nomadic Fulani, ownership of the tent, its structure, internal furniture and fittings belong to the woman, who assembles and dismantles the home. It is the woman who either makes the mats and tapestries or who has them provided by her family as a dowry. As the Fulani settled in the cities the long Hausa traditions of building permanent structures were accepted by them. With such acceptance the woman lost 'ownership' and control of the home, but retained ownership of the interior furnishings making up her dowry.

Since external mud decoration is regarded as man's work among the Hausa, it is not known to what extent women—Fulani, Hausa or of other Nigerian peoples—have been cultural agents, introducing to husbands, or passing on to children elements of their own cultural traditions in decorative treatment. Since women control children during the early formative years, some perceptual traditions are probably transmitted in this way. It is interesting to note that the 'Bori', a ceremony usually associated with animism, is controlled and run by Hausa women. This cult is still widely practised although it has been strongly condemned since the jihad a hundred and seventy years ago. It illustrates the strength of women's influence, simply in maintaining an irregular practice.[23] However, the only overt sign of women's influence in the decoration of Hausa buildings is the placing of a brass bowl at the intersection of mud arches. One theory for this custom is a structural one: it is thought that when the plate loosens and falls the arches are no longer stable. Whatever the reason, it seems that the idea may have come initially from the women's method of decorating their huts, and in buildings where plates are not used for this purpose, the junction of the arches is often emphasized with a circular mud pattern.

Examples of 20th century decoration

The gradual relaxation of extreme sanctions against display by the indigenous merchant class, the example of foreign traders and the growing wealth of the new Hausa middle class stimulated a proliferation of decorated houses in the Hausa settlements this century. The new burst of decoration was characteristic of the nouveau riche—the prosperous trader or wealthy prostitute, rather than members of the royal families or growing administrative class. Wealthy members of the royal families still followed the pattern set by their ancestors, confining decoration to small areas of the interior; the new administrative class have demonstrated position and prestige by building permanent structures, owning more comfortable furnishings and investing in a car.[24]

Leary has noted that external decoration dating from the first two decades of this century consisted of simple patterns made up from triangles and circles: he quotes particularly the

7.36 *Emir's Palace, Kano, Soron Giwa*

7.37 *Emir's Palace, Kano, Soron Giwa*

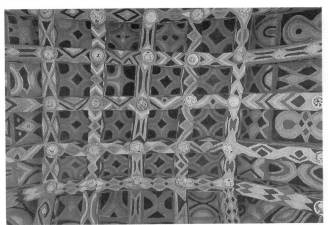

7.38 *Emir's Palace, Kano, Soron Ingila*

7.39 *Emir's Palace, Kano, Soron Ingila*

decoration on piers in the market stalls, Zaria, designed in 1912–13 by Maigidado dan Ubaniya, chief builder to the Emir and grandson of the builder of the Zaria Mosque.[25] Similar simple patterning can be seen on the buildings of the Christian Mission in Wusasa, just outside Zaria. Some of those buildings were designed and built by Galadima 'Umaru ibn Dahiru, another grandson of Mallam Mikaila. According to Leary,

'Umaru ibn Dahiru is responsible for other decorations of the 1920s and 1930s, 'all based on simple combinations of triangles and circles, slightly more complex than their predecessors but by no means exuberant'.[26]

Since the 1930s decoration has become more complex. Ornate designs in the 1930s and 1940s can still be seen in the Emir's Palace in Kano. (See Figures 7.36 to 7.39.) A house in

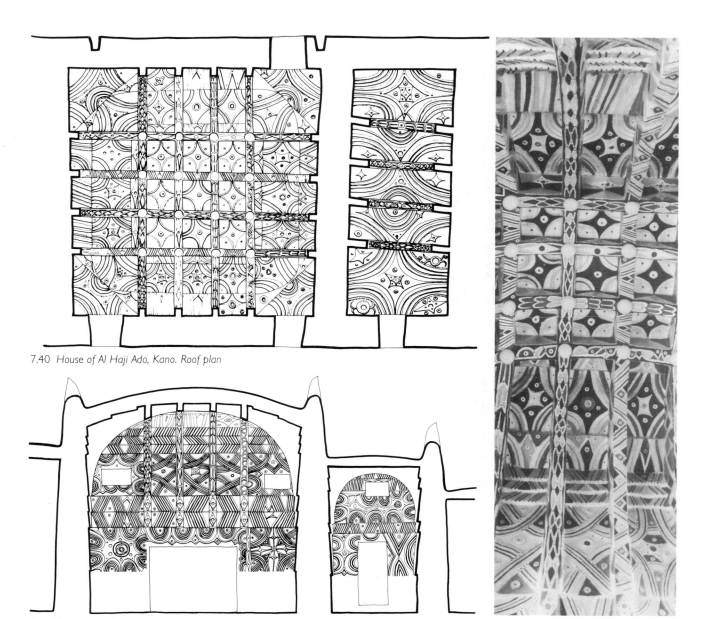

7.40 *House of Al Haji Ado, Kano. Roof plan*

7.41 *House of Al Haji Ado, Kano. Section*

7.42 *House of Al Haji Ado, Kano*

7.43 *Bicycle House, Zaria. Decoration by Jibrilu Dan Abubaker*

7.44 *Bicycle House, Zaria. Detail*

7.45 *Bicycle House, Zaria. Doorway*

Kano—Alhaji Ado's—in the same style as the palace buildings has unfortunately been demolished. (See Figures 7.40 to 7.42.) Here mud decoration was taken to its utmost limits: shapes within the room were lost in a vast web of interlacing designs, the exuberance of the pattern being further emphasized by the use of black, silver, red and blue paints. One of the most elaborate façades in Zaria, the so-called 'bicycle house' was decorated by Jibrilu dan Abubaker, great-grandson of Mallam Mikaila, in the 1940s. (See Figures 7.43 to 7.45.) Another interesting decorated interior in the style of Jibrilu is the

7.46 *House of Tafida, Sokoto, Wall I*

7.48 *House of Tafida, Sokoto, Wall 3*

7.47 *House of Tafida, Sokoto, Wall 2*

7.49 *House of Tafida, Sokoto, Wall 4*

7.50 *Zaria, decoration by Haruna*

7.52 *Zaria, decoration by Haruna*

7.51 *Zaria, decoration by Haruna*

7.53 *Zaria, decoration by younger brother of Haruna*

7.54 *Geometrical decoration: Zaria*

7.55 *Geometrical decoration: Zaria*

7.56 *Geometrical decoration: Zaria*

house of Tafida in Sokoto.[27] (See Figures 7.46 to 7.49.) These buildings seem to herald the beginning of a major period of elaborate internal and external decorative work throughout Hausaland.

The tradition of decorative work was carried on in the 1950s and early 1960s by a number of craftsmen, foremost among them Haruna dan Buhari, the great-great-grandson of the builder of the mosque and the current *sarkin magina*. In the early 1950s he decorated the extension to the palace in Zaria, the first time such a building was treated in this manner. Thus, the final bastion of conservatism was breached by the new style, legitimizing the changing views of *kunya*, the sense of propriety, with regard to ostentatious external decoration. *Sarkin* Haruna dan Buhari no longer decorates houses in Zaria, for this means of displaying *azziki* (prosperity) is no longer fashionable. However, he has been engaged in building at Jos museum in an effort to preserve this art form for posterity. Some of Haruna's work in Zaria is illustrated in Figures 7.50 to 7.52.

During the 1950s and early 1960s two quite distinct types of wall decoration were carried out by two very different sorts of builders. First there was traditional Hausa ornamentation which can be traced as far back as the late eighteenth century;

then, a new sort of repetitive pattern executed by *shegege* builders. Traditional ornament was executed by men who were members of long-established families of builders, where knowledge was passed down from father to son. Although this decoration did change over two centuries, such changes were slow and cumulative: the style developed to keep pace with the needs of society. While the decorations of the present

7.57 *Hausa embroidery*

sarkin magina, Haruna, and particularly those of the former chief builder, Jibrilu, are different from those of their common ancestor, Mallam Mikaila, they remain within the same school of design and are closer in character to this work of a century ago than to the patterns made by the other school of decorators illustrated in Figures 7.54 to 7.56.

The decorations of Haruna are non-representational, with the exception of the use of the crown and sceptre as symbols of royal power. Whether for a royal or non-royal patron his decorations are predominantly geometric, following tradition. Leary believes this may be because Haruna and his patrons are all members of a group directly related to the Emir through traditional clientship links.[28] The strong linear character of this decoration led Kirk-Greene to suggest an origin in the Sudan and the Middle East, the designs being brought to Hausaland by pilgrims returning from Mecca with intricately designed leatherwork.[29] Leary believes that the decorations used by builders in Hausaland and the spirals and interlacing knots typical of embroidered patterns on the rich garments of rulers and officials have much in common.[30] Prussin believes much of the impetus for Hausa decoration, and particularly its symbolism, are derived from Islamic sources.[31] Certainly it is true that Hausa leatherwork and embroidery use patterns

7.58 *Carved timber doorway, Nnewi*

similar to the mud decorations of 1930 to 1965, and that North African Islamic influence must have played some part in their development; yet in character and spirit Hausa mud decoration of this period is African. (See Figure 7.57.) The linear quality of mud patterning can be seen in the carved timber panels used in Igbo buildings, for instance, and the basic elements that make up these patterns—the triangle, lozenge and circle—are common throughout Nigeria.[32] (See Figure 7.58.)

In Zaria and other Hausa cities, it appears that a number of builders who were not members of the established families of builders have worked for some time this century. They have been recruited into the craft and are termed *shegege*: they have less prestige and are not eligible for higher office within the Hausa system of clientage. Judging by the quality and form of their work, the starting point in design appears to be Jibrilu's 'bicycle house' (Jibrilu being the most innovative of the traditional school of builders).

Wall decoration of the *shegege* builders is not confined to the doorway but extends over the whole façade. Motifs include the patterns common in Haruna's work and also representations of the ablution kettle (*buta*), Koranic slate (*allo*), and other artefacts associated with Islam. The house owner's profession may be indicated by depicting a lorry, sewing machine or motor car in the decoration, a visit to Mecca by an aeroplane. The proud owner of a car may have his registration number recorded in the pattern, a devout Muslim a pious saying in Arabic. Highly modelled decoration is still associated with the entrance and main parts of the elevation, but other sections of the wall have a cheaper form of repetitive patterning, cut into the mud while it is damp, or traced on to it with cement. The decoration usually consists of a broad pattern imitating the jointing in stone or brick construction. The rectangles formed in this way may be further geometrically sub-divided, or have small formalized flowers placed within them. The corners of buildings, the parapet and the junction of rooms are often picked out in white, the flowers or other smaller designs in pale pastel colours. The total effect of this decorative treatment is very pretty when seen against the grey-brown background of the laterite walls.[33]

These styles of mud decoration were in profusion during the mid-1960s, but as an art form they are rapidly dying out, the remaining examples being washed away by the rains, to be replaced by a simple mud coating on the entire wall or by concrete block work. The introduction of concrete block walls no doubt played a part in the demise of mud relief work. Attempts to recreate it in cement mortar were unsuccessful.

Wall decoration has not entirely disappeared, however. A new form of mural painting is in evidence which consists of more naturalistic themes painted on to the surface of the wall. (See Figures 7.22 to 7.24.) To what extent this form of wall decoration will catch the imagination of the Hausa and become common it is not possible to say, but although it is not in the local tradition of *sarkin maigina* Haruna or the *shegege* builders, it is more suitable to the new building technology and therefore has a greater chance of survival.

Conclusion

It is all too easy to conclude, as Kirk-Greene does, that:

> Despite the temptation to interpret these mural designs at their face value, I do not think many of them are symbolic or representative in the way that shapes and patterns so often 'mean' something to the European mind. They are attractive, yes, catching the eye and imagination, but with no deeper significance.[34]

Indeed, when asked to describe motifs in their decoration builders use the term *zane zane*, which simply means 'marks' or 'patterns': they can give no suggestions of their meaning. Names given to designs are usually associative. The circle, for instance, is called *fai-fai* which is also the name of a circular woven cover for a calabash and gramophone record.

Yet it is clear that Hausa wall decoration has been used to emphasize the opening to the compound and ownership of boundary walls. From time to time the stature and personality of the occupant of the house have been expressed both by the exuberance and the motifs of the decoration. Within this developing art form individual craftsmen (both traditional and of the *shegege* school), in addition to serving the clients' needs, have developed personal, distinctive styles of self expression. However, they have used symbols and motifs which may have their roots in an animistic past together with Islamic spiritual symbols.

The Hausa builders have been subject to outside influences: Fulanis, traders from North Africa, captives from the middle-belt of Nigeria and, later, Europeans. The development of decoration has varied according to the depth to which these influences have penetrated. In general terms it is possible to distinguish two main styles of Hausa decoration corresponding to the architectural styles of the north and south. The northern style is lighter, the decoration appearing like ribbon applied to the surface, while the southern style is bolder, deeply incised with a tendency to greater freedom and exuberance. The Hausa building industry, being in the hands of certain families, tends towards conservatism and it is not surprising to find that traditional forms used in decoration have developed slowly over the years. Only minor changes in composition or refinement of technique have occurred during any given period. The pace of change quickened during the last burst of wall decoration this century with the growth of the *shegege* class of builders.

Decoration and construction are part of the same process and it is not difficult to imagine a builder turning to the structure for decorative inspiration. The patterns made by the *azara* reinforcement before it is covered in mud, or before it is plastered, makes interesting shapes which may suggest motifs for use in the final design. The horizontal lines on the underside of an arch could well be a repetition on a smaller scale of the *azara* corbelling, while the patterning of the *azara* in ceiling panels produces coffering whose shapes are similar to those used in even the most complex Hausa designs. In part of the house built by Mohamadu Mazawachi, the first Emir of Kazaure, there is an old room where the ceiling coffering is carried down part of the wall, which may be an experiment in the use of this type of patterning on wall surfaces. (See Figure 7.59.)

It is not suggested that the development of structural features is the full explanation of Hausa decoration during the last two hundred years. A knowledge of Babban Gwani Mallam Mikaila and his work would quickly dispel such oversimplification. But it does seem that an appreciation of structural shapes and the building process may have had some effect on decoration.

It is not possible to determine with any accuracy the origin and meaning of much of the symbolism in Hausa wall decoration during the last two centuries, but it must be emphasized that it is possible to distinguish the style of individual artist craftsmen. They have used the motifs in their own ways, some experimenting and outdoing their contemporaries in the production of designs. Mallam Mikaila was able to do this in the last century and Mallam Jibrilu, his great-grandson, achieved a similar breakthrough a hundred years later. Mallam Mikaila derived his inspiration from the structure; Mallam Jibrilu consciously accepted Islamic and Western symbols as a starting point for pattern making. He used these symbols in a distinctive way to produce powerful patterns which engulf and overpower the structure, unlike the designs of his great-grandfather which are subsidiary to the structure and emphasize its main forms.

7.59 *House of Tafida, Sokoto, wall 2*

8. Architectural derivatives: The process of acculturation

Introduction

The Hausa system of mud construction is based upon an empirical knowledge of the strength of materials and a method of sizing building elements based on the scale of the human body and building techniques. The limit set by these design parameters has resulted in a series of building sizes that correspond closely to a broad band of normal dimensions which could almost be described as modular.[1] This does not mean that each dimension of a building is determined accurately according to some system of proportion, but rather that sizes are an inherent part of the system, and failure to observe normal rules of good building results in collapse or requires a change of technology.

The environment and technology set the limits within which Hausa architecture developed. Social and economic requirements influenced the spatial arrangement of the various architectural elements to serve the needs of the community. The organic nature of Hausa architecture is a reflection of the structure of society. In the past, the impermanent nature of the building materials made it possible for the total amount of accommodation and its disposition within the settlements to vary rapidly, keeping pace with the organic nature of the extended family system. So far this quality has not been disrupted by the introduction of more permanent structures: such structures which are still a small proportion of the total building stock.

The Hausa have developed an architecture using materials found in their locality and have adopted, adapted or invented systems of constructions that take these materials to their structural limits. In adapting impermanent and relatively unsuitable building materials to a climate which has periods of heavy rainfall the Hausa have created an extremely attractive built environment composed of buildings whose sculptural forms give expression to the plastic nature of mud. Within the limits set by the structural possibilities of the materials the buildings provide shelter from the extreme conditions of the climate.

Although there are similarities between Hausa architecture and that of other parts of West and North Africa it has a distinct character of its own which is the product of a cohesive and definable culture. The form of Hausa architecture, like the structure of Hausa society, has undergone a long process of change and development with new ideas from outside the area being introduced from time to time. The present building forms cannot be fully appreciated without an understanding of the effect of culture contact between the Hausa and neighbouring states. The process of acculturation has been a long one; the early influences on the Nok who occupied the area prior to the establishment of the Hausa states are unknown, but it is possible to be more certain of the effects of culture contact closer to modern times.

It is interesting to speculate on the influence of Pharaonic Egypt on West Africa. But speculation it must be, because there is very little evidence. We may note the similarities in character between the building forms of the Egyptians and the older mosques of Hausaland, but this could be explained simply as similar roofing problems giving rise quite independently to similar structural solutions.

Building types in West Africa

In the area of West Africa between the Sahara and the forest zone the chief building type is made entirely from vegetable material—that is some sort of thatching fixed on to a timber frame.[2] The predominance of this building type indicates that it may be the indigenous form of structure for this climatic zone. In the West African Sudan there are three areas where this possible indigenous structure does not predominate: around the great northern bend of the Niger, Hausaland and the Chad area[3]—the West African termini of the Saharan caravan routes and consequently the areas that had most contact with North African and Nilotic cultures. In the Chad area and Hausaland the main hut type is the structure with mud walls and thatched roof (*dakuna*); close to the northern bend of the Niger the all-mud structure (*soro*) predominates.

The mud wall may have been developed in the West African Sudan but is more likely to have been imported from more advanced cultures. As a technique it may even have been introduced by the legendary first rulers of the Hausa states who, according to custom, arrived in their present location after travelling from the east through Bornu, but coming originally from further north.[4] There is less doubt about the origin of the rectangular room with mud walls and mud roof. Its introduction was late: in the fifteenth century Leo Africanus described Timbuktu as consisting of thatched houses, and there is a description of the building of a mud-roofed mosque in Bornu in the twelfth century which seems to indicate that it was something of an extraordinary occurrence in that area too at that time.[5]

It seems that the rectangular room of mud walls and mud roof was an unusual structural form around Timbuktu until the fifteenth century, and that in the Chad area it has never replaced the older huts as the dominant house form. The rectangular mud structure was possibly introduced into Hausaland from Mali at about the same time as Islam, in the fourteenth century.[6] However, until the seventeenth century this architecture remained an alien and exotic form, used only for mosques and the houses of foreign traders. From about this time direct contact between Hausaland and North Africa was first established yet travellers in Hausaland as late as the nineteenth century still described the Hausa settlements as a mixture of *soro* and *dakuna* building types. Lugard, writing in 1904, described Kano as the southern limit of the *soro*, or

nothern type of architecture, and he wrote that *soro* buildings were used in Zaria only by the chiefs and the Emir.[7]

Barth's portrait of Kano in the 1850s reveals a mixture of *soro* and *dakuna* building types. He gave detailed descriptions of the various quarters of the town which show quite clearly that the majority of the new ruling class, the Fulani, lived in the simpler *dakuna*. Barth found one exception to this rule, the Emir, who occupied a large mud palace. According to him the defeated Habe still occupied their *soro* buildings, but as the century wore on the Fulani were influenced by the Arabs and by the defeated Habe and they too began to live in houses built in the *soro* style.[8] It was not until the British occupation of Hausaland, which broke the autocratic power of the Fulani, that greater numbers of Hausa traders of the *talakawa* class became wealthy and were permitted to display their wealth by the building of *soro* houses. The British occupation and the new emphasis on trade encouraged the rapid growth of a class of wealthy merchants, who were both willing and able to invest in building forms which were formerly beyond their means and probably regarded as the prerogative of the ruling class.

Before discussing possible alien influences on the form, layout and detail of buildings, it is necessary to trace the origin and development of the two main building types, the *soro* and the *dakuna*. It is not known for certain how or when the *dakuna* hut was first introduced into the Sudan and Hausaland. It may have been developed in this region, but it is more likely that the all-grass hut is the indigenous form of semi-permanent structure associated with the area and that the *dakuna* hut was introduced with other technological innovations such as smelting at the time of the Nok culture. New building techniques were brought to the eastern and western Sudan from North Africa between the fourth and twelfth centuries, among them the use of burnt bricks, introduced into Mali during the fourteenth century by Al Saheli. This material was used at Gambaru in the Bornu-Kanem area in the sixteenth century by Mairam Aisa Kili N'girmaram.[9]

The brick buildings in Mali and Bornu-Kanem were unusual and exotic structures unsuitable for wholesale use in the Western Sudan, but they may by their form have acted as a stimulus to the development of a rectilinear architecture in mud, a material more suited to curvilinear shapes. However, the evidence suggests that few if any of these ideas reached Hausaland or had any significant impact upon local building technology until the seventeenth century. Then Hausaland was in direct contact with the Arab world of North Africa and came under its influence; the Habe, or ruling class, adopted the North African style of architecture. During the nineteenth century the Fulani conquerors of Hausaland adopted the architectural style of the defeated Habe as they too came within the sphere of influence of North Africa.[10] It was due to the constant cultural contact between Hausaland and North Africa in the three centuries before the British occupation, that the art of mud building became established among the leading families of the emirate cities of Hausaland. But it is only since the beginning of this century that the *soro* style has become available for all those who can afford it.

The *dakuna* remains the building type in general use by the *talakawa*, especially in rural areas, although many of the peasant class, particularly in the urban centres, still build the *zaure* from mud and may indeed have other rooms in this style. Nowadays they tend to invest in more permanent modern structures. The compounds of the ruling families contain *dakuna*, *soro* and 'modern' buildings, so that in Hausaland building styles are freely mixed. A man decides which type of hut to build after considering such factors as the use to which it will be put, its position in relation to the main courtyard and the cost.

The courtyard plan

The courtyard, in one form or another, is a universal plan type in West Africa. At its most simple form it is either a group of huts forming the walls of an irregular enclosed space, or a group of huts scattered within a circular containing wall. It probably evolved in the same natural way as the round hut itself, and may well be the product of the culture of early sedentary agriculturalists. As such it probably developed quite naturally or independently in Hausaland.

The rectangular courtyard figures in many pre-dynastic Egyptian hieroglyphics, and together with the rectangular room is either a product of a technological advance requiring the use of tools to shape and frame timber members, or the natural outcome of building with burnt bricks.[11] The rectangular courtyard house was used throughout Egyptian times and was in use in the Middle East when Mohammed built his home at Mecca. Today the courtyard house, using rectangular rooms and rectangular external spaces, is to be found in many areas of the Middle East. (See Figure 8.1.)

The rectangular courtyard house was probably introduced into Hausaland at the same time as *soro* building. In a Hausaman's description of the setting out of a building, the rectangular compound is shown to be an ideal type and many houses do indeed have courtyards that approximate to a rectangular shape:

> When they are about to lay the foundations of the wall, it would be best if Tanko gave them ropes and pegs to set up. They should tie the rope to the pegs and align the sides lest they be crooked, or lest one be longer than the other. It is best that the compound should be exactly rectangular. The plan of the house is best if laid out in this way.[12]

To judge from the buildings I have measured, the right angle appears to be unknown in Hausaland, although most buildings have floor plans that are trapezoidal or, as in the case of the Friday Mosque in Zaria, approximating to a parallelogram. Despite the probability that Al-Saheli brought the knowledge of the right angle to the Sudan from Egypt there seems little evidence of its use, although the opposite sides of buildings and spaces are often approximately equal, possibly due to their being set out using ropes of the same length. This lack of knowledge, or at least use of the right angle, is most surprising considering the close contact between Hausaland and North Africa. When Clapperton visited Sokoto in the 1820s he noted that Sultan Bello had a copy of Euclid, and he saw a mosque being constructed which had been designed by a man from Zaria whose father, also a builder, had studied 'Moorish' architecture in Egypt.[13] It appears that if the right angle was known to the Habe builders then they saw no good reason to use it.

Although the right angle was not used by the Hausa, the main buildings are formal compositions. For example, the visual effect of the Friday Mosque in Zaria is one of sobriety, and this is confirmed by a study of its plan and roof plan. The regularity of the plan is self evident, most elements correspond about a series of axes and sub-axes. The symmetrical composition of the Mosque, however, is not that artificial symmetry associated with the 'Beaux Arts' period in Europe, but a lively discipline where corresponding forms vary slightly, either by accident or design or because of the nature of the building materials. Such accidents of detail add charm to the design: because the visual structure of the composition is strong they are able to fall into place without disrupting the overall effect. In designing the Mosque in this orderly way, the architect, Mallam Mikaila, was following in the tradition of Hausa building, for as we have seen it is Hausa custom to build as regularly as building and constructional techniques permit. This tradition is probably a result of the ideas that came to West Africa from North Africa or Egypt where regularity of design was the result of a more precise building technology.

The development of the mosque

The first mosque in Islam, according to Cresswell, was the converted home of Mohammed at Madikia.[14] As in other cultures the religious buildings of Islam initially took the form of the standard home, and the mosques in North Africa still show the effect of this early influence of the house plan. Mosques in Hausaland have taken the standard Islamic form of a building within a walled area, but unlike those in North Africa the courtyards are not surrounded by covered arcades. The Hausa mosque may be free-standing within the courtyard but is entered through small gatehouses used as ablution chambers, a form closer to the house plan of the Hausa than to the fully-developed Egyptian mosques. It is interesting to note the marked differences between the present day Sudanese house in Khartoum and the Hausa house. (See Figure 8.1.) Although both have been designed to achieve privacy, particularly for the women of the household, the Hausa link between the private world of the house and the public world of

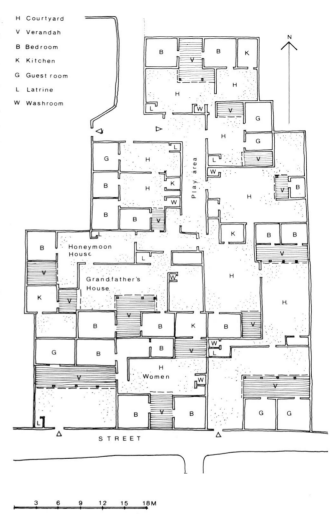

H Courtyard
V Verandah
B Bedroom
K Kitchen
G Guest room
L Latrine
W Washroom

8.1   Sudanese house plan. The house of the Awad El-Kerimi family. Khartoum

the street is an entrance hut (*zaure*); in Khartoum the link is the entrance courtyard (*hosh*).

The Friday Mosque in Zaria, for example, uses ablution chambers as a buffer between the courtyard of the mosque and the busy street; the Emir's entrance through the *Shari'a* court and a series of other rooms and courtyards is a planning solution very close to that of the normal Hausa home. Figure 3.15 is a plan of the home of the direct descendants of Mallam Mikaila in Zaria, and is said to have been built by him. The entrance *zaure* is certainly similar in style and feeling to the *Shari'a* court of the Friday Mosque and makes an interesting comparison with his more prestigious work.

Since the beginning of the nineteenth century the Hausa mosque has changed in two important ways. In Habe times, prior to the jihad, there was a tower (*sumi'a* or *hasumiya*) attached to each mosque. Towers from this period can still be seen in Katsina and Bauchi (see Figures 4.65 to 4.67), although there is evidence that the present tower in Katsina was rehabilitated at the beginning of the present century.[15] In Habe times the mud tower was a feature both of the mosque and the houses of emirs and chiefs.

According to Clapperton, such towers were built for defence.[16] Since Leo Africanus did not comment on mud towers in Hausaland, it is safe to assume that they were first introduced directly from North Africa in the seventeenth century or later. It seems possible that the tower was introduced to improve the defences of Kano and Katsina in their struggle to control the southern terminus of the central Saharan trade route. From old sketches and photographs, it can be seen that the now demolished *sumi'a* of Kano mosque had many small, slit-like windows. It appears ideally suitable as a retreat from which to make a last stand against the enemy. Whatever the reason for building towers in the seventeenth and eighteenth centuries, they are similar in form to the minarets of such mosques as that of Ahmad Ibn Tulun (built A.D. 876–9) in Cairo,[17] or the Great Mosque in Qairawan[18], and to the defensive towers of the Dades Valley in Morocco. The Friday Mosques in Zaria and Kazaure and others built since the jihad have no tower which may indicate that it had less significance during the comparatively peaceful times in the latter part of the nineteenth century.[19]

The development of arch construction

Another change in the form of the mud mosque was the replacement of the trabeated system of construction by the use of arches. The first account of such a mosque is given in Clapperton's journal, a record of his second visit to Hausaland in 1828. As mentioned above, the mosque being built in Sokoto was designed by a man from Zaria whose father, also a builder, had studied 'Moorish' architecture in Egypt.[20] Clapperton noted that the design of Bello's main suite of reception rooms was the same as the houses of all the most important families in Hausaland. He described one of Bello's rooms as being about 9m. square and requiring eight arches to support the domed roof. This does not represent an early formative stage in the development of the arch, but is the maximum size for a square room using this system of construction. So it may be argued that by the end of the second decade in the eighteenth century the fully developed Hausa architectural style already existed. It is possible to form some idea of the type of houses in which the Habe rulers of Hausaland lived by studying the *zaure* of the Emir's palace in Daura. This simple structure, which is whitewashed and has very little decoration, is a very beautiful example of the type of building which was to be found in Hausaland in the late eighteenth century. (See Figures 4.36 to 4.43.)

Since the arch is a latent possibility of the Hausa structural system and is in effect a series of corbels it may well be a product of a slow development. On the other hand, its introduction may be due to the skill and knowledge of the Zaria builder who had studied in Egypt, returning home perhaps full of new ideas with which he experimented. Even if the invention of the arch is not due entirely to the efforts of one man, it seems likely, since his son was invited to Sokoto to build an important mosque, that he was a leading exponent of its use. He may well have been the first builder to realize the full potential of the arch and to use it in more daring ways.

The Friday Mosque in Zaria, built by Babban Gwani Mallam Mikaila for Emir Abdulkarim in the 1830s, is very similar to the one described by Clapperton, and so close in time to it that it is more than likely that the two mosques were built by the same man, or at least by close relatives of the same family of builders.[21] The post of chief builder (*sarkin maigina*) is still held by the direct male descendant of Babban Gwani, which seems a good reason to believe that the chief builder of Zaria before Babban Gwani was a more senior male member of his family.[22]

Structurally and from an aesthetic point of view, the Mosque in Zaria went further than most contemporary buildings. Its main arches are coupled and sweep right down to the floor; those of the Daura Palace and the Sokoto Mosque, which Clapperton described, rest on columns, a solution which represents a transitional stage between the spanning of a space using straightforward corbels and a lintel, and Babban Gwani's complete arch form. The Zaria Mosque is perhaps the high point of Hausa architecture, but it is said that Babban Gwani built one more mosque for the Emir of Birnin Gwari which, although smaller, was as fine as his earlier building.[23] On the completion of his mosque, the Emir of Birnin Gwari seized Babban Gwani and had him executed so that no mosque would ever be built to equal the one in Birnin Gwari.[24] Judging Babban Gwani only on the one work in Zaria, discounting both this last folk tale and the possibility that he may have built an equally fine mosque in Sokoto, it is evident that he made a major contribution to the art of Hausa building.

The roots of Hausa architecture are lost in antiquity, but it is possible that it shares a common ancestry with the great buildings of Pharaonic Egypt. Some of the early pre-dynastic hieroglyphics depict houses with small pinnacles similar to the *zankwaye* that decorate Hausa buildings. The whole character of the Egyptian house drawings resembles that of the architecture of both present day Nubia and Hausaland. (See Figure 8.2.) Pre-dynastic reed architecture of Egypt similar to that of the Marsh Arabs of Iraq may have been the forerunner for both the mud architecture of Sudan and that of Pharaonic Egypt.[25]

The *zankwaye* or pinnacles constructed on top of Hausa walls are found in the architecture of many other parts of the Sudan. They may have originated in North Africa and found their way into Hausaland from the seventeenth century onwards. However, between Wa in the north of Ghana and

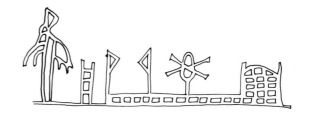

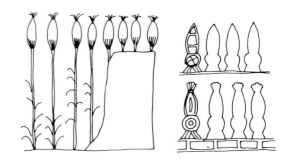

8.2 *House forms and hut shrines in pre dynastic Egypt. (E.B. Smith, Egyptian Architecture New York 1938)*

Timbuktu in Mali there are many mosques whose walls are a striking series of pointed buttresses (see Figure 8.3). The buttresses are totally unnecessary to resist lateral thrust, since the structure consists of simple columns and beams. This particular building form is similar to the huge termite nests in the same region, a natural form for mud structures, their battered wall surfaces following the line of slip for laterite. Since they have no horizontal surfaces the effect of erosion by rainfall is minimized. It is not suggested that the mosques of Northern Ghana are a conscious copy of the termite nest, but their forms are similar and may have been developed partly for climatic reasons. The buttresses are possibly the mud versions of an older structural form associated with buildings made from local vegetation. Whatever the origin of these intriguing mosques, the projecting buttresses in some cases become simple pinnacles similar to the Hausa *zankwaye*.

The mud arch and the arch used in Egyptian Islamic architecture, from which it was derived, are the same shape as the reed arches of the Marsh Arabs. When loaded, the bundles of reeds which form the arches take the shape of a horseshoe and again suggest a link between mud architecture and an earlier form of reed structure. Reed arches are not unknown in the Western Sudan, for they are used by the Buduma people who inhabit the islands of Lake Chad and have a similar technology to the Marsh Arabs.[26] A less likely reason for the shape of the mud arch may be the simple practicalities of building an arch on to a battered wall; the arch may simply follow the line of the wall until the first *azara* is placed in position, when the angle of the arch automatically changes. However, because of its horseshoe shape the arch merges beautifully with the general line of the wall and is far more pleasing in its monolithic mud form than its more sophisticated cousin made in stonework where the voussoirs are emphasized. The horseshoe arch may in fact have undergone three phases of development from a reed, to a mud and finally to a stone structure.

The male descendants of Babban Gwani are today the leading family of builders in Zaria, their knowledge having been passed down to them from their ancestors. Clapperton's

8.3 *Mosque, Northern Ghana*

account of his meeting with the builder of the Sokoto Mosque shows that this family tradition of building existed early in the last century. The Hausa builders are members of the old Habe families. So it would seem quite wrong to assume, as Crowder has, that 'this restraining influence [the simplicity of the Fulani] on the crude art of the Hausas combined with wider Arab influence to produce an unusual style of architecture'.[27] On the contrary, it seems that the structural techniques developed by the Habe have given the architecture its simplicity and dignity. The Habe, over many hundreds of years, have assimilated the North African influence, producing an architecture quite different from that of the Songhai, the Bornu, or the North African states. The period of contact with other cultures was long and the process of adaptation of indigenous architecture slow, being the work of families of builders who passed their skills from father to son, and who adapted new ideas as and when necessary in the developing society. Such ideas were not altogether alien, and were probably a development of the same original culture, and thus quite compatible with the forms and ideas existing in the West African Sudan.

9 Conclusion

Introduction

The creation of the built environment in Hausaland is the core of this study. So far the concern has been to discover how and why a particular built environment came to be. As expected there is confirmation that the built environment is in a constant process of change. In Hausaland the rate of change appears to be accelerating. While accepting that change is both inevitable and in some cases desirable this final chapter intends to show that these changes can be brought about without destroying the great traditions of Hausa city building. No matter which set or sets of development policies are adopted to solve urban problems those policies result in the built environment. It is with this aspect of the development process, particularly in Hausaland, that this part of the study deals. It is not the intention, therefore, to develop ideas or policies for dealing with the vast web of interconnected developmental problems. Nor, is a single panacea offered which, if applied, will magically dispel the horrendous conditions of the squatter camps surrounding the great cities of Africa, India, South America and Asia. It will, however, be shown that the Hausa people and their urban areas need not follow others down this cul-de-sac of environmental squalor and degradation.

The 1960s and early '70s saw many attempts at solving third world housing problems using mass housing techniques. Even the more human low rise comprehensive developments seem, in general terms, to have failed; the housing need being too great for the available resources and the cost of individual units being beyond the resources of the vast majority of those in housing need. Attempts in the 1970s and '80s to spread the capital outlay so that more people would benefit from the development encouraged ideas such as site-and-service schemes and self-help housing. Such schemes also have a high rate of failure; standards set for self-help housing still being too high for the poor in the developing world. Corruption too has sometimes led to the appropriation of sites by the more affluent as second homes and for renting and investment. Current conventional wisdom, however, would still have us believe that the housing problems of the third world urban poor can be solved through self-help schemes given security of tenure for the owner builder. The concept of autonomous housing, which maximises the constructional contribution of the participants and his degree of self-government, while minimising the investment by the sponsor or government agency, is seductively simple, holding out, as it does, the possibility of solving one of the world's most intractable problems and at a minimal cost to the wealthy nations.[1] A study conducted in Nairobi suggested that this particular solution may lead to further benefits for the wealthy squatter landlords and more expensive housing for the poor.[2] It seems that the squatter landlord, the 'corporations' as they are known locally in Nairobi, are important agents of informal development: any proposal not taking their interests into consideration would founder. It seems that solutions for the housing problems of the low income groups should be tailored to suit individual conditions of place and people.

The Hausa settlements in common with urban centres in the rest of Nigeria and in other parts of the developing world have grown rapidly in the last twenty-five years. Conditions, however, within the traditional parts of the settlements and in areas occupied by the Hausa where traditional building methods are still practised do not exhibit the squalor to be found in those areas occupied by 'strangers'. Within the traditional areas there has certainly been a loss of environmental quality: this survey has recorded the loss of many fine decorated murals, an increase in the use of the ubiquitous tin roof, an increase in the quantity of badly designed and constructed concrete block structures and the penetration of the car into previously pedestrianised areas. Such losses have compensations in the expansion of piped water, electricity and the growing convenience of the transportation system. Despite the loss of some environmental quality Hausa settlements nevertheless present to the world a dignified and human appearance in contrast to the sordid squatter settlements of the third world. By careful development of Hausa building traditions it is possible to retain the best of both worlds, the necessary and much valued modern facilities together with the highest traditions of urban quality, and this despite the mounting population pressures and the luring chimera of fashionable architectural ideas from the western world.

Hausaland

Any set of policies for developmental purposes require to be linked to a specific place and people. This study relates to one group of people occupying *Kasar Hausa*, the land where Hausa is spoken. The Hausa states developed initially in an area which can be defined as a geographical and environmental unit. Within this isolated and self-contained region the Hausa have developed a quite distinctive culture with their own strong traditions. They have, to some extent, been contained within their present boundaries by the inhospitable environmental conditions in the Sahara to the north and the middle belt to the south. To the east and west Hausaland was polarised for many centuries between its more powerful neighbouring states centred at Chad and the great northern bend of the Niger. To some extent this situation was fossilized at the time of the colonial occupation and partition of West Africa.

Clearly, conditions are not quite as neat and simple as this description of *Kasar Hausa* portrays. The Hausa have indeed over-spilled from their heartland into the surrounding less promising regions and their cultural traditions have affected peoples in adjoining areas. Within *Kasar Hausa* there are two quite distinct sub-regions or two broad ecological zones having quite distinct soil types, variations in climate and vegetation. To some extent these ecological variations are mirrored in the regional variation in architectural style; the

north being more Saharan, lighter in structure, appearance and decoration; the southern style being more African in appearance; massive, bolder in structural design while decoration is deeply incised and flamboyant. The two styles reflect the character of the two ethnic components which have combined to form the Hausa people. The northern style of architecture is more completely influenced by the ruling Fulani — originally a nomadic people with deep cultural roots in Islam — and ideas of the Islamic world of the Mediterranean, while the south of Hausaland still retains many of its African traditions kept alive by the Habe, the other ethnic component of the Hausa.

The formulation of development policies, particularly those concerned with the built environment, appropriate to a given situation clearly requires an understanding of the cultural history of the community for whom such policies are designed. In the case of the Hausa the environment has provided the backcloth against which culture has developed. Man, however, is not simply a passive actor in the process of development reacting to environmental stimuli. The environment itself has been modified by cultural development: technological advances, changes in economic, social and religious institutions have themselves conditioned the way in which the built environment has evolved.

The Hausa states emerged, firstly, from the revolutions in agriculture and iron smelting, and secondly because of the population movements to the south of Hausaland which led to the need to develop strongly fortified centres. The communities within these highly nucleated settlements developed complex political and administrative structures of city and state government in response to the expanding trans-Saharan trading connections. On sites with plentiful water supplies, good agricultural land, a defensible position and imbued with ancient religious meaning, the Hausa built great fortified mud cities dominating a landscape of smaller dependent settlements. The territorial organisation closely reflects the political and religious structures of the Hausa community. It was this organisation which made it possible for them to take advantage of the inherent qualities of the environment. Although there have been changes in the political and administrative structures in Hausaland since independence the Emir and local elders still retain influence within the old settlements while Islam retains its dominant force in the Hausa community. Future development will of necessity reflect changes in the power structure, but while this extremely conservative society accepts the traditional leadership of the Emirs and respects the teachings and institutions of Islam, changes in urban form may be slow and self-analytical thereby avoiding the great damage inflicted upon many third world cities.

The forces stimulating structural change in Hausa settlements are the increasing urban populations, a demand for improved road systems for vehicular circulation, the need to improve services such as water and electricity, the land requirements of the new uses associated with a modern state such as office development, industrial estates and shopping facilities, and finally the changing attitude that now considers land a commodity to be bought and sold. Clearly, a plan of action for Hausa settlements which ignored this dynamic for change would be totally ineffective. Nevertheless, strong persistent cultural traditions can be harnessed to give direction to change so that city building in this part of the world may reach the heights of an art form rather than a total submission to alien economic and technological forces resulting in a formless, inhuman landscape of poverty and dependence.

Among those features of Hausa settlements which may give direction to future development is the idea of place associated with ethnic group, common trade or common ancestor. Such a concept could form the basis for future urban growth; city additions taking the form of beads upon a string – the vehicular spine also being the routes for the essential modern services. Agricultural produce is an important contribution to many family incomes amongst the Hausa at the moment. Urban farms are an important feature of some third world cities and are a far more effective use of land than the incidental open space surrounding current low cost housing schemes such as the ones in Kano.[3] With a little imagination at the design stage such incidental open space could be reorganised to form the basis of urban farmland. A delightful feature of the present Hausa city is the structure of spaces – linking the most public meeting place, the *dendal*, through the space at the neighbourhood centre associated often with the ward head's home, to the semi private space that links neighbouring homes and leads on finally to the privacy and seclusion of the courtyard in the *cikin gida*. Future city extensions could conform to this healthy tradition with little effort; where each such addition would comprise a small community with a physical identity, some agricultural land and a spatial structure of narrow shaded pedestrian routes connecting centre to home. In such communities there would be minimal penetration by motor vehicles as most people would commute, as they do at present, by minibus.

The concept of the home and indeed the family is quite different from the western model. Generally speaking the home in western society, sometimes even referred to as a 'unit of accommodation', consists of a fixed amount of space. Family mobility is high, homes being bought and sold or exchanged in other ways during the lifespan of the family to suit its changing accommodation needs. In contrast, the Hausa family, once established retains its location. The home expands and contracts to suit changing needs over several generations. Hausa newcomers to a community obtain unused (therefore unowned) land on which to build their homes: a civilised method of dealing with the 'housing problem'. The land ownership question is therefore of vital importance to the future of Hausa cities. Traditional attitudes to land, for housing purposes, that is, security of tenure and free access to land, is essential for future developmental purposes. Bureaucratic procedures associated with land nationalisation and other similar administrative actions in developing countries inevitably lead to corruption, lengthy delays, higher housing costs and attempts by the state to build large housing schemes to solve the housing problem, a problem in part created by these very procedures.

The principles of the Islamic way of life guide the present planning and design of housing in this society: these principles should be formally embodied into the system of by-laws which govern housing development in the traditional centres of the Hausa community. Amongst these principles, for example, 'privacy' and 'wife seclusion' are extremely important and it is difficult to imagine dramatic changes in this aspect of community life in the near future. It follows that buildings should be designed so that they do not overlook others, entrances to homes require careful positioning in relation to neighbouring buildings and some form of external perimeter wall is essential. Such requirements rule out flats of any description and indeed the western type villa as models for house designs.

The present system of Hausa construction has produced a dignified built environment with many fine buildings of architectural merit. Fashions, however, are changing and it is not the intention here to advocate a return to a 'glorious past', such a romantic notion would be a great dis-service to the Hausa. Culture is forever changing and the rate of change in Hausaland is accelerating. It is nevertheless appropriate to examine current building practice to see if it can be made to serve this society's future.

The Hausa still build most houses from local building materials using traditional constructional techniques on a self-help basis assisted by local building specialists. While self-help is being urged on other developing countries as an alternative to mass housing, in Hausaland it is common practice in urban areas. Most developing countries are concerned about foreign exchange and the reduction of imports. It can be argued, therefore, that the continuing use of building materials found in the local environment is a significant contribution to a reduction of national indebtedness.

Mud buildings are comfortable and elegant surroundings in which to live. The work of Foyle in illustrating some of the buildings occupied by Europeans and the writings of Musson support this claim.[4] While a visit to some of the property belonging to the Christian community in Wusasa shows how such property can be properly maintained and adapted for modern living conditions. For example the houses have been wired for electricity; have a water supply, water-borne sanitation and a hygienic kitchen. These lovely houses combine the best of two worlds – the dignity of fine traditional buildings whose forms have evolved over many generations to suit a rigorous climate and the modern amenities to which the Hausa quite justifiably aspire.

Traditional building techniques will, no doubt, continue to be used in most rural areas and small settlements without Government action and possibly in spite of such action. However, if this traditional method of house building is to survive in urban areas certain official actions are necessary. The large borrow pits located in cities, from which material is taken for building purposes, are clearly a health hazard: their closure and sealing as in Zaria is a natural precaution any local Government is required to take. However, the official action of closing the borrow pits has led to an increase in the cost of building materials making them less competitive with imported materials. The siting and location of borrow pits in relation to housing is of prime importance in planning future settlement extensions so that distances are not excessive but that no health hazard is caused. Secondly, *azara* the main component in reinforced mud is in great demand for urban housing. Government action is necessary therefore to ensure both the conservation and the replanting of the dumi palm in sufficient quantity to meet the demand at reasonable cost. Finally, the training of builders in traditional skills may require formal organisation to ensure that such builders are able to organise and control the specialist trades required for service installation. The establishment of a school for traditional builders, the 'barefoot builder', who both understands his own technological traditions but is also capable of experimenting with new techniques would be an effective counterbalance to those Nigerian schools of architecture modelled on Western ideas of architectural education stressing service through lucrative consultancy work.

The Hausa community faces inevitable change. In this period of rapid change it is important to re-appraise those cultural traditions out of which grew a pleasant and urbane landscape: the worthy setting for many lovely buildings. An understanding of the qualities of Hausa architecture is an essential foundation for the development of architectural forms suitable for use by this community at the end of this century. Slums similar to those of Calcutta, Nairobi and Lagos, which ignore their respective indigenous traditions are the depressing alternative to sensitive development based on a thorough appreciation of the cultural traditions that inspired a great work of architecture such as the Friday Mosque in Zaria designed by Mallam Mikaila, who became known as *Babban Gwani*, the 'Great Builder'.

Notes

Introduction

1 Christopher Alexander, *A Pattern Language* (New York, Oxford University Press, 1977).

2 Centre national d'art et de culture Georges Pompidou, *Down to Earth*, tr. Ruth Eaton (London, Thames and Hudson, 1982).

3 F.W. Schwerdtfeger, *Traditional Housing in African Cities* (New York, John Wiley, 1982).

4 Hasan Fathy, *Architecture for the poor* (London, University of Chicago Press, 1973).

5 Amos Rappoport, *House Form and Culture* (Englewood Cliffs, Prentice-Hall, 1969) and *Human Aspects of Urban Form* (Oxford, Pergamon, 1977).

6 Akin Mabogunje, 'The Land and Peoples of West Africa', in J.F.A. Ajayi and Michael Crowder (eds), *History of West Africa* (London, Longman, 1971), vol.1.

7 For the general history of the Hausa states I am indebted particularly to S.J. Hogben and A.H.M. Kirk-Greene, *The Emirates of Northern Nigeria* (London, Oxford University Press, 1966) and Abdullahi Smith, 'The Early States of the Central Sudan', in Ajayi and Crowder, *History of West Africa*, op. cit. M.G. Smith's work gave valuable insights into the way of life and organization of the settlements; see particularly M.G. Smith, *Government in Zazzau* (London, Oxford University Press, 1960) and *The Economy of the Hausa Communities of Zaria*, Colonial Research study No.16 (London, H.M.S.O., 1955).

8 The chapter is based mainly upon M.J. Mortimore (ed.), *Zaria and its Region* (Zaria, Ahmadu Bello University, Dept. of Geography, 1970); A.W. Urquhart, *Planned Urban Landscapes* (Zaria, Ahmadu Bello University, 1977), and G. Nicolas, 'Essai sur les structures fondamentales de l'espace dans la cosmologie Hausa', *Journal de la Société des Africanistes* vol.36, 1966, which is a fascinating account of pre-Islamic symbolism in settlement layout.

9 The section on the family compound owes much to the work of Schwerdtfeger's analysis of the relationship between kinship pattern, its growth and development and the effects on the physical form of the compound. See Schwerdtfeger, *op. cit.* Taylor and Webb's translation of *Labarun Al' Adun Hausawa Da Zantatukansu* (London, O.U.P., 1932), gives a first-hand account of the building operation. While not agreeing with some of Labelle Prussin's conclusions, I found her insights into architectural meaning in African societies of great interest. See Labelle Prussin, 'Fulani-Hausa Architecture', *African Arts*, vol.X (October 1976), no.1.

10 For an analysis of Hausa construction see A.E. Daldy, *Temporary Buildings in Northern Nigeria*, Technical Paper no.10 (Public Works Department, Nigeria, 1945).

11 This section of the study owes a great deal to the theoretical statements in O.H. Koenigsberger, *et al.*, *Manual of Tropical Housing and Building: Part 1, Climatic Design* (London, Longman, 1974).

12 I am greatly indebted to the work of Allan Leary for many of the ideas contained in this section, in particular his article 'A Decorated Palace in Kano', and his unpublished paper, 'Social and Economic Factors in the Development of Hausa Building Decoration', Jan. 1975.

1 Environment and Settlement Pattern

1 A more correct translation of *Kasar Hausa* is 'the land where the Hausa language is spoken'. Fig. 1.1 shows the area in Nigeria occupied by the Hausa people whose mother tongue is Hausa. However, it should be noted that Hausa is the most widely spoken African language in Nigeria. Not shown in Fig. 1.1 are the areas in Niger occupied by the Hausa.

2 A.T. Grove, *Africa South of the Sahara*, 2nd edn. (London, Oxford University Press, 1970), pp.2, 3.

3 J.N. Paden, *Religion and Political Culture in Kano* (Berkeley, University of California Press, 1973), p.46.

4 K.M. Buchanan and J.C. Pugh, *Land and People in Nigeria* (London, University of London Press, 1955), pp.1–12.

5 The area provided many slaves for the trans-Saharan trade, and it has been suggested that this denudation of the population may be the cause of a major colonization of the area by the tsetse fly. See R.J. Harrison Church, *West Africa*, 8th edn. (London, Longman, 1980), p.172.

6 *Ibid.*, pp.22–3.

7 Buchanan and Pugh, *op. cit.*, pp.12–14.

8 R.M. Prothero, *Migrant Labour from Sokoto Province Northern Nigeria* (Kaduna, Government Printer, 1958), p.3.

9 Derwent Whittlesey, 'Kano: A Sudanese Metropolis', *Geographical Review*, vol.27 (1937), p.179.

10 M.J. Mortimore, 'Settlement Evolution and Land Use' in *Zaria and its Region*, ed. M.J. Mortimore (Zaria, Ahmadu Bello University, Dept. of Geography, 1970), pp.102–122.

11 A.T. Grove, 'The Ancient Erg of Hausaland, and Similar Formations on the South Side of the Sahara', *Geographical Journal*, Dec. 1958, p.528.

12 M.J. Mortimore and J. Wilson, *Land and People in the Kano Planning Authority* (Zaria, Ahmadu Bello University, Dept. of Geography, March 1965), p.4.

13 R.K. Udo, *Geographical Regions of Nigeria* (London, Heineman, 1970), pp.157–8.

14 G.W. Lawson, *Plant Life in West Africa* (London, Oxford University Press, 1966), pp.5–9.

15 *Ibid.*, pp.33–6; Buchanan and Pugh, *op. cit.*, pp.35–6.

16 R.W.J. Keay, *An Outline of Nigerian Vegetation* (Lagos, Federal Government Printer, 1959); G. Jackson, 'Vegetation around the city and nearby villages of Zaria', in M.J. Mortimore (ed.), *Zaria and its Region*, *op. cit.*, pp.61, 80.

17 M.J. Mortimore, 'Settlement Evolution and Land Use', *op. cit.*, pp.102–22.

18 Keay, *op. cit.*, pp.26–7.

19 Lawson, *op. cit.*, pp.38–9.

20 Akin Mabogunje, 'The Land and Peoples of West Africa', in J.F.A. Ajayi and Michael Crowder, *History of West Africa* (London, Longman, 1971), vol.1, p.5.

21 Mabogunje, *op. cit.*, p.5.

22 G.P. Murdoch, *Africa, its Peoples and their Culture History* (New York, McGraw-Hill, 1959), p.6.

23 R.H. Dyson, 'Archeology and the Domestication of Animals in the Old World', *American Anthropologist*, 1953, pp.661–73. According to Dyson the 'true horse' may have been introduced into Africa much later than the other basic domesticated neolithic animals.

24 Thurston Shaw, 'The Prehistory of West Africa', in Ajayi and Crowder, *History of West Africa*, vol.1, pp.38–44.

25 Mabogunje, *op. cit.*, pp.7–9.

2 The Evolution of Settlement

1 Thurston Shaw, 'The Prehistory of West Africa' in J.F.A. Ajayi and Michael Crowder (eds.), *History of West Africa* (London, Longman, 1971), vol.1, p.64.

2 J.D. Fage, *A History of West Africa*, 4th edn. (London, Cambridge University Press, 1969), pp.6–10; R.A. Oliver and J.D. Fage, *A Short History of Africa* (Harmondsworth, Penguin, 1962), pp.44–52.

3 Robin Horton, 'Stateless Societies in the History of West Africa' in Ajayi and Crowder, *History of West Africa*, vol.1, pp.109–13.

4 *Ibid.*, p.110.

5 E.W. Bovill, *The Golden Trade of the Moors* (London, Oxford University Press, 1958), pp.16–30.

6 S.J. Hogben and A.H.M. Kirk-Greene, *The Emirates of Northern Nigeria* (London, Oxford University Press, 1966), p.51.

7 Nehemia Levtzion, 'The Early States of the Western Sudan to 1500', in Ajayi and Crowder, *History of West Africa*, vol.1, pp.114–51.

8 Hogben and Kirk-Greene, *op. cit.*, pp.89–98.

9 E.J. Arnett (tr.) 'A Hausa Chronicle', *Journal of the African Society*, vol.9 (1910), pp.161–7.

10 Fage, *A History of West Africa*, *op. cit.*, pp.31–4.

11 Abdullahi Smith, 'The Early States of the Central Sudan', in Ajayi and Crowder, *History of West Africa*, vol.1, pp.181–6.

12 A.T. Grove and A. Warren, 'Quarternary Landforms and Climate on the South Side of the Sahara, *Geographical Journal*, vol.CXXXIV (1968) 2, pp.194–208.

13 *Ibid.*

14 This description of the formation of the Hausa states and their early history is owed to Abdullahi Smith's chapter in Ajayi and Crowder, *History of West Africa*, vol.1, pp.152–95.

15 Joseph Greenberg, *The Influence of Islam on a Sudanese Religion* (New York, J.J. Augustin, 1946).

16 Abdullahi Smith, 'Some Notes on the History of Zazzau under the Hausa Kings', in M.J. Mortimore (ed.) *Zaria and its Region* (Zaria, Ahmadu Bello University, Dept. of Geography, 1970), pp.82–101.

17 *Ibid.*

18 This section on medieval Hausaland is owed to the work of Abdullahi Smith in Mortimore, *Zaria and its Region*.

19 Sultan Bello, quoted in Hogben and Kirk-Greene, *The Emirates of Northern Nigeria, op. cit.*, p.217.

20 M.G. Smith, *Government in Zazzau* (London, Oxford University Press, 1960), p.84.

21 A.W. Urquhart, *Planned Urban Landscapes* (Zaria, Ahmadu Bello University Press, 1977), p.10.

22 Greenberg, *The Influence of Islam, op. cit.*

23 Tradition suggests that Islam was introduced into Hausaland by merchants from Mali and that this occurred some time in the fourteenth century. See Greenberg, *The Influence of Islam*. Smith suggests that the date of the first appearance of Muslims in Hausaland is unknown, but their effect on government in the area probably does not pre-date the last part of the fifteenth century. See

Abdullahi Smith in Ajayi and Crowder, *History of West Africa, op. cit.*, vol.1, p.190.

24 Bovill, *op. cit.*, pp.86–92; Fage, *A History of West Africa, op. cit.*, pp.23–6.

25 Abdullahi Smith in Ajayi and Crowder, *History of West Africa, op. cit.*, vol.1, p.192.

26 Michael Crowder, *The Story of Nigeria* (London, Faber & Faber, 1962), p.36; Hogben and Kirk-Greene, *op. cit.*, p.313.

27 Arnett, 'A Hausa Chronicle', *op. cit.* Hausa tradition mentions seven bastard Hausa states (*banza bakwai*) in addition to the seven true states (*Hausa bakwai*) founded by Bayejida. The *banza bakwai* included Zamfara, Kebbi, Nupe, Gwari, Yaura, Yoruba and Kororofa, all of which probably came under the influence of Hausa culture.

28 Hogben and Kirk-Greene, *op. cit.*, pp.99–105; Hunwick, 'Songhay, Borno and Hausaland in the Sixteenth Century', in Ajayi and Crowder, *History of West Africa*, vol.1, pp.274–80.

29 R.A. Adeleye, 'Hausaland and Bornu, 1600–1800', in *ibid.*, pp.556–60.

30 For a description of the jihad and the effect it had on Hausaland see Crowder, *The Story of Nigeria, op. cit.*, pp.78–95; Hogben and Kirk-Greene, *op. cit.*, pp.116–30.

31 R.A. Adeleye, *op. cit.*

32 A.W. Urquhart, *op. cit.*, pp.69–71.

33 H. Barth, *Travels and Discoveries in North and Central Africa* (London, Longman, 1857–8), vol.11, pp.32–41.

34 Gavin McDonnell, 'The Dynamics of Geographic Change: The case of Kano', *Annals of the Association of American Geographers*, vol.54, no.3, Sept. 1964, p.369.

35 *Ibid.*, p.362.

3 The Structure of Hausa Settlements

1 E.J. Arnett (tr.) 'A Hausa Chronicle', *Journal of the African Society*, vol.9 (1910), pp.161–7.

2 S.J. Hogben and A.H.M. Kirk-Greene, *The Emirates of Northern Nigeria* (London, Oxford University Press, 1966), p.149.

3 Abdullahi Smith, 'The Early States of the Central Sudan', in J.F.A. Ajayi and Michael Crowder (eds.), *History of West Africa* (London, Longman, 1971), vol.1, p.186.

4 A.W. Urquhart, *Planned Urban Landscapes of Northern Nigeria* (Zaria, Ahmadu Bello University Press, 1977), pp.69–74. Caliphate cities were also established in Yorubaland at Ilorin and in the Nupe town of Bida, both of which are outside Hausaland and not within the scope of this work.

5 Frank Heath (tr.), *A Chronicle of Abuja* by Alhaji Hassan and Mallam Shuaibu Na'lbi (Ibadan, Ibadan University Press, 1952).

6 The populations for 1963 were taken from Government of Nigeria, Federal Office of Statistics, *Population Census of Nigeria* (Lagos, Government of Nigeria, 1963). Zaria is estimated to have had a population of about 238,000 in 1980: Hassan Bedawi, *Housing in Zaria* (Zaria, Ahmadu Bello University, Dept. of Urban and Regional Planning, 1977), p.8.

7 J.C. Moughtin, 'The Traditional Settlements of the Hausa People', *Town Planning Review*, vol.xxxv (April 1964), no.1, p.23.

8 Heinrich Barth, *Travels and Discoveries in North and Central Africa* (London, Longman, 1857–8), vol.2, pp.303–5; vol.3, pp.388–9.

9 Hogben and Kirk-Greene, *op. cit.*, pp.50–51.

10 Michael Crowder, *The Story of Nigeria* (London, Faber & Faber, 1962), pp.31–4.

11 C.K. Meek, *Land Tenure and Land Administration in Nigeria and the Cameroons* (London, H.M.S.O., 1957), pp.113–7, 163–6. In a traditional sense ownership of land is non-existent in Hausaland, but Blair found that in some districts of Kano houses were bought and sold, and family tenure was being substituted by individual tenure. See T.L.U. Blair, 'Giant of the North. In the Midst of Change', *West Africa*, 8 June 1963, p.627.

12 Barth, *op. cit.*, vol.2, pp.120–22.

13 A.W. Urquhart, *op. cit.*, p.25.

14 Colonial Reports, Northern Nigeria, 1904.

15 Barth, *op. cit.*

16 H.L.B. Moody, 'Ganuwa, The Walls of Kano City', *Nigeria Magazine*, vol.92 (1967), p.26.

17 J.S. Trimingham, *Islam in West Africa* (Oxford, Clarendon Press, 1959), pp.21–40.

18 G. Nicolas, 'Essai sur les structures fondamentales de l'espace dans la cosmologie Hausa', *Journal de la Société des Africanistes*, vol.36 (1966), pp.65–107.

19 *Ibid.* I am indebted to Nicolas for the details of Hausa spatial symbolism which follow. See also his article: 'Un système numérique symbolique Hausa: le trois et le sept dans la cosmologie d'une société hausa (vallée de Maradi)', *Cahiers d'études Africaines*, vol.8 (1968), pp.568–616.

20 G. Nicolas, 1966, *op. cit.*, and Polly Hill, *Population, Prosperity and Poverty: Rural Kano 1900 and 1970* (Cambridge University Press, 1977).

21 Urquhart, *op. cit.*, p.13.

22 Abdullahi Smith, 'History: Some Notes on the History of Zazzau under the Hausa Kings', in M.J. Mortimore (ed.), *Zaria and its Regions* (Zaria, Ahmadu Bello University, Dept. of Geography, 1970), p.93.

23 Urquhart, *op. cit.*, pp.13–15

24 Abdullahi Smith, *op. cit.*

25 Nicolas, 1966, *op. cit.*, pp.72–2. Translated for me by Catherine McMahon.

26 Trimingham, *op. cit.*

27 Abdullahi Smith, 'Some Considerations Relating to the Formation of States in Hausaland', *Journal of the Historical Society of Nigeria*, vol.v, (Dec. 1970), no.3, p.340.

28 M.J. Mortimore, 'Settlement Evolution and Land Use', in M.J. Mortimore (ed.), *Zaria and its Regions*, *op. cit.*, p.110.

29 Abdullahi Smith, 'History: Some Notes on the History of Zazzau under the Hausa Kings', *op. cit.*, p.89.

30 Urquhart, *op. cit.*, p.7.

31 H.R.J. Davies, 'Zaria and its Hinterland', in M.J. Mortimore (ed.), *Zaria and its Region*, *op. cit.*, p.134.

32 Urquhart, *op. cit.*, p.14.

33 Told to the author by the present chief builder of Zaria, Mallam Haruna, a descendent of Alhaji Mikaila.

34 Moughtin, 'The Traditional Settlements of the Hausa People', *op. cit.*

35 Blair, *op. cit.*, p.627.

36 Urquhart, *op. cit.*

37 H. Clapperton, 'Captain Clapperton's Narrative', *Missions to the Niger*, vol.4, 'The Bornu Mission 1822–25', Part 3 (London, Cambridge University Press, The Hackluyt Society, 1966), p.701.

38 *Ibid.*

39 Urquhart, *op. cit.*, p.34.

40 F.J.D. Lugard, *The Dual Mandate in British Tropical Africa* (London, 1922).

41 Moughtin, 'The Traditional Settlements of the Hausa People', *op. cit.*

4 The Architectural Programme

1 J.F. Harbeson, *The study of Architectural Design* (New York, Pencil Points Press, 1926), pp.8, 9.

2 Labelle Prussin, 'An Introduction to Indigenous African Architecture', *Society of Architectural Historians Journal*, vol.33, Oct. 1974, pp.182–205.

3 *Ibid.*, and see, for example, the diagram 'The Tree of Architecture', in Banister Fletcher, *A History of Architecture*, 15th edn. (London, Batsford, 1950).

4 Paul Oliver (ed.), *Shelter in Africa* (London, Barrie and Jenkins, 1978).

5 For example, see Udo Kuttermann, *New Architecture in Africa* (London, Thames & Hudson, 1963).

6 From October 1981 to February 1982 the Centre Georges Pompidou in Paris held an exciting exhibition entitled 'Des Architectures de Terre', on traditional architectural forms built of earth from many parts of the world. Ruth Eaton Trns., *Mud Architecture: an old idea, a new future: Down to Earth* (London, Thames and Hudson, 1982).

7 Amos Rapoport, *House Form and Culture* (Englewood Cliffs, Prentice-Hall, 1969).

8 Susan Denyer, *African Traditional Architecture* (London, Heinemann, 1978), and Labelle Prussin, *op. cit.*

9 'The original meaning of the word *gandu* is tribute, as from an Emir to the Sultan of Sokoto. Gradually the word came to denote the land from which the tribute was collected since the tribute largely consisted of agricultural produce. From here the meaning of the word may have been extended to mean those people who work on the land to get the tribute. From here it is a small step to the meaning of an arrangement whereby two or more married adults work together on a common farm.' See B.J. Buntjer, 'Rural Society', in M.J. Mortimore (ed.), *Zaria and its Region* (Zaria, Ahmadu Bello University, Dept. of Geography, 1970), p.158, and R.C. Abraham, *Dictionary of the Hausa Language* (University of London Press, 1962), p.296. Here Buntjer's meaning of *gandu* is used: i.e. 'two or more married males working together on a common farm in a single authority unit', with the proviso that agriculture may not necessarily be the only economic activity of the group.

10 The relationship of the cyclic nature of family growth and decline to house form has been documented in Friedrick Schwerdtfeger, 'Housing in Zaria', in Oliver, *Shelter in Africa, op. cit.* See also J.C. Moughtin, 'The Traditional Settlements of the Hausa People', in *Town Planning Review*, vol.xxxv (April 1964), no.1, p.23.

11 See Chapter 3, pp.60–73.

12 G. Nicolas, 'Essai sur les structures fondamentales de l'espace dans la cosmologie Hausa', *Journal de la Société des Africanistes*, vol.36 (1966), p.78. Translated for me by Catherine McMahon.

13 M.G. Smith, *The Economy of the Hausa Communities of Zaria* (London, H.M.S.O., Colonial Research Study no.16, 1955), p.50.

14 Schwerdtfeger, 1971, *op. cit.*, p.62. If this is true then it would appear that the scheme for setting out the house in pre-Islamic Hausa societies documented by Nicolas was never rigorously applied throughout the region.

15 *Ibid.*, p.65.

16 Joseph Greenberg, 'The Influence of Islam on a Sudanese Religion', in Marion Smith (ed.), *Monographs of the American Ethnographical Society* (New York, J.J. Augustin, 1946), p.17.

17 Polly Hill, 'Big Houses in Kano Emirates', *Africa*, vol.xliv (April 1974), no.2, pp.1–135.

18 M.G. Smith, *Government in Zazzau, 1800–1950* (London, Oxford University Press, 1960), p.102.

19 When this building was surveyed in 1962 its population was reported to me as greater than 100; the same number was given on my second visit in 1980. On further enquiry in 1980, by having the individuals named in each *sassa*, the actual population turned out to be 79; the figure 100 simply meant 'many'. My impression is of a greater population in the compound in 1982, which bears out the evidence of the physical survey.

20 For an account of living in this house see Margaret Mussom, 'The Desert at their Door', *Nigeria*, no.39, pp.266–8; see also A.M. Foyle, 'European Houses in Mud, Kano', *Nigeria*, no.39, pp.261–265.

21 Christopher Alexander, *et. al.*, A Pattern Language: Towns, Buildings and Construction (New York, Oxford University Press, 1977).

22 Peter Marris, *Family and Social Change in an African City* (London, Routledge, 1961).

23 Adepoju Onibokun, 'Low Cost Housing: An Appraisal of an Experiment in Nigeria', *Journal of Administration Overseas*, 16 (April 1977), no.2, pp.118–9.

24 J.C. Moughtin, 'Settlements and Housing in an Arid-zone Developing Country: Case Study in Hausaland, Northern Nigeria', in Gideon Golany (ed.), *Desert Planning* (London, Architectural Press, 1982), pp.145–59.

25 Allen Leary, 'A Decorated Palace in Kano', *AARP*, no.12, Dec. 1977, pp.11–17.

26 Schwerdtfeger, 'Housing in Zaria', *op. cit.*

27 Captain Hugh Clapperton, 'Journal of an Excursion from Kouka in Bornu, through Sudan to Soccatoo, the Capital of Bello, Sultan of the Felatahs', in E.W. Bovill (ed.), *Missions to the Niger*, vol.IV, *The Bornu Mission 1922–25* (Cambridge University Press, 1966), p.713.

28 Leary, 'A Decorated Hausa Palace', *op. cit.*

29 A.H.M. Kirk-Greene, *Barth's Travels in Nigeria* (London, Oxford University Press, 1962), p.106.

30 Leary puts a date of 1825 on the council chamber (*majalisa*), which though not drawn in this figure is part of the building complex. Leary, *op. cit.*

31 Clapperton, *op. cit.*, pp.676, 679, 687, 698.

32 *Ibid.*, p.651.

33 Tradition has it in Zaria that the mosque was built for Emir Abdulkarim who reigned from 1834 to 1846.

34 This is according to Alhaji Haruna, the present chief builder.

35 J.C. Moughtin and A.H. Leary, 'Hausa Mud Mosque', *Architectural Review*, vol.137 (Feb. 1965), no.816, pp.155–8.

5 Architectural Construction

1 Heinrich Barth, *Travels and Discoveries in North and Central Africa* (London, Longman, 1857–8), vol.3, p.389; vol.2, p.226.

2 In 1962 there was a brickworks between Maiduguri and Dikway. Bricks were burnt in the same way as pots, stacked beneath a bonfire of wood.

3 F.W. Taylor and A.G.G. Webb (tr.),*Labarun Al' Adun Hausawa Da Zantatukansu* (London, Oxford University Press, 1932), pp.171–2.

4 *Ibid.*, p.171.

5 In Zaria the timber taken from the *dumi* palm is also called *azara*.

6 Based on table in A.F. Daldy, *Temporary Buildings in Northern Nigeria* (Nigeria, Public Works Department, 1945), pp.4, 5.

7 J.C. Moughtin, 'The Friday Mosque, Zaria City', *Savanna*, vol.1 (Dec. 1972), no.2, pp.143–63.

8 For details of arch construction see also Daldy, *op. cit.*

9 Leary notes that the largest ceiling vault in the palace at Kano consists of twenty arches: 'The ceiling vault of the largest, *Soron Ingilia*, is an elaborate form of *daurin guga* construction, of a type referred to as *kafa ashirin* (twenty half-arches) or *rijiya* (*goma*) *sha shida* (sixteen 'wells' or coffers, between arch crossings).' Leary, 'A Decorated Palace in Kano', *AARP*, Dec. 1977, no.12, p.14.

10 Moughtin, 'The Friday Mosque, Zaria City', *op. cit.*, pp.149–50.

11 Taylor and Webb, *Labarun Al' Adun Hausawa Da Zantatukansu, op. cit.*, p.181.

12 Daldy states that: 'This continuation of the arch is done partly for effect, but mainly it is a legacy from the past. Until the last fifty years there was always a pillar projecting from the wall under each arch; then it was realised that this pillar had no structural value, and it was gradually left out; the lengthening of the arch is the last trace of this pillar.' Daldy, *op. cit.*, pp.11, 12. In the Friday Mosque, Zaria, built some hundred years before Daldy wrote his text, Mallam Mikaila was using the type of arch described by him as a relatively recent innovation.

13 J.C. Moughtin, 'The Traditional Settlements of the Hausa People', *Town Planning Review*, vol.xxxv (April 1964), no.1, p.29.

14 Taylor and Webb (trs.), *op. cit.*, p.177.

15 *Ibid.*, pp.185–7.

16 The *bagaruwa* tree, sometimes called the *gabaruwa*, is the Egyptian mimosa, *Acacia arabica*, the original source of gum arabic.

17 Daldy, *op. cit.*, p.22, suggests that *makuba* is less susceptible to attack from white ant and still retains its waterproofing qualities if '4 cigarette tins full of solignum to 2 headpans of *makuba* and 12 headpans of red earth' are mixed together.

18 Taylor and Webb (trs.), *op. cit.*, pp.187–9

6 Climate and Built Form

1 Carlos Monge, 'Biological basis of human behaviour', in A.L. Kroeber *et al, Anthropology Today* (Chicago, University of Chicago, 1953), pp.127–44.

2 For analytical purposes the climate of Hausaland has been described according to its extremes. The Hausa themselves, however, distinguished four seasons in the year—*bazara* from mid-February to mid-May which is the hot dry season of the harmattan; *damima* from mid-May to the end of August, the rainy season; *kaka*, from the beginning of September to the end of November, the harvest season; and lastly, *rani*, from the end of November to mid-February, the cold dry season of the harmattan which is the building season.

3 This discussion of design for climate in Hausaland is based upon and owes much to the more general theoretical propositions in O.H. Koenigsberger *et al, Manual of Tropical Housing and Building, Part 1: Climatic Design* (London, Longman, 1974), ch.7, pp.203–33.

4 For an analysis of traditional architecture in similar climatic conditions in other parts of Africa, see Miles Danby, 'Building design in hot, dry climates', in Gideon Golany (ed.), *Desert Planning* (London, Architectural Press, 1982), pp.113–23, and W.J. Kidd, 'The influence of arid-zone climate on house design in Sudan', *ibid.*, pp.137–44.

5 See Ch.4, p.??

6 Alexander uses the term 'pattern language'. See C. Alexander *et al.*, *The Oregon Experiment* (New York, Oxford University Press, 1975).

7 Architectural Decoration

1 Allan Leary, 'A Decorated Palace in Kano', *AARP*, Dec. 1977, no.2.

2 Morris, *The Biology of Art* (London, Methuen, 1962).

3 Labelle Prussin, 'An Introduction to Indigenous African Architecture', *Society of Architectural Historians Journal*, Oct. 1974, vol.33, pp.183–203.

4 H.R. Palmer, 'Notes on Traces of Totemism and Some Other Customs in Hausaland', *Man*, vol.10 (1910), no.40, pp.72–76.

5 R.T.D. Fitzgerald, 'The Dakarkari Peoples of Sokoto Province, Nigeria', *Man*, vol.42 (1942), no.19, pp.25–36.

6 *Ibid*.

7 Leary, *op. cit.*, and A.J. Arkell, 'Forms of the Talhakim and Tanaghilit as Adopted from the Tuareg by Various West African Tribes', *Journal of the Royal Anthropological Institute*, vol.65 (1935), pp.307–10.

8 Labelle Prussin, 'Fulani-Hausa Architecture', *African Arts*, vol.X (Oct. 1976), no.1, pp.8–19.

9 J.S. Trimingham, *A History of Islam in West Africa* (London, Oxford University Press, 1962), p.232.

10 R.A. Bravmann, *Islam and Tribal Art in West Africa* (Cambridge University Press, 1974), p.26.

11 A.H. Leary, 'Social and Economic Factors in the Development of Hausa Building', unpublished paper, dated Jan. 1975; and M.G. Smith, 'The Hausa System of Social Status', *Africa*, vol.29, 1959, pp.239–52.

12 A.H.M. Kirk-Greene, *Decorated Houses in a Northern City* (Kaduna, Baraka Press, 1963).

13 Leary, *op. cit.*

14 A.G. Hopkins, *An Economic History of West Africa* (New York, Columbia University Press, 1973).

15 J.C. Moughtin and A.H. Leary, 'Hausa Mud Mosque', *Architectural Review*, vol.137 (Feb. 1965), no.818, pp.155–8.

16 Captain Hugh Clapperton, 'Journal of an Expedition from Kouka in Bornu, through Soudan to Soccatoo, the Capital of Bello, Sultan of the Felatahs', in E.W. Bovill (ed.), *Missions to the Niger*, vol.IV, *The Bornu Mission, 1822–25* (Cambridge University Press, 1966), p.698.

17 A.H.M. Kirk-Greene (ed.), *Barth's Travels in Nigeria* (London, Oxford University Press, 1962), p.106.

18 Quoted in Leary, 'A Decorated Palace', *op. cit.*

19 F.D. Lugard, 'Northern Nigeria', *Geographical Journal*, vol.23 (Jan. 1904), pp.1–29.

20 Clapperton, *op. cit.*, pp.693–4.

21 N.W. Thomas, 'Decorative Art among the Edo-speaking People of Nigeria; 1, Decoration of Buildings', *Man*, vol.10 (1910), article 37, pp.65–6.

22 Prussin, *op. cit.*

23 A.J.N. Tremearne, *The Ban of the Bori* (London, Frank Cass, 1968).

24 A.H.M. Kirk-Greene (1963), *op. cit.*

25 Leary (1975), *op. cit.*, p.13.

26 *Ibid.*, p.15.

27 The chief builder to the caliphate, being descended from the father of Mallam Mikaila, a devoted follower of Shehu Uthman dan Fodio, resides in the family home in Zaria. The *sarkin magina* is commissioned to execute works in all the cities of the caliphates. So Tafida's house may be the work of Jibrilu.

28 Leary (1975), *op. cit.*

29 Kirk-Greene (1963), *op. cit.*

30 Leary (1975), *op. cit.*

31 Prussin (1976), *op. cit.*

32 The differences between Hausa mud patterning and that of other cultures should not be underestimated. For example Igbo mud

patterning may owe a great deal to the transposition of techniques from the craft of woodcarving while Hausa work may owe more to the transposition of ideas from embroidery, the other great craft of the culture.

33 For a description of the work of a *shegege* builder, Ango Tukr Tukr see Leary's unpublished essay, 1975, *op. cit.*

34 Kirk-Greene, *op. cit.*

8 Architectural Derivatives:

1 J.C. Moughtin, 'The Traditional Settlements of the Hausa People', *Town Planning Review*, vol.xxxv (April 1964), no.1, pp.21–34.

2 Office de la Recherce Scientifique (avec la collaberation de H. Labouret), *L'Habitation en Afrique Occidentale et Centrale; Fornie et Materiaux, Essai*. Bureau des Études Humaines, 1948. This is probably still true except in the large urban centres, despite the introduction of modern building types.

3 *Ibid*.

4 Alhaji Hassan and Na'ibi Shuaibu, *A Chronicle of Abuja* (Lagos, African Universities Press, 1962), pp.1–3. See also Abdullahi Smith, 'The Early States of the Central Sudan', in J.F.A. Ajayi and Michael Crowder (eds.), *History of West Africa* (London, Longman, 1971), vol.1, pp.157–8.

5 Leo Africanus, *The History and Description of Africa* (London, Hakluyt Society, 1896), vol.3, p.824, and H.R. Palmer, *The Bornu Sahara and Sudan* (London, Murray, 1936), p.9.

6 Joseph Greenberg, 'The Influence of Islam on a Sudanese Religion', in Marion W. Smith (ed.), *Monographs of the American Ethnological Society* (New York, J.J. Augustin, 1946).

7 F.D. Lugard, 'Northern Nigeria', *Geographical Journal*, vol.23 (1904),
8 Heinrich Barth, *Travels and Discoveries in North and Central Africa*, 2nd edn. (London, Longmans, 1857–8), vol.2, pp.121–3.

9 H.R. Palmer, *Sudanese Memories* (Lagos, Government Printer, 1928), p.1.

10 This appears to be a more reasonable explanation than that of Labelle Prussin who believes that Hausa architecture is the result of Fulani influence. Labelle Prussin, 'Fulani-Hausa architecture', *African Arts*, vol.x (1976), Part 1, pp.8–19.

11 The change from curvilinear to rectilinear structures has been associated with the technological innovations that occurred at the time of the changes in the organization of the structure of society from a matriarchal to a patriarchal system. See Lewis Mumford, *The City in History* (Harmondsworth, Penguin, 1966).

12 F.W. Taylor and A.G.G. Webb (trs.), *Labarun Al'Adun Hausawa Da Zantatukansu* (London, Oxford University Press, 1932), p.179.

13 Hugh Clapperton, *Journal of a Second Expedition into the Interior of Africa* (London, Murray, 1829), pp. 198–9; and Dixon Denham and Hugh Clapperton, *Narratives of Travels and Discoveries in Northern and Central Africa in the Years 1822, 1823 and 1824* (London, Murray, 1826), vol:2, p.103.

14 K.A.C. Cresswell, *Early Muslim Architecture* (Oxford, Clarendon, 1932), vol.1, pp.1–20.

15 S.J. Hogben and A.H.M. Kirk-Greene, *The Emirates of Northern Nigeria* (London, Oxford University Press, 1966), p.162.

16 Clapperton (1829), *op. cit.*, p.165.

17 Cresswell (1940), *op. cit.*, vol.II, pp.332–60.

18 *Ibid.*, vol.I (1932), pp.325–8, and vol.II (1940), pp.208–26.

19 One exception to this generalisation is the mosque constructed in Sokoto which Clapperton described.

20 Clapperton (1829), *op. cit.*, pp.103.

21 Hogben and Kirk-Greene (1966), *op. cit.*, p.223; and D.E. Awani 'Zaria City Mosque', *Nigercol* (Feb. 1959), p.20. (According to Awani the Mosque is dated to 1824 which does not accord with the local tradition that it was built, as Awani agrees, during the time Abdulkarim was Emir of Zaria.)

22 Mallam Mikaila, according to the current chief builder in Hausaland, Sarkin Maigina Haruna, was a devoted follower of Shehu 'Uthman Dan Fodio, being rewarded by him with a flag of office as chief builder after the successful jihad.

23 J.C. Moughtin and A.H. Leary, 'Hausa Mud Mosque', *Architectural Review*, vol.137 (Feb. 1965), no.816, pp.155–8.

24 Awani (1959), *op. cit.*, p.23.

25 Wilfred Thesiger, *The Marsh Arabs* (London, Longmans, 1964).

26 Olive Macleod, *Chiefs and Cities of Central Africa* (London, Blackwood, 1912), pp.212–37.

27 Michael Crowder, 'The Decorative Architecture of Northern Nigeria', *African World* (Feb. 1956), p.9.

9 Conclusion

1 J.F.C. Turner, *Housing by People* (London, Marion Books, 1976).

2 Denis Kabagambe and Cliff Moughtin, 'Housing the Poor, A case study in Nairobi', *Third World Planning Review*, vol.5 (August 1983), no.3, pp.227–248.

3 J.C. Moughtin, 'Settlements and housing in arid-zone developing country: case study in Hausaland, Northern Nigeria', in Gideon Golany (ed.), *Desert Planning* (London, Architectural Press, 1982).

4 A.M. Foyle, 'European Houses in Mud, Kano', *Nigeria*, no.39, pp.261–265, and Margaret Mussom, 'The Desert at their Door', *Nigeria*, no.39, pp.266–68.

Bibliography

R.C. Abraham, *Dictionary of the Hausa Language*, 2nd Edition (London, University of London Press, 1962).

R.A. Adeleye, "Hausaland and Bornu 1600–1800", in J.F.A. Ajayi and Michael Crowder (eds), *History of West Africa* (London, Longman, 1971), vol.1.

J.F.A. Ajayi and Michael Crowder, *History of West Africa* (London, Longman, 1971).

Leo Africanus, *The History and Description of Africa* (London, Hakluyt, 1896).

Christopher Alexander *et al.*, *The Oregon Experiment* (New York, Oxford University Press, 1975).

Christopher Alexander *et al.*, *A Pattern Language: Towns, Buildings and Construction* (New York, Oxford University Press, 1977).

Henriette Alimen, *The Prehistory of Africa* Trns. A.H. Brodrick (London, Hutchinson, 1957).

A.J. Arkell, "Some Tuareg ornaments and their connection with India", *Journal of the Royal Anthropological Institute*, vol.65, 1934, pp.297–307.

A.J. Arkell, "Forms of the Talhakim and Tanaghilit as adopted from the Tuareg by various West African tribes", *Journal of the Royal Anthropological Institute*, vol.65, 1934, pp.307–311.

E.J. Arnett (trns), "A Hausa Chronicle", *Journal of the African Society*, vol.9, no.34, 1910, pp.161–167.

E.J. Arnett, *Gazetteer of Sokoto Province* (London, Waterlow and Sons, 1920).

D.E. Awani, "Zaria City Mosque", *Nigercol*, Feb., 1959.

Heinrich Barth, *Travels and Discoveries in North and Central Africa* 5 vols. (London, Longman, 1857–8).

W.R. Bascom and M.J. Herscovits (eds), *Continuity and Change in African Cultures* (Chicago, Chicago University Press, 1963).

Hassan Badawi, *Housing in Zaria* (Zaria, Ahmadu Bello University, Dept. of Urban and Regional Planning, 1977).

T.L.U. Blair, "Giant of the North. In the Midst of Change", *West Africa*, 8 June 1963.

Paul Bohannan, "Beauty and Scarification Amongst the Tiv', *Man*, vol.56, 1956, pp.117–121.

E.W. Bovill (ed), *The Bornu Mission, 1822–25*, vols.2 and 4 (Cambridge, Hakluyt Society, Cambridge University Press, 1966).

E.W. Bovill, *The Golden Trade of the Moors* (London, Oxford University Press, 1958).

R.A. Bravmann, *Islam and Tribal Art in West Africa* (Cambridge, Cambridge University Press, 1974).

K.M. Buchanan and J.C. Pugh, *Land and People in Nigeria* (London, University of London Press, 1955).

B.J. Buntjer, "Rural Society" in M.J. Mortimore (ed), *Zaria and its Region* (Zaria, Ahmadu Bello University, Dept. of Geography, 1970).

Centre National d'art et de culture George Pompidou, *Down to Earth*, trns. Ruth Eaton (London, Thames and Hudson, 1982).

R.J.H. Church, *West Africa*, 8th edn. (London, Longman, 1980).

Captain Hugh Clapperton, *Journal of a second Expedition into the Interior of Africa, from the Bight of Benin to Soccatoo* (London, John Murray, 1829).

K.A.C. Cresswell, *Early Muslim Architecture*, vols.1 and 2 (Oxford, Clarendon Press, 1932).

Michael Crowder, "The Decorative Architecture of Northern Nigeria", *African World*, Feb., 1956, pp.9–10.

Michael Crowder, *The Story of Nigeria* (London, Faber, 1962).

A.E. Daldy, *Temporary Buildings in Northern Nigeria*, Technical paper no.10 (Nigeria, Public Works Department, 1945).

Miles Danby, "Building in hot, dry climates", in Gideon Golany (ed), *Desert Planning: International Lessons* (London, Architectural Press, 1982).

H.R.J. Davis, "Zaria and its hinterland" in M.J. Mortimore (ed), *Zaria and its Region*, (Zaria, Ahmadu Bello University, Dept. of Geography, 1970).

Major Dixon Denham, Captain Hugh Clapperton and Doctor Walter Oudney, *Narrative of Travels and Discoveries in Northern and Central Africa in the years 1822, 1823 and 1824* (London, John Murray, 1826).

P.W.C. Dennis, "The District around Zaria, Northern Nigeria", *Scottish Geographical Magazine*, vol.60, June 1944, pp.15–19.

Susan Denyer, *African Traditional Architecture* (London, Heinemann, 1978).

T.O. Elias, *Nigerian Land Law and Custom*, 3rd Edition (London, Routledge, 1962).

E.E. Evans-Pritchard, *The Position of Women in Primitive Societies* (London, Faber, 1965).

J.D. Fage, *An Introduction to the History of West Africa* (Cambridge, Cambridge University Press, 1956).

J.D. Fage, *A History of West Africa* (London, Cambridge University Press, 1969).

Bernard Fagg, "The Nok Culture", *West African Review*, Dec., 1956, pp.20–24.

Bernard Fagg, "A life-size Terra-Cotta Head from Nok", *Man*, vol.56, 1956, p.89.

Bernard Fagg, "An outline of the Stone Age of the Plateau Minesfield", in *Proceedings of the Third International West African Conference in Ibadan, 1949* (Lagos, 1956).

William Fagg, "The Study of African Art" in Simon and Phoebe Ottenberg (eds), *Cultures and Societies of Africa* (New York, Random House, 1960).

Hassan Fathy, *Architecture for the Poor* (Chicago, University of Chicago Press, 1973).

Federation of Nigeria, *Digest of Statistics*, vol.12, no.4 (Lagos, Oct., 1963).

R.T.D. Fitzgerald, "The Dakakari Peoples of Sokoto Province, Nigeria", *Man*, vol.42, 1942, pp.25–36.

Sir Banister Flight Fletcher, *A History of Architecture on the Comparative Method*, 15th Edition (London, Batsford, 1950).

A.M. Foyle, "The House of a Merchant in Kofarmata Street, Kano", *Nigeria*, no.37, 1951, pp.29–35.

A.M. Foyle, "European Houses in Mud, Kano", *Nigeria*, no.39, 1952, pp.261–266.

A.M. Foyle, "Some Aspects of Nigerian Architecture", *Man*, vol.53, 1953, pp.1–3.

Leo Frobenius, *The Voice of Africa*, vols.1 and 2 (London, Hutchinson, 1913).

Joseph Greenberg, *The Influence of Islam on a Sudanese Religion* (New York, J.J. Augustin, 1946).

A.T. Grove, "The Ancient Erg of Hausaland, and similar formations on the south side of the Sahara", *Geographical Journal*, vol.124, 1958, pp.528–533.

A.T. Grove, "Population and Agriculture in Northern Nigeria", in K.M. Barbour and R.M. Prothero (eds), *Essays on African Population* (London, Routledge, 1961).

A.T. Grove and A. Warren, "Quarternary landforms and Climate on the south side of the Sahara", *Geographical Journal*, vol.134, 1968, pp.194–208.

Alhaji Hassan and Shuaibu Na'Ibi, *A Chronicle of Abuja*, trns. Frank Heath (Lagos, African University Press, 1962).

Polly Hill, "Big Houses in Kano Emirate", *Africa*, vol.XLIV, no.3, April 1974, pp1–135.

Polly Hill, *Population prosperity and poverty: Rural Kano 1900 and 1970* (Cambridge, Cambridge University Press, 1977).

Thomas Lionel Hodgkin, *Nigerian Perspectives: An Historical Anthology* (London, Oxford University Press, 1960).

S.J. Hogben, *Muhammaden Emirates of Nigeria* (London, Oxford University Press, 1930).

S.J. Hogben and A.H.M. Kirk-Greene, *The Emirates of Northern Nigeria* (London, Oxford University Press, 1966).

A.G. Horton, *An Economic History of West Africa* (New York, Columbia University Press, 1973).

Robin Horton, "Stateless Societies in the History of West Africa", in J.F. Ajayi and Michael Crowder (eds), *History of West Africa*, vol.1 (London, Longmans, 1971).

J.O. Hunwick, "Songhay, Borno and Hausaland in the sixteenth century", in J.F.A. Ajayi and Michael Crowder (eds), *History of West Africa*, vol.1, (London, Longman, 1971).

G. Jackson, "Vegetation around the city and nearby villages of Zaria", in M.J. Mortimore (ed), *Zaria and its Region* (Zaria, Ahmadu Bello University, Dept. of Geography, 1970).

R.W.J. Keay, *An Outline of Nigerian Vegetation* (Lagos, Federal Government Printer, 1959).

W.J. Kidd, "The Influence of Arid-Zone Climate on House Design in Sudan", in Gideon Golany (ed), *Desert Planning: International Lessons* (London, Architectural Press, 1982).

A.H.M. Kirk-Greene, *Adamawa past and present* (London, Oxford University Press, 1958).

A.H.M. Kirk-Greene, "Decorated Houses in Zaria", *Nigeria*,

no.68, March 1961, pp.53–78.

A.H.M. Kirk-Greene (ed), *Barth's Travels in Nigeria: Extracts from the journals of Heinrich Barth's travels in Nigeria, 1850–1855* (London, Oxford University Press, 1962).

A.H.M. Kirk-Greene, *Decorated Houses in a Northern City* (Kaduna, Baraka Press, 1963).

O.H. Koenigsberger *et al.*, Manual of Tropical Housing and Building, Part 1, Climate Design (London, Longman, 1974).

Udo Kultermann, *New Architecture in Africa* (London, Thames and Hudson, 1963).

R.L. Lander and J. Lander, *Journal of an Expedition to Explore the Course and Termination of the Niger, with a narrative of a voyage down that river to its termination*, vols.1, 2 and 3 (London, John Murray, 1832).

G.W. Lawson, *Plant Life in West Africa* (London, Oxford University Press, 1966).

A.H. Leary, "A Decorated Palace in Kano", *AARP*, no.12, Dec., 1977, pp.11–17.

A.H. Leary, *Social and Economic Factors in the Development of Hausa Building Decoration*, Unpublished paper, Jan., 1975.

Nehemia Levtzion, "The Early States of the Western Sudan to 1500" in J.F.A. Ajayi and Michael Crowder (eds), History of West Africa, vol.1 (London, Longmans, 1971).

F.J.D. Lugard, "Northern Nigeria", *Geographical Journal*, vol.23, 1904, pp.1–29.

F.J.D. Lugard, *The Dual Mandate in British Tropical Africa*, 5th Edition (London, Cass, 1965).

Akin Mabogunje, *Urbanization in Nigeria*, (London, University of London Press, 1968).

Akin Mabogunje, "The Land and Peoples of West Africa" in J.F.A. Ajayi and Michael Crowder (eds), *History of West Africa*, vol.1 (London, Longmans, 1971).

Frank Mbanefo, "The Iba House in Onitsha", *Nigeria*, no.72, 1962, pp18–25.

Gavan McDonnell, "The Dynamics of Geographic Change: The Case of Kano", *Annals of the Association of American Geographers*, vol.54, no.3, Sept., 1964, pp.355–371.

Olive Macleod, *Chiefs and Cities of Central Africa* (London, Blackwood, 1912).

Peter Marris *Family and Social Change in an African City* (London, Routledge, 1961).

C.K. Meek, *Land Tenure and Land Administration in Nigeria and the Cameroons* (London, HMSO, 1957).

C.M. Meek, *The Northern Tribes of Nigeria*, vols.1 and 2 (London, Humphrey Milford, 1925).

R. Miller, "Katsina, A City of the Desert Border", *Geography*, vol.22, 1937, pp.283–292.

R. Miller, "Katsina, A Region of Hausaland", *Scottish Geographical Magazine*, vol.54, 1938, pp.203–219.

Carlos Monge, "Biological Basis of Human Behaviour" in A.L. Kroeber *et al.* (ed), *Anthropology Today* (Chicago, University of Chicago, 1953).

H.L.B. Moody, "*Ganuwa*, The Walls of Kano City", *Nigeria Magazine*, vol.92, 1967, p.26.

Desmond Morris, *The Biology of Art* (London, Methuen, 1962).

M.J. Mortimore and J. Wilson, *Land and people in the Kano close-settled zone* (Zaria, Ahmadu Bello University, Dept. of Geography, 1965).

M.J. Mortimer (ed), *Zaria and its Region* (Zaria, Ahmadu Bello University, Dept. of Geography, 1970).

J.C. Moughtin, "The Traditional Settlements of the Hausa People", *Town Planning Review*, vol.35, no.1, April 1964, pp.21–34.

J.C. Moughtin and A.H. Leary, "Hausa Mud Mosque", *Architectural Review*, vol.137, no.816, Feb., 1965, pp.155–158.

J.C. Moughtin, "New Homes for Old Societies", *Proceedings of the Town and Country Planning Summer School*, 1968, pp.1–5.

J.C. Moughtin, "The Friday Mosque, Zaria City", *Savanna*, vol.1, no.2, Dec., 1972, pp.143–163.

J.C. Moughtin, "Building Materials in the Third World", *Proceedings of the Town and Country Planning Summer School*, 1976, pp.70–75.

J.C. Moughtin, "Settlement and Housing in an Arid Zone Developing Country: Case Study in Hausaland" in Gideon Golany (ed), *Desert Planning: International Lessons* (London, Architectural Press, 1982).

J.C. Moughtin, "Settlements and buildings as the physical expression of a culture: a case study in Nigeria" in K.J.

Miller (ed), *International Karakoram Project*, vol.1 (Cambridge, Cambridge University Press, 1984).

Lewis Mumford, *The City in History* (London, Secker and Warburg, 1961).

G.P. Murdock, *Africa, its Peoples and their Culture History* (New York, McGraw-Hill, 1959).

Margaret Mussom, "The Desert at their Door", *Nigeria*, no.39, pp.266–288.

G. Nicolas, "Essai sur les structures fondamentales de l'espace dans la cosmologie Hausa", *Journal de sociétié des Africanistes*, vol.36, 1966, pp.65–107.

G. Nicolas, "Un système numérique symbolic: le trois et le sept dans la cosmologie d'une sociétié hausa (vallée de Maradi)", *Cahiers d'études Africaines*, vol.8, 1968, pp.568–616.

C.R. Niven, "Kano in 1933", *Geographical Journal*, vol.82, 1933, pp.336–343.

Office de la Recherce Scientifique (avec la collaberation de H. Labouret), *L'Habitation en Afrique Occidentale et Centrale; Fornie et Materiaux*, Essai, Bureaux des Études Humaines, 1948.

Paul Oliver (ed), *Shelter in Africa* (London, Barrie and Jenkins, 1978).

R.A. Oliver and J.D. Fage, *A Short History of Africa* (Harmondsworth, Penguin Books, 1962).

Adepoju Onibokun, "Low Cost Housing: An appraisal of an Experiment in Nigeria", *Journal of Administration Overseas*, 16, no.2, April 1977, pp.114–120.

J.N. Paden, *Religion and Political Culture in Kano* (Berkley, University of California Press, 1973).

H.R. Palmer, "Notes on traces of totemism and some other customs in Hausaland", *Man*, vol.10, 1910, pp.72–76.

H.R. Palmer, *Sudanese Memoires* (Lagos, Government Printer, 1928).

H.R. Palmer, *The Bornu, Sahara and Sudan* (London, John Murray, 1936).

Mungo Park, *Travels of Mungo Park*, ed. Roland Miller (London, J.H. Dent and Sons, 1954).

R.M. Prothero, "Land use at Soba, Zaria Province, Northern Nigeria", *Economic Geography*, vol.33, Jan.,1957, pp.72–86.

R.M. Prothero, "Heinrich Barth and the Western Sudan", *Geographical Journal*, vol.124, 1958, pp.326–337.

R.M. Prothero, *Migrant Labour from Sokoto Province, Northern Nigeria* (Kaduna, Government Printer, 1959).

Labelle Prussin, "An Introduction to Indigenous African Architecture", *Society of Architectural Historians Journal*, vol.33, Oct., 1974, pp.182–205.

Labelle Prussin, "Fulani-Hausa Architecture", *African Arts*, vol.x, no.1, Oct., 1976, pp.8–19.

Amos Rapoport, *House Form and Culture* (Englewood Cliffs, Prentice-Hall, 1969).

Amos Rapoport, *Human Aspects of Urban Form* (Oxford, Pergamon, 1977).

C.H. Robinson, *Hausaland: Fifteen Hundred Miles Through the Central Sudan* (London, 1896).

F.W. Schwerdtfeger, "Housing in Zaria" in Paul Oliver, (ed) *Shelter in Africa*, (London, Barrie and Jenkins, 1978).

F.W. Schwerdtfeger, *Traditional Housing in African Cities* (Chichester, John Wiley and Sons, 1982).

Thurston Shaw, "The Prehistory of West Africa' in J.F.A. Ajayi and Michael Crowder (eds), *History of West Africa*, vol.1 (London, Longmans, 1971).

Abdullahi Smith, 'Some notes on the history of Zazzau under the Hausa Kings" in M.H. Mortimore (ed), *Zaria and its Region* (Zaria, Ahmadu Bello University, Dept. of Geography, 1970).

Abdullahi Smith, "Some considerations relating to the formation of states in Hausaland", *Journal of the Historical Society of Nigeria*, vol.V, no.3, Dec., 1970.

Abdullahi Smith, "The early states of central Sudan" in J.F.A. Ajayi and Michael Crowder (eds), *History of West Africa*, vol.1 (London, Longmans, 1971).

Mary F. Smith, *Baba of Karo* (London, Faber and Faber, 1954).

M.G. Smith, *The Economy of Hausa Communities of Zaria Province*, Colonial Research Publication no.16 (London, HMSO, 1955).

M.G. Smith, "The Hausa system of social status", *Africa*, vol.29, 1959, pp.239–252.

M.G. Smith, *Government in Zazzau 1800–1950* (London, Oxford University Press, 1970).

P.A. Talbot, "Note on Ibo Houses", *Man*, vol.xiv, 1916, p.129.

F.W. Taylor and A.G.G. Webb (trns), *Labarun Al'Adun Hausawa Da Zantatukansu* (London, Oxford University Press, 1932).

Wilfred Thesiger, *The Marsh Arabs* (London, Heinemann, 1964).

N.W. Thomas, "Decorative Art among the Edo-speaking People of Nigeria; 1, Decoration of Buildings", *Man*, vol.10, 1910, pp.65–66.

A.J.N. Tremearne, *The Ban on the Bori* (London, Frank Cass & Co, 1968).

A.J.N. Tremearne, "Hausa Houses", *Man*, vol.x, 1910, pp.117–180.

J.S. Trimingham, *Islam in West Africa* (Oxford, Clarendon Press, 1959).

J.S. Trimingham, *A History of Islam in West Africa* (London, Oxford University Press, 1967).

R.K. Udo, *Geographical Regions of Nigeria* (London, Heineman, 1970).

A.W. Urquhart, *Planned Urban Landscapes of Northern Nigeria* (Zaria, Ahmadu Bello University Press, 1977).

James Walton, "Corbelled Stone Huts in Southern Africa", *Man*, vol.L1, 1951, pp.45–48.

Derwent Whittlesey, "Kano: A Sudanese Metropolis", *Geographical Review*,. vol.27, 1937, pp.177–199.

Index

Trade
  local 10, 20, 24, 42, 52
  trans-Saharan 4, 16, 25,
    26
Trimingham, J.S 40, 133
Tsetse fly 13
Tubali 110, 112, 113
Tunisia 18

Ulama 24
Urban communities 16
  development 15
Urbanization 15, 71
Urquhart 36, 38
Urvoy 30
Uthman dan Fodio 25–30,
  34, 63, 133, 134

Vegetation 11
Verandah 119, 121
von Thunen 12
Village 15

Wall construction 101, 115
Walled towns 21
  city 26
Wards 44
Water 10
  table 10
Weathering 7, 111
Western concept of home
  70
Wusasa Church 114

Yo River 24
Yoruba 8, 53
Yola 26

Zaghawa 30
Zaria 10, 12, 21, 51
  province 12
  Emir's Palace 74, 80

Friday Mosque 91, 95,
  111
Zaure 48, 57, 60, 67, 134
Zazzau18, 21, 22, 24

Zazzau 18, 21, 22, 24